FOOL'S PARADISE
A CAREY McWILLIAMS READER

A CALIFORNIA LEGACY BOOK

Santa Clara University and Heyday Books are pleased to publish the California Legacy series, vibrant and relevant writings drawn from California's past and present.

Santa Clara University—founded in 1851 on the site of the eighth of California's original 21 missions—is the oldest institution of higher learning in the state. A Jesuit institution, it is particularly aware of its contribution to California's cultural heritage and its responsibility to preserve and celebrate that heritage.

Heyday Books, founded in 1974, specializes in critically acclaimed books on California literature history, natural history, and ethnic studies.

Books in the California Legacy series appear as anthologies, single author collections, reprints of important books, and original works. Taken together, these volumes bring readers a new perspective on California's cultural life, a perspective that honors diversity and finds great pleasure in the eloquence of human expression.

Series editor: Terry Beers
Publisher: Malcolm Margolin
Advisory Committee: Stephen Becker, William Deverell, Peter Facione, Charles Faulhaber, David Fine, Steven Gilbar, Dana Gioia, Ron Hansen, Gerald Haslam, Robert Hass, Jack Hicks, Timothy Hodson, James Houston, Jeanne Wakatsuki Houston, Maxine Hong Kingston, Frank LaPena, Ursula K. Le Guin, Jeff Lustig, Tillie Olsen, Ishmael Reed, Alan Rosenus, Robert Senkewicz, Gary Snyder, Kevin Starr, Richard Walker, Alice Waters, Jennifer Watts, Al Young.

Thanks to the English Department at Santa Clara University and to Regis McKenna for their support of the California Legacy series.

FOOL'S PARADISE

A CAREY McWILLIAMS READER

Edited by Dean Stewart and Jeannine Gendar
Foreword by Wilson Carey McWilliams
Introduction by Gray Brechin

Santa Clara University ‖ Santa Clara
Heyday Books ‖ Berkeley

© 2001 by Clapperstick Institute

Library of Congress Cataloging-in-Publication Data

McWilliams, Carey, 1905-
  Fool's paradise : a Carey McWilliams reader / foreword by Wilson Carey McWilliams ; introduction by Gray Brechin.
     p. cm. — (A California legacy book)
  ISBN 1-890771-41-4 (pbk.)
  1. California—History. 2. California—Social conditions. 3. California—Politics and government. I. Title. II. Series.
  F861.5 .M39 2001
  979.4—dc21

                          2001002416

Cover Art: "Working on a Farm" by Henry Sugimoto. Gift of Madeleine Sugimoto and Naomi Tagawa, Japanese American National Museum (92.97.110)
Cover Design: Rebecca LeGates
Interior Design: Jeannine Gendar
Printing and Binding: Publishers Press, Salt Lake City, UT
Orders, inquiries, and correspondence should be addressed to:
     Heyday Books
     P.O. Box 9145
     Berkeley, CA 94709
     (510) 549-3564, fax (510) 549-1889
     www.heydaybooks.com

Printed in the United States of America

10 9 8 7 6 5 4 3 2 1

CONTENTS

Acknowledgments

THE EDITORS wish to thank California Legacy series editor Terry Beers for his considerable assistance with this book, as well as Dana Wolfe of Santa Clara University and Jared Stanley of Heyday Books for help with research and production. As always, the help that the staff of the Bancroft Library at the University of California, Berkeley, has given us has been invaluable. Thanks also to Craig Tenney of Harold Ober Associates and to *The Nation*.

Carey McWilliams at *The Nation*. Courtesy of The Bancroft Library (77/140c).

Foreword

In *The Education of Carey McWilliams,* my father spoke of his life as having taken place in five "worlds," (1) his boyhood in a cattle-ranching family in northwest Colorado, (2) his more or less literary 1920s in California, (3) his turn to politics in the 1930s, (4) his varying involvements in the "War Years," down to 1950, and (5) his nearly thirty-year stint as editor of *The Nation.*

The asymmetry is evident: every decade of his California years counted as a "world," three times as important as his time in New York, and his early years in Colorado—he left the state, expelled from Denver U., when he was still in his teens—enjoy a similar standing. New York, in other words, consumed *time* (and takes up slightly more than half the pages of *The Education*), but the *place* touched him relatively little. The New York chapters of *The Education* are almost entirely devoted to his work on *The Nation,* and it wouldn't be far off the mark to describe him as a migrant laborer in New York, always planning to return to California. And as much as he remained a Californian at heart, he was even more a Westerner, disposed to distinguish his Western radicalism from what he saw as the sectarian, Eurocentric Left of the East. As that suggests, he was more tied to his past than he sometimes let on.

He cherished a sense of himself as one of a kind, the product of a very personal "education," a reflection on circumstances that were as much a matter of chance as of necessity—open-ended, a work in progress, like his America, subject to redefinition and reform.

He was, moreover, no admirer of "identity politics," as we call it nowadays: speaking of the work of his friend John Fante, he once referred to the "new ethnicity" in literary criticism as an "intellectual fad." Fante, he said, was "as American as Huckleberry Finn."

Now, in a sense, this assertion is bizarre: Fante was turbulently but profoundly Catholic and much caught up with his family and his heritage. Yet my father's judgment was also shrewd: John Fante was a Denver boy and a baseball adept, with a remarkable feeling for the sounds and silences of American English, and to treat him as an "Italian American" novelist would risk losing sight not only of Fante's very personal talent, but the universalities of his insight. In criticism as in politics, my father saw "tribalism" as too inclined to focus on human constructs as opposed to human fundamentals. His belief in equality and his sense of possibility disposed him to discount the past, if only for effect, as in his claim that family influences and "tribal loyalties" had no effect in shaping his political convictions.

It is true that his parents, and theirs before them, held more or less mainstream or conservative views. And certainly, my father didn't share the militant Scots-Irish Protestantism of the McWilliams clan (although for that matter, neither did his father: both my grandparents were, at most, lightly churched; my grandmother's parents, born into Catholic families, had settled into Episcopalianism; my grandfather, hedging his bets, gave money to all the local churches). Yet the heritage showed in obvious ways: what was virtually my father's only firsthand reporting on foreign affairs dealt, almost inevitably, with Northern Ireland. That he sympathized, predictably, with Bernadette Devlin and the largely Catholic movement for equal rights would have scandalized his Missouri relatives, but he was more than proportionately amused by the numbers of distant kinfolk in Ulster who sought to enlist him in their cause. He might *side* with the rebels (and other reasons aside, he loved Yeats), but he was called by the old quarrels.

And in every way that matters, my father was a cultural Calvinist. He did his share of hell-raising—John Fante, admiringly, once called him an "evil companion"—but he mirrored his parent's reserve and their devotion to work and self-reliance enough so that he could refer to dependence on others as "degrading" and "morally disintegrating."

Most important, my father's parents were moralists (so, for that matter, were pretty much all his relatives). They knew the grays of life in practice, and they were capable of humor and mercy, but they were guided by an inner map demarcating right and wrong. My father rejected any number of their precepts; he retained their stance. He was deeply troubled, for example, by the decline of the "Protestant ethic" under the impact of postwar consumerism, pointing so insistently to things like quiz-show frauds, employee theft, and corporate shams that *The Nation*, by his admission, often sounded like a "nineteenth-century scold." And he was amused, but not displeased, when a reporter compared him to Billy Graham.

He acknowledged being drawn to moral critics like Ambrose Bierce, Henry and Brooks Adams, and John Jay Chapman: his own primary concern, he said, was with "values," asserting the moral dimension of human life, the claim of right to judge practice. In that, he cultivated the status of an outsider. Idealism, he remarked, is bound to be compromised or ineffective in political life: in the first place, idealists do not agree with one another, and even if they did, practice always constrains and mires theory. But, *contra* Machiavelli, he held that idealism still matters. Its office is critical, its duty to remind us of our moral shortcomings and the inadequacy of our justice, a Jeremiad informed by faith in the possibility of improvement. In such sentiments, it is impossible not to hear at least the echo of my father's Covenanter ancestry.

His family also taught him that citizenship matters and that politics is a worthy endeavor. Both my grandparents were voters and partisans, and almost the only disagreements between them that my father or my uncle Casley remembered were political. (The daughter of a Union veteran, grandmother was a solid Republican; my grandfather, like all the McWilliamses, was an undeviating Democrat.) And when my grandfather was elected to the Colorado State Senate, politics took up even more of the stage, especially since my father, bored with school in Denver, found relief in listening to legislative debates and exploring the state capitol.

It was a privileged childhood. My grandparents were gentry in Steamboat Springs, my grandfather a dominating figure who "did pretty much as he pleased." In the winter, my grandmother moved into town with the boys to make it easier for them to attend school and to enjoy the advantages of society; during legislative sessions in Denver, the family stayed in the Brown Palace Hotel, still a monument of elegance, and my father and his brother attended the very tony—if educationally inadequate—Wolfe Hall Military Academy.

That life, in the aristocracy of the stockmen's West, had at least two abiding influences on my father. In the first place, the rhythm of cattle ranching in northwest Colorado was shaped by the land and the seasons, cattle being fed in feedlots during the winter, driven west into open range in the spring, and up into the mountains for the summer. Nature was fundamental and the land a presence. It helped that my father loved geography, his atlas opening the door to fantasy and theory. In any event, he learned to see the land as an inescapable counterweight to human designs, an understanding evident in his recognition that, while the West is linked to the East by law and custom, the corridors of the land run north and south, connecting the West to Mexico, a geographic gravitation working to wear down contrary contrivances. In the aftermath of his family's economic ruin, Colorado helped instill the lesson that the "authority of the land," and of nature generally, is more basic and enduring than human societies or ways of life.

That fallen society, however, had taught its own lessons. Inequalities of wealth and power there were, and evident enough, and Steamboat was overwhelmingly white and Christian, but cattle country—in my father's eyes, at any rate—was a social democracy, a rough equality of dignity. Employers like his father were not necessarily or ordinarily exploiters (although there was unmistakable class conflict in the mines nearby). In Steamboat's very small world, respectable ladies and merchants and cowhands had their distinct and recognized places, as did the whores and saloon keepers in "Brooklyn" across the Yampa; all were parts of a whole, playing their roles in the drama of the common life. Remembered with a hint of rose, Steamboat's society taught him that with equal dignity, other inequalities may not be galling, just as without it, even material equality is likely to seem hollow. Francis Carney is probably right to argue that the insight gave him an inoculation against Marxism, but even more certainly, it helped him focus, as his friend Edmund Wilson did, on the human need for recognition.

The charm of his life as a princeling made it only more shattering when the cattle kingdom fell. World War I had brought boom years; the end of the war found my grandfather overextended, and with stunning rapidity he went broke, suffered a nervous collapse, and died. My grandmother moved to Los Angeles, where a brother was living; the boys eventually followed. It was truly a world's end: aristocrats in Colorado, in California the family scrabbled to hold onto the lower edge of the middle class.

My father would have been a rebel in any event, but whatever faith he had in authority was a casualty of his family's catastrophe. He was bound to hold his father somewhat accountable: the man knew better, after all, even leaving his sons the advice "do not speculate or seek to get rich too quickly." But my father's love for his father made him readier to fault the system, the market and the government that had urged ranchers on and left them in the lurch, to say nothing of Woodrow Wilson, whose failure to live up to his high promises my father experienced as a betrayal.

"I was not in a state of depression or despair," my father wrote in his *Education*, "I was rebellious." He may have wanted to remember his mood in that way, but his writings in the early twenties strike at least a pose of world-weariness with an edge of disgust, and his dissent was primarily literary and aesthetic. Inevitably, he was drawn to F. Scott Fitzgerald and was at least half taken by Robinson Jeffers's argument that World War I marked civilization's ending and that the United States was a perishing republic. Sometimes, he was moved by political events—his outrage over Sacco and Vanzetti stayed with him all his life—but like that roaring generation, he lived much of the decade as a rebel without a cause.

Still, he was attracted to H. L. Mencken's rollicking impieties precisely because Mencken spoke to the more political dimension of his soul. A "libertarian, but never a liberal" and more or less immune to political enthusiasms, Mencken also was never tempted by romantic alienation. He was vastly entertained by American politics and delightedly contemptuous of the American public, always mocking but very much in the stew. And for all his anti-democratic posturing, Mencken was "a notably democratic person," open to all kinds and all voices, an intellectual echo of frontier democracy. Mencken encouraged my father as a writer—urging him, among other things, to write a book, his first, about Ambrose Bierce—and he reciprocated by imitating Mencken's hairstyle (parted straight down the middle) and his drinking habits (bourbon Manhattans). They had a falling out over politics in the thirties, but my father always acknowledged his debt to Mencken's patronage and example.

He found another saving grace in the 1920s in the beginnings of his love affair with Los Angeles and with California. At first, comparing L.A. to Denver, he found it inferior, a "city of strangers, of milling marauders," anonymous, without order, muddled and incomplete. But he knew that the Denver he remembered was part of a vanishing order of things, and he came to love L.A. for the openness of the place, its numberless improbabilities always hinting at great possibilities.

It was then a rather provincial, boosterish city and its intellectuals formed a relatively small circle. He met adherents of offbeat religions, like the venerable Hamlin Garland, or utopians, like Upton Sinclair, but what really mattered were the younger writers like Louis Adamic, John Fante, and William Saroyan, and the bookmen like Jake Zeitlin. They formed a sizzling sort of fellowship, a Smart Set West, given to long, convivial conversations about art, philosophy, and human folly.

Among his friends from those roistering years, Fante stands out because (unlike Adamic, for example), he never shared my father's taste for politics and even thought him a "sucker" for indulging it. "My business in life," Fante said, "is to save myself," a conviction which, his immediately personal dramas aside, pointed him to the Big Questions. He was, as I've indicated, involved in a lover's quarrel with the Church; at first attracted and later repelled by Nietzsche, he knew the spell of Plato and he thought Augustine or Aristotle superior to Marx or Mussolini—or so he wrote Mencken, who probably detested all four—in their understanding of human yearning. Conversation with Fante, in other words, gave my father a reminder, a voice of theory against the claims of practice, some protection against losing himself in the political thickets.

In fact, although—or *because*—he distrusted abstractions, my father's radicalism reflected a theorist's disposition. Convinced that all humans are caught up in pretense, he distrusted all conventions and customs and appearances, all official myths and explanations. That skepticism extended to ideologies, even those on the Left. Like everyone else in the thirties, he wrote, he was interested in Marxism, but he "never succeeded in mastering the sacred texts." Actually, he had a fairly good command of Marxist teaching, appreciating Marxism's critique of capitalism, though not its "scientific" socialism: it was the *sanctity* of the texts that eluded him, the ideologist's conviction of an infallible blueprint for Utopia. He was, in one sense, a thoroughgoing naysayer, an enemy of orthodoxies. But he was also something more: he insisted on holding conventions to the mirror of nature, hoping to enable things "to be called by their right names." Radicalism, in his understanding, was simply another term for a determination to get to the truth, as in the proposition that, in reality, we are "brothers under the skin."

He was persuaded that all human societies rely on deceptions, more or less effective, hiding secrets that are embarrassing if not guilty. There is always "evil in paradise," even if it is ordinarily seamy and pathetic rather than grandly wicked. Southern California, without adequate harbors or water, so dependent on convention in the effort to keep a step ahead of ever present nature, was just as determined to conceal its economic underside— the poor, of course, but also the people my father met when he worked in the advertising office of the *Los Angeles Times*, deadbeats and fly-by-nights, purveyors of exotic arts, "two-bit predators out to con the ignorant and fleece the innocent," all petty signs of sleaziness on a grander scale.

The prevailing disposition in Los Angeles through all my father's California years was resolutely self-deceived, living out a strange, Protestant fantasy—the "last trek" of the "Aryan race," Harry Carr called it—facing West toward the ocean, determined, often cruelly, to hide or minimize Mexicans, African Americans, and Asians, reminding Catholics of their marginality, and, since Jews intruded on this urban idyll, disposed to a more or less respectable anti-Semitism.

From the twenties onward, California sharpened his focus as a social critic, heightening his appreciation for the less visible signs of power—the politics of water, for example—and for the lonely and ignored, the inhabitants of "Shadow America." But it was the thirties, of course, that moved him into full-fledged political engagement, driven by a sense of moral necessity to do more than observe, and drawn by the political romances and excitements of the time.

California politics in the thirties, like my father's description of Los Angeles, was a "circus without a tent," made desperately serious by the depression. All kinds of nostrums got a hearing, movements like Utopia, Inc. and Ham 'n Eggs, while the promise to End Poverty in California made Upton Sinclair a credible Democratic candidate for governor in 1934.

My father worked actively for Sinclair, but he recognized in these stirrings the gasping of an older political world, decisively Protestant and middle class, inadequate to an industrial society in which even agriculture was increasingly dominated by "factories in the field," and organization on a grand scale had become essential to economic justice and democratic citizenship.

The labor movement was democracy in a new mode, multi-ethnic and based on the injuries of class, especially in Los Angeles, an open-shop city with a history of labor violence. When he spoke to a meeting of women walnut-shellers in 1937, he was struck by their diverse languages, united, it seemed, only by the word "Organize!" and he felt like a "white-faced anemic flunky of the upper classes," exhilarated, despite that discomfort, at being part of a great democratic struggle.

It was characteristic that he valued the labor movement for its contributions to the moral education of autonomous citizens. He worried that the depression was escalating a sense of dependence and a kind of hopeless passivity, and he argued that, above all, the jobless—like working Americans generally—needed "a set of ideas and a fight" to "stiffen their character."

As that may suggest, his political convictions had a touch of syndicalism, a concern to empower citizens rather than to do for them. An abiding critic of authority, he was no enthusiast for the state, for bureaucracy, or for any structure of power: he saw the need for central planning and he supported the liberal orthodoxies in public policy, but never without a watchful uneasiness.

In the same way, his commitment to labor did not blind him to the fact that the leadership of any large organization tends to grow away from the rank and file, so that organized labor, too, had its guilty secrets, its deals with corrupt politicians, and its racketeers like Willie Bioff.

Still, he was happy to invoke state power to make it easier for people to help themselves. That dedication, applied to the varying exploitation of Filipinos, Mexicans, and "Okies" of California's agricultural working class, made him a splendidly controversial Commissioner of Immigration and Housing in the administration of Governor Culbert Olson (1939–1943), so detested by the Right and by organized agriculture that Earl Warren, who defeated Olson in his bid for reelection, pledged to make firing my father his first official act. Even the most savage criticism, however, never had much power to deter him.

More skeptical than any ideology, his "native American radicalism" was also more idealistic, more thoroughgoing in its devotion to the goal of a self-governing citizenry. The politics he valued was a sphere of associations and meetings, of speeches and arguments, a matter of public places and many voices. My father was among the first to point to the political rise of public relations firms and political consultants, like California's Clem Whitaker and Leone Baxter, precisely because he saw, even in those early manifestations, the danger to democratic civic life of a politics of media and mass.

His devotion to democratic civility made him a champion of civil rights, understood as the affirmative duty of government to defend the equal dignity of citizens. Through the thirties, he was involved with issues of racial and ethnic inequality, but he was moved to what amounted to full-time concern with civil rights by the internment of Japanese Americans and by instances of racism like the Sleepy Lagoon case. Reflection on such events, seemingly so paradoxical during World War II, that "people's war," contributed to *Brothers Under the Skin*, with its then exceptional argument that the government has a magisterial obligation to promote civic equality. He added a special dimension to that case a few years after the war with his treatment of Mexican Americans in *North from Mexico*, a work that now has many of the marks of prophecy.

But the coming of the war also marked the increasing salience of foreign policy, the rise of America as an imperial republic. International politics was not my father's forte, and not just because it involved matters distant from his experience. It made him morally uneasy, especially in the years before World War II. He was, he said, a "pacifist by conviction," made even more suspicious of the state by World War I, who knew that in international practice both dispositions may have to be set aside. In the prewar years, he was anti-fascist but largely opposed to intervention, looking for an evanescent third way. Still, dragging his feet, he came reluctantly to support something like the administration's position: his account in the *Education of Carey McWilliams* likens his position to that of Humphrey Cobb, the bitterly antiwar author of *Paths of Glory*, who hated fascism even more savagely than he hated war.

The Cold War was different. With some justification, my father was convinced that America's conflict with the Soviet Union could have been much softened, a persuasion given added impetus by the danger it posed for democracy at home. He never doubted the need for an opposition sufficiently forceful to compel the government to make its case in democratic argument, a necessity emphasized by the fact that so much of Cold War politics was covert, tending to reduce public life to a charade. The greater part of his last three decades was spent challenging McCarthyism and the Cold War consensus, and more fundamentally, the apparatus of organized power and moral relativism that threatens to eclipse both citizenship and democratic life.

He lived long enough to see some of his old causes victorious and himself regarded as a sage by a number of old enemies. (The *Los Angeles Times*, for example, took to priding itself on his years as an employee.) But for every old battle won, he found two new ones worth fighting. He was a sardonic Galahad, constant to the democratic Grail, and there is more than a little of him in Orwell's imagined description of Dickens:

> Laughing, with a touch of anger in his laughter, but no triumph, no malignity…a man who is always fighting against something, but who fights in the open and is not frightened…a free intelligence, a type hated with equal hatred by all the smelly little orthodoxies now contending for our souls.

WILSON CAREY McWILLIAMS
May 2001

Introduction

Artist Frank Du Mond painted the kind of California history that most of us learned in high school. In one panel painted for San Francisco's 1915 Panama-Pacific International Exhibition, youthful pioneers leave the elderly behind on New England's cold and rocky shores. In its companion, they enter the Golden State, capes billowing, as an allegorical figure of California and a joyous chorus of native sons welcome them to a promised land replete with oranges, grapes, and gold. Playing the losers in this pageant, natty Spanish explorers and a pious padre bring up the rear. California Indians and Asians have fallen out of the picture frame altogether.

Inspired by depictions of Roman triumphal marches, Du Mond's figures in these two panels are overwhelmingly Anglo-Saxon and predominately male. He gives viewers an ascensional view of history, imbuing the present state of California—and the nation to which it nominally belongs—with the legitimacy and mythic destiny of heroic argonauts. No conflict mars the westward course of empire.[1]

Carey McWilliams filled in the many omissions from that kind of comforting history. Had *he* painted those murals, they would have featured not a march but a rout of races and classes in a land beleaguered by their growing demands upon it. More than anyone of his time, McWilliams peeled back the giddy and gaudy orange-crate label of official state history to reveal the disturbing reality of what California is and has been for those not included in Du Mond's parade.

That he did so *when* he did yanks the rug from beneath an argument dear to cultural reactionaries—namely, that historians should not attempt to impose the values of a presumably more enlightened age upon the benighted past. McWilliams's prodigious output of writing demonstrates that the demand for social justice is nothing new, that radical voices in the past sought the root cause and remedy of social problems then as they do today. And just as they are today, such voices were usually maligned and marginalized by those who, through their ownership of the mass media, determined where the mainstream would flow. For those of us who lean unapologetically to the left as it flows ever farther to the right, encountering the writings of Carey McWilliams is like running into an old friend in a foreign city.

If I were to paint the unruly and often pugnacious procession to which McWilliams belongs, I would include Josiah Royce, Henry George, John Muir, Fremont Older, Charlotte Perkins, Upton Sinclair, Delilah Beasley, Lincoln Steffens, and Robinson Jeffers. Each in his or her own way courageously challenged received wisdom and common practice, and most paid a price for doing so. Doubtless there were many more, such as the Yurok champion of Indian rights Lucy Thompson, whose race or class or inarticulateness in English denied them the public forum. Socialist Michael Harrington wrote that such people constitute the secret history of the United States.

McWilliams wrote much of that history, giving voice to the voiceless and holding a mirror up to a state which, like Norma Desmond, the faded star in *Sunset Boulevard*, had convinced itself that it was just as lovely and alluring as yellowing press clips said it was. No one in California (and few, if any, on the national scene) could match McWilliams for his rare combination of intellect and scholarship informed by an ethical vision and conveyed with impassioned eloquence. Like Tocqueville, he was capable of piercing cant and fashion to analyze the broader forces of the dream-driven culture that surrounded him. Why, for example, are Anglos driven to project an Hispanic Shangri-la onto the California they took from Mexico? Could they, he wondered, be attempting to flee from what they had made of the spoils of war? Of an elite group of Santa Barbara *caballeros* called the *rancheros visitadores*, McWilliams noted: "Ostensibly a gay affair, the annual ride represents a rather grim and desperate effort to escape the bonds of a culture that neither satisfies nor pleases. Actually there is something rather pathetic about the spectacle of these frustrated businessmen cantering forth in search of ersatz weekend romance, evoking a past that never existed to cast some glamour on an equally unreal today."[2]

This collection documents the astonishing array of topics tackled by McWilliams. Issues of race and class, the oppression of labor, and the structural causes of endemic poverty and hunger in a land so apparently rich fascinated him. In his essay on utopian movements, he introduces us to a bizarre cast of charismatic characters and their followers, attempting to explain why California has provided such fertile soil for cults, and to determine which of those movements might sprout bona fide fascism. McWilliams found such leaders as Aimee Semple McPherson and Guy W. Ballard to be far less dangerous than the men who occupy executive suites: "The real crackpots of Los Angeles in the thirties were the individuals who ordered tons of oranges and vegetables dumped in the bed of the Los Angeles River, while thousands of people were unemployed, hungry, and homeless."[3] More potentially dangerous still, he felt, were the politicians who served those men and had their support: "A dapper little man with an astonishing capacity for petty malice, Nixon might best be described as a distinctly third-rate Tom Dewey. In his campaign he enjoys the support of virtually every newspaper in the state."[4]

He understood the indignities and violence faced daily by Asians, Mexicans, blacks, and Okies, as he did the powerful political and economic interests which the scapegoating of those groups served. He knew how such animosities led to individual and collective debasement, and on to further violence. The bombing of Pearl Harbor and the war in the Pacific were at least partly the result a long history of racial provocation of which few Americans were aware: "Once America was committed to a policy of discrimination based on race, national self-consciousness was stimulated throughout the Far East."[5] From that point, collective violence became inevitable.

McWilliams had a keen sensitivity to the peculiarities of the California land and climate, to its limitations as well as its bounty and its beauty. One might call him a proto-environmentalist, for he knew that land—and land *value* in a monopolized market economy—is essential for understanding the state and the ways in which it has shaped and been shaped by the myriad peoples who have sought to own it. Newcomers, he observed, "have never understood the crucial importance of water," for that would suggest a limit that "Southern California has always been extremely reluctant to discuss [as] its basic weakness."[6] The myth of boundless abundance so necessary to lure more immigrants to California might well be the state's undoing, he predicted, for there is a nearly perfect correlation between California's steady increase in population and the number of forest fires, floods, and other such "natural" disasters.

Like a psychiatrist seeking the root causes of family dysfunction, Mc-Williams plunged deeper into issues of land ownership in his attempt to understand and explain California's turbulent history. He knew that shortly after the Gold Rush, a very few individuals had used whatever means necessary to transfer immense tracts of the public domain to themselves and to their heirs and corporations, and that clandestine land monopoly had continued to decisively shape California. The plantation economy of the Deep South was therefore reproduced in the Far West, with the same deep division between a privileged oligarchy and its landless peasantry further complicated by racial animosity. With that division came a reign of rural and urban terror necessary to keep the powerless in their place—lynchings, beatings, night riders, enforced ignorance, and genuine concentration camps suggesting tendencies to a native fascism—that, like the shortage of water, belied the popular image of California as the happiest place on earth.

McWilliams further proposed that the ties between the South and West were political as well as cultural. In "The Long-Suffering Chinese," he brilliantly analyzed how an axis of leaders in both regions collaborated to blackmail the federal government into condoning the legal suppression of blacks in the South and Asians on the Pacific Coast. Twenty-three years later, writing for *The Nation*, he decoded the political rhetoric of a pivotal election and concluded that thinly veiled racism pervaded campaign rhetoric: "Most [Californians] won't talk about it at all if they can escape it. They don't want the nation to know—they don't want to admit to themselves—that the number-one state may elect Ronald Reagan Governor in order to 'keep the Negro in his place.'"[7] Here was the Southern Strategy *in utero*.

It is as a public intellectual that I most admire McWilliams, for he sought not only to analyze problems but to move his readers to remedy them, and for that he needed a large audience. Unlike the hermetic academic prose of today, his writing is as clear as it is impassioned and informed, masterfully incorporating anecdote and telling quotations to engage the interest and concern of middle-class readers even in such seemingly remote subjects as the working conditions of Mexican migrant workers. The French agricultural economist Jean-Pierre Berlan wrote that he had, after discovering *Factories in the Field*, "quickly realized that there was more theoretical depth in this book than in all the doctoral dissertations of the Department of Agricultural Economics at the University of California!"[8] For all that theoretical depth, McWilliams's eloquence made *Factories* a best-seller when it was published in 1939.

The depression, McWilliams wrote in his autobiography, radicalized him as it did so many others, and by the time *Factories in the Field* appeared, that group of men and women were not just documenting current events but actively shaping them. Kevin Starr describes the dense synergies in which McWilliams played such a crucial role:

> [Agricultural economist] Paul Taylor went into the field at about the same time that Carey McWilliams went into the archives. Taylor, in turn, recruited Dorothea Lange as a photo-reporter. Lange's photographs, in turn, stimulated Steinbeck's investigations and helped him frame his perspective. Carey McWilliams, meanwhile, was having his perspective shaped by Steinbeck's strike novel *In Dubious Battle* (1936) and Steinbeck's reportage as well as by Lange's photographs. John Ford, in turn, obtained the black-and-white look of his film version of *The Grapes of Wrath* from the Farm Security Administration photographs taken by Lange and others. In 1940 the Public Affairs Committee of New York issued Paul Taylor's collected reports under the title *Adrift on the Land,* illustrating it with stills from John Ford's film. In *Adrift on the Land,* Taylor refers to both Steinbeck and McWilliams as parallel commentaries and partial sources. It was now time for government reports to participate in this synergy—to rise to the level of documentary art.[9]

We will never know what might have become of that progressive movement reborn with the enabling momentum given it by Roosevelt's New Deal, for like the first wave of progressivism, it was aborted by the outbreak of war and the Red Scare that followed. Nonetheless, McWilliams continued to play a vitally important role from New York as editor of *The Nation,* while his books went on to teach and to guide those who believe, as did he, that the ideal of justice and security as human birthrights was worth working toward. Among others, they inspired a Mexican field hand named César Chévez, who recalled:

> Although I had been a farmworker traveling the migrant streams for many years and knew through bitter experience what prejudice and discrimination were, these books gave

me whole new insights into the forces that create wealth and poverty. They provided a link to the past and helped me to focus my determination to improve the lives of the farmworkers into strategies and tactics and a plan for action.[10]

An inscription on the frieze of the old state courts building in Sacramento enjoins those who enter to "bring me men to match my mountains." Frank Du Mond painted those men in his equally inspirational—and equally facile—murals. McWilliams, by contrast, goads us to grow up. California could not, he believed, produce anything meriting the term of civilization until it acknowledged the dark complexities of its past, the injustices of its present, and the severe limitations of a future predicated on the infantile fantasy of endless growth. "California needs men who can see beyond its mountains," he wrote, "men who can see the entire West and who realize that, as with all good things, there comes a time when the gold runs out."[11] We had such a man in Carey McWilliams; he remains the mountain to match.

GRAY BRECHIN

June 2001

ENDNOTES

1. Du Mond's murals were moved to San Francisco's Main Library when the fair closed. They were removed when the Asian Art Museum gutted that building and, like so much of the Panama-Pacific International Exhibition art, are now in permanent storage.
2. "The Growth of a Legend," p. 14 of this volume.
3. "The Politics of Utopia," p. 61 of this volume.
4. "Bungling in California," p. 229 of this volume.
5. *Brothers under the Skin,* by Carey McWilliams (Boston: Little, Brown & Co., 1946).
6. Water! Water! Water!" p. 156 of this volume.
7. "How to Succeed With the Backlash," p. 252 of this volume.
8. "Carey McWilliams," by Ralph Engelman in *Dictionary of Literary Biography,* vol. 137: American Magazine Journalists, 1900–1960, ed. Sam G. Riley. The Gale Group, 1994.
9. *Endangered Dreams: The Great Depression in California*, by Kevin Starr (New York: Oxford University Press, 1996).
10. *California: The Great Exception,* ed. Carey McWilliams (Berkeley: University of California Press, 1998).
11. Ibid.

1

MECCA OF THE MIRACULOUS

…into a Limbo large and broad, since called the Paradise of Fools, to few unknown…

—John Milton, "Paradise Lost"

The Growth of a Legend

1946

CONSIDERING the long, dark record of Indian mistreatment in Southern California, it is difficult to account for the curious legend that has developed in the region about the well-being of the natives under Mission rule. According to this legend, the Missions were havens of happiness and contentment for the Indians, places of song, laughter, good food, beautiful languor, and mystical adoration of the Christ. What is still more astonishing is the presence in the legend of an element of masochism, with the Americans, who manufactured the legend, taking upon themselves full responsibility for the criminal mistreatment of the Indian and completely exonerating the Franciscans. "In the old and happy days of Church domination and priestly rule," writes one Protestant historian, "there had been no 'Indian question'! That came only after American 'civilization' took from the red men their lands and gave them nothing in return."

Equally baffling, at first blush, is the intense preoccupation of Southern California with its Mission-Spanish past. Actually, one of the principal charms of Southern California, as Farnsworth Crowder has pointed out, is that it is not overburdened with historical distractions. "As against any European country, certain parts of the United States and even neighboring Mexico," writes Mr. Crowder, "human culture has left relatively few marks, monuments, and haunts over the vast virginal face of the state. Almost any square block of London is more drenched with flavors of the past than the whole of Los Angeles. The desert areas and valleys cannot evoke any such awareness of human antiquity and the genesis of great religions and civilizations as can

3

the borderlands of the Mediterranean. No Wordsworths, no Caesars, no Pharaohs have made their homes here. The Californian simply cannot feed upon the fruits and signs of yesterday as can a Roman, a Parisian, an Oxonian." And yet this is precisely what he attempts to do. The newness of the land itself seems, in fact, to have compelled, to have demanded, the evocation of a mythology which could give people a sense of continuity in a region long characterized by rapid social dislocations. And of course it would be a tourist, a goggle-eyed, umbrella-packing tourist, who first discovered the past of Southern California and peopled it with curious creatures of her own invention.

"H.H."

Someday the Los Angeles Chamber of Commerce should erect a great bronze statue of Helen Hunt Jackson at the entrance to Cajon Pass. Beneath the statue should be inscribed no flowery dedication, but the simple inscription: "H. H.—In Gratitude!" For little, plump, fair-skinned, blue-eyed Helen Hunt Jackson, "H. H." as she was known to every resident of Southern California, was almost solely responsible for the evocation of its Mission past, and it was she who catapulted the lowly Digger Indian* of Southern California into the empyrean.

    Born in Amherst on October 15, 1830, Helen Maria Fiske became a successful writer of trite romances and sentimental poems quite unlike those written by her friend and neighbor Emily Dickinson. She was married in 1852 to Lieutenant Edward Bissell Hunt of the Coast Survey, who died a few years after the marriage. In later years, she married William Sharpless Jackson, a wealthy banker and railroad executive of Colorado Springs. It is rather ironic to note that Mrs. Jackson, who became one of the most ardent freelance apologists for the Catholic Church in America, was a confirmed anti-Papist until she visited California. As might have been expected, she first became interested in Indians while attending a tea party in Boston. At this tea, she met Standing Bear and Bright Eyes, who were lecturing on the grievous wrongs suffered by the Poncas tribe. At the time of this meeting, Mrs. Jackson was forty-nine years of age, bubbling with enthusiasm, full of rhymes. Quick to catch the "aboriginal contagion," which had begun to spread among

---

* There is no tribe of "Digger" Indians; the term was applied to California Indians during the Gold Rush era, presumably because digging sticks were a ubiquitous tool for gathering food. The term has lasted into the 21st century but is now considered derogatory.

the writers of American romances, she immediately usurped the position of defender of the Poncas tribe and thereafter no more was heard of Standing Bear and Bright Eyes. In 1881 *Harper's* published her well-known work, *A Century of Dishonor*, which did much to arouse a new, although essentially spurious, interest in the American Indian.

In the spring of 1872, Mrs. Jackson had made a brief visit, as a tourist, to the northern part of California. Later she made three trips, as a tourist, to Southern California: in the winter of 1881–1882, the spring of 1883, and the winter, spring, and summer of 1884–1885. It scarcely needs to be emphasized that her knowledge of California, and of the Mission Indians, was essentially that of the tourist and casual visitor. Although she did prepare a valuable report on the Mission Indians, based on a field trip that she made with Abbot Kinney of Los Angeles, most of her material about Indians was second-hand and consisted, for the greater part, of odds and ends of gossip, folk tales, and Mission-inspired allegories of one kind or another.

She had originally been sent to Southern California by *Century* magazine to write some stories about the Missions, which, according to the illustrator who accompanied her, were to be "enveloped in the mystery and poetry of romance." In Southern California she became deliriously enamored of the Missions, then in a state of general disrepair and neglect, infested with countless swallows and pigeons, overrun by sheep and goats, and occasionally inhabited by stray dogs and wandering Indians. "In the sunny, delicious, winterless California air," these crumbling ruins, with their walled gardens and broken bells, their vast cemeteries and caved-in wells, exerted a potent romantic influence on Mrs. Jackson's highly susceptible nature. Out of these brief visits to Southern California came *Ramona*, the first novel written about the region, which became, after its publication in 1884, one of the most widely read American novels of the time. It was this novel which firmly established the Mission legend in Southern California.

When the book was first published, it provoked a storm of protest in the Southland. Egged on by various civic groups, the local critics denounced it as a tissue of falsehoods, a travesty on history, a damnable libel on Southern California. But the book was perfectly timed, providentially timed, to coincide with the great invasion of homeseekers and tourists to the region. As these hordes of winter tourists began to express a lively interest in visiting "Ramona's land," Southern California experienced an immediate change of attitude and, overnight, became passionately Ramona-conscious. Beginning about 1887, a Ramona promotion of fantastic proportions began to be organized in the region.

Picture postcards by the tens of thousands were published showing "the school attended by Ramona," "the original of Ramona," "the place where Ramona was married," and various shots of the "Ramona country." Since the local chambers of commerce could not, or would not, agree upon the locale of the novel—one school of thought insisted that the Camulos rancho was the scene of the more poignant passages, while still another school insisted that the Hacienda Guajome was the authentic locale—it was not long before the scenic postcards depicting the Ramona country had come to embrace all of Southern California. In the eighties, the Southern Pacific tourist and excursion trains regularly stopped at Camulos so that the wide-eyed Bostonians, guidebooks in hand, might detrain, visit the rancho, and bounce up and down on "the bed in which Ramona slept." Thousands of Ramona baskets, plaques, pincushions, pillows, and souvenirs of all sorts were sold in every curio shop in California. Few tourists left the region without having purchased a little replica of the "bells that rang when Ramona was married." To keep the tourist interest alive, local press agents for fifty years engaged in a synthetic controversy over the identities of the "originals" for the universally known characters in the novel. Some misguided Indian women began to take the promotion seriously and had themselves photographed—copyright reserved—as "the original Ramona." A bibliography of the newspaper stories, magazine articles, and pamphlets written about some aspect of the Ramona legend would fill a volume. Four husky volumes of Ramonana appeared in Southern California: *The Real Ramona* (1900), by D. A. Hufford; *Through Ramona's Country* (1908), the official, classic document, by George Wharton James; *Ramona's Homeland* (1914), by Margaret V. Allen; and *The True Story of Ramona* (1914), by C. C. Davis and W. A. Anderson.

From 1884 to date, the Los Angeles Public Library has purchased over 1,000 copies of *Ramona*. Thirty years after publication, the same library had a constant waiting list for 105 circulating copies of the book. The sales to date total 601,636 copies, deriving from a Regular Edition, a Monterey Edition (in two volumes), a De Luxe Edition, a Pasadena Edition, a Tourist Edition, a Holiday Art Edition, and a Gift Edition. Hundreds of unoffending Southern California babies have been named Ramona. A townsite was named Ramona. And in San Diego thousands of people make a regular pilgrimage to "Ramona's Marriage Place," where the True Vow Keepers Clubs—made up of couples who have been married fifty years or longer—hold their annual picnics. The Native Daughters of the Golden West have named one of their "parlors," or lodges, after Ramona. The name Ramona appears in the corporate title of fifty or more businesses currently operating in Los Angeles. Two of Mrs. Jackson's articles for *Century*, "Father Junipero and His Work" and "The Present Condition of the Mission Indians of Southern California," were for years required reading in the public schools of California. Reprints of Henry Sandham's illustrations for *Ramona* are familiar items in Southern California homes, hotels, restaurants, and places of business. In 1914 one of the Ramona historians truthfully said that "Mrs. Jackson's name is familiar to almost every human being in Southern California, from the little three-year-old tot, who has her choice juvenile stories read to him, to the aged grandmother who sheds tears of sympathy for Ramona." Two generations of Southern California children could recite from memory the stanzas from Ina Coolbrith's verses to Helen Hunt Jackson, often ornately framed on the walls of Southern California homes:

> There, with her dimpled, lifted hands,
> Parting the mustard's golden plumes,
> The dusky maid, Ramona, stands,
> Amid the sea of blooms.
> And Alessandro, type of all
> His broken tribe, for evermore
> An exile, hears the stranger call
> Within his father's door.

Translated into all known languages, *Ramona* has also been dramatized. The play based on the novel was first presented at the Mason Opera House in Los Angeles on February 27, 1905, the dramatization having been written by Miss Virginia Calhoun and General Johnstone Jones. Commenting upon Miss Calhoun's performance in the role of Ramona, the *Los Angeles Times* reported that "in the lighter parts she held a fascination that was tempered with gentleness and playfulness. Her slender figure, graceful and pliant as a willow, swayed with every light touch of feeling, and the deeper tragic climaxes she met in a way to win tears from the eyes of many." Over the years, three motion-picture versions of the novel have appeared. In 1887, George Wharton James, who did much to keep the Ramona promotion moving along, "tramped every foot of the territory covered by Mrs. Jackson," interviewing the people she had interviewed, photographing the scenes she had photographed, and "sifting the evidence" she had collected. His thick tome on the Ramona country is still a standard item in all Southern California libraries. For twenty-five years, the chambers of commerce of the Southland kept this fantastic promotion alive and flourishing. When interest seemed to be lagging, new stories were concocted. Thus on March 7, 1907, the *Los Angeles Times* featured, as a major news item, a story about "Condino, the newly discovered and only child of Ramona." In 1921 the enterprising chamber of commerce of Hemet, California, commissioned Garnet Holme to write a pageant about Ramona. Each year since 1921 the pageant has been produced in late April or early May in the heart of the Ramona country, by the chamber of commerce. At the last count, two hundred thousand people had witnessed the pageant.

The legendary quality of Mrs. Jackson's famous novel came about through the amazing way in which she made elegant pre-Raphaelite characters out of Ramona and "the half-breed Alessandro." Such Indians were surely never seen upon this earth. Furthermore, the story extolled the Franciscans in the most extravagant manner and placed the entire onus of the mistreatment of the Indians upon the noisy and vulgar gringos. At the same time, the sad plight of Ramona and Alessandro got curiously mixed up, in the telling, with the plight of the "fine old Spanish families." These fine old Spanish families, who were among the most flagrant exploiters of the Indian in Southern California, appeared in the novel as only slightly less considerate of his welfare than the Franciscans. Despite its legendary aspects, however, the *Ramona* version of the Indians of Southern California is now firmly implanted in the mythology of the region. It is this legend which largely accounts for the "sacred" as distinguished from the "profane" history of the Indian in Southern California.

It should be said to Mrs. Jackson's credit, however, that she did arouse a momentary flurry of interest in the Mission Indians. Her report on these Indians, which appeared in all editions of *A Century of Dishonor* after 1883, is still a valuable document. As a result of her work, Charles Fletcher Lummis founded the Sequoya League in Los Angeles in 1902, "to make better Indians"; and, through the activities of the league, the three hundred Indians who were evicted from the Warner Ranch in 1901 were eventually relocated on lands purchased by the government. Aside from the relocation of these Indians, however, nothing much came of Mrs. Jackson's work in Southern California, for the region accepted the charming Ramona as a folk figure but completely rejected the Indians still living in the area. A government report of 1920 indicated that 90 percent of the residents of the sections in which Indians still live in Southern California were wholly ignorant about their Indian neighbors and that deep local prejudice against them still prevailed.

At the sacred level, it is the half-breed Alessandro who best symbolizes the Indian heritage of Southern California. At the secular level, however, one must turn to the local annals to select more appropriate symbols. There is, for example, the character Polonia, an Indian of great stature and strength, whose eyes had been burned out of their sockets. Clad in a tattered blanket, this blind Indian was a familiar figure on the dusty streets of Los Angeles in the 1850s and 1860s. And there was Viejo Cholo, or Old Half-Breed, who wore a pair of linen pantaloons and used a sheet for a mantle. His cane was a broom handle; his lunch counter, the swill basket. Viejo Cholo was succeeded, as the principal Indian eccentric of Los Angeles, by another half-breed, Pinikahti. A tiny man, Pinikahti was only four feet in height. Badly pock-marked, he had a flat nose and stubby beard. He was generally attired, notes Harris Newmark, "in a well-worn straw hat, the top of which was missing, and his long, straight hair stuck out in clumps and snarls. A woolen under-shirt and a pair of overalls completed his costume, while his toes, as a rule, protruded from his enormous boots." Playing Indian tunes on a flute made out of reeds from the bed of the Los Angeles River, Pinikahti used to dance in the streets of the town for pennies, nickels, and dimes, or a glass of aguardi ente. Polonia, Viejo Cholo, and Pinikahti, these are the real symbols of the Indian heritage of Southern California.

REDISCOVERY OF THE MISSIONS

With the great Anglo invasion of Southern California after 1880, the Spanish background of the region was, for a time, almost wholly forgotten. "For many years," wrote Harry Carr, "the traditions of Los Angeles were junked by the scorn of the conquering gringos. When I was a schoolboy in Los Angeles, I never heard of Ortega or Caspar de Portolá or Juan Bautista de Anza." And then, with the publication of *Ramona*, the Spanish background began to be rediscovered, with the same false emphasis and from the same crass motives that had characterized the rediscovery of the Indian. Both rediscoveries, that of the Indian and that of the Spaniard, occurred between 1883 and 1888, at precisely the period when the great real-estate promotion of Southern California was being organized.

Insofar as the Spanish saga is concerned, it all began in 1888, when, as John A. Berger has written, "the romantic people of Southern California," under the leadership of Charles Fletcher Lummis, formed an Association for the Preservation of the Missions (which later became the Landmarks Club). With the gradual restoration of the Missions, a highly romantic conception of the Spanish period began to be cultivated, primarily for the benefit of the incoming tides of tourists, who were routed to the Missions much as they were routed to the mythical site of Ramona's birthplace. A flood of books began to appear about the Missions, with Mrs. Jackson's *Glimpses of California and the Missions* (1883) being the volume that inspired the whole movement. It was followed, after a few years, by George Wharton James's *In and Out of the Old Missions*, which, for a quarter of a century, was the "classic" in this field. My own guess would be that not a year has passed since 1900 without the publication of some new volume about the Missions. Not only has a library of books been written about the Missions, but each individual Mission has had its historians. Books have been written about the architecture of the Missions, about the Mission bells, about the Franciscans (notably Father Junipero Serra, a popular saint in Southern California), and about the wholly synthetic Mission furniture. In fact, the Mission-Spanish background of the region has been so strongly emphasized that, as Max Miller has written, "The past is almost as scrambled as the present, and almost as indefinite…the whole thing got mixed up." With each new book about the Missions came a new set of etchings and some new paintings. In 1880, William Keith painted all of the Missions of California. He was followed by the artist [Henry Chapman] Ford of Santa Barbara, who, in 1890, completed his etchings of the Franciscan establishments. Since 1890, the Missions have been painted by Jorgenson, Edward Deakin, Alexander F. Harmer, William Sparks, Gutzon Borglum, Elmer Wachtel, Minnie Tingle, and a host of other artists.

In 1902, Frank Miller, owner of the Glenwood Cottage Inn at Riverside, with funds provided by Henry Huntington, began to construct the famous Mission Inn. Designed by Myron Hunt, the Mission Inn was built wing by wing around the old adobe Glenwood Cottage, until the new structure covered an entire block. Once completed, the inn gave the initial fillip to Mission architecture, so called, and soon Missionesque and Moorish structures began to dot the Southern California landscape. It was here, in the Mission Inn, that John Steven McGroarty wrote the *Mission Play*, for which he was deservedly decorated by the Pope. The play had its premiere at San Gabriel on a warm spring evening, April 29, 1912, under the sponsorship of the Princess Lazarovic-Hrebrelanovic of Serbia, with a cast of "one hundred descendants of the Old Spanish families." On the opening night, "queer chugging noises filled the air and the acrid smoke from burnt gasoline floated over the ancient Mission and the little adobes that nestled around it. It was the first big outpouring of automobiles that San Gabriel had ever had." The elite of Southern California turned out, en masse, for the premiere. The play, of course, was an enormous success. McGroarty boasted that it had been seen by 2.5 million people, a world's record. During the sixteen consecutive seasons that it played at San Gabriel Mission, over 2,600 performances were recorded. Later the play was institutionalized, under official sponsorship, and became an enormous tourist attraction. A tourist who went to California and failed to see Catalina Island, Mt. Wilson, and the *Mission Play* was considered to have something wrong with his head. In recognition of his great services to Southern California, "Singing John" [McGroarty], the songster of the green Verdugo hills, was made poet laureate of California on May 17, 1933. Needless to say, the play perpetuated the Helen Hunt Jackson version of the Indians, the Spanish dons, and the Franciscans.

As a curious postscript to the growth of this amazing legend, it should be pointed out that the Catholic Church played virtually no role whatever in the Ramona-Mission revival in Southern California, which, from its inception, was a strictly Protestant promotion. As a matter of fact, Abbot Kinney, who took Mrs. Jackson through the Indian country in the eighties, later wrote that "the archbishops, bishops, and priests of those days were not, as a rule, much concerned about the condition of the Indians [theoretically still wards of the church] and the old Mission churches. Many of them were Catalans, who had little or no sympathy with the high ideals of the noble Franciscans. We actually found some of these priests, or those in higher authority, selling part of the lands that had originally been held by the Franciscans in trust for the Indians—not one foot of which belonged to the Church." With the exception of a few Irish priests, such as Father Joseph O'Keefe and Father John O'Sullivan, the Catholic Church did not figure prominently in the movement to restore the Missions. Even today the expensively restored Missions, as J. Russell Smith has pointed out, are "little more than carefully preserved historical curiosities and penny-catchers." Since McGroarty was a converted Catholic, however, it can be said that through this faithful son the Church did exert considerable influence on the formation of the Mission legend.

"Why is it," asked James L. Duff some years ago in *Commonweal*, "that such a distinctly non-Catholic city as Los Angeles should evince such a consistent emotional preoccupation with its Catholic past?" Scrutinizing the local directory, Mr. Duff reported that the word "mission" was to be found as part of the corporate name of over a hundred business enterprises in Los Angeles. He was also surprised to find that such expressions as "in the days of the dons" and "in the footsteps of the padres" had become community colloquialisms in Southern California. The dominantly Catholic city of San Francisco, with its Mission Dolores, has never been greatly interested in the Missions. The incongruity is only greater by reason of the fact that Los Angeles is not merely non-Catholic; it can scarcely be called a California city, except in a geographical sense. It is a conglomeration of newcomers and has always had the lowest percentage of native-born Californians of any city in the state. Paradoxically, the less Catholic a community is in Southern California, the more the Mission past has been emphasized. The incongruity, however, is never noticed. Not one of the numerous Pope-baiting fundamentalist pastors of Southern California has ever objected to this community-wide adoration of the Missions. "Here," writes Mr. Duff, "is a city that is almost militantly non-Catholic, audaciously energetic, worshipping Progress, adulating the tinseled world of motion pictures, yet looking with dreaming eyes upon a day and a philosophy of life with which it has neither understanding nor communion, vaguely hoping that the emotion it is evoking is nostalgic."

Not only is Los Angeles a non-Catholic city, but, popular legend to the contrary, it is not a city of churches. Recently, the *Los Angeles Times* published an editorial under the caption "What! No Church Bells?" The occasion was the May 13, 1945, celebration of V-E Day when, much to the astonishment of the *Times*, it was discovered that "church bells are exceedingly scarce in Los Angeles." At the present time, a movement is under way, sponsored by the *Times*, to bring church bells to Los Angeles, so that "thousands of residents of Los Angeles who formerly lived in Eastern and Midwestern states" may, "on the clear Sabbath mornings," be called to worship by the pealing of bells. "To hear that call again," comments the *Times,* "in their new home, would tend to keep them in touch with their childhood and with the simple, comforting faith with which childhood is blessed, but which sometimes is neglected and all but forgotten," particularly in Southern California.

With the rediscovery of the Catholic-Mission past, the same split occurred in the Spanish tradition of the region that had occurred in relation to its Indian background. Just as Ramona and Alessandro became the sacred symbols of the Indian past, so the Spanish dons, rather than the Mexicano *paisanos*, became the sacred symbols of the Spanish past. A glance at almost any of the popular novels of Stewart Edward White will show, for example, how the romantic side of this tradition has been emphasized to the detriment—in fact, to the total neglect—of its realistic latter-day manifestations. Despite all the restorations, revivals, pageants, plays, paintings, museum collections, and laboriously gathered materials about this Spanish past, it was not until 1945 that a serious effort was launched to teach Spanish, as a language of the region, in the public schools.

Today there is scarcely a community in Southern California, however, that does not have its annual "Spanish fiesta," of which the Santa Barbara fiesta is the most impressive. Attending one of the early Santa Barbara fiestas, Duncan Aikman reported that "every man, woman, and child who owed any allegiance to Santa Barbara was in costume....Shoe salesmen and grocery clerks served you with a bit of scarlet braid on their trouser seams. Paunchy realtors and insurance solicitors full of mental mastery dashed about town in gaudy sashes. Deacons of the total immersion sects sported, at the least, a bit of crimson frill around their hatbands. High-school boys scurried by, their heads gorgeously bound in scarfs and bandanas...The very street-car conductors wore Spanish epaulettes and earrings and a look of grievance even more bitter than usual. Women wore mantillas and an apparently official uniform in the way of a waist of yellow, black, and scarlet, so universally that you could tell the outland females by their native American costumes. The Mexican population dug up its old finery and musical instruments and paraded the sidewalks with the timid air of reasserting their importance after long abeyance." Once the fiesta is over, however, the Mexicans retreat to their *barrios*, the costumes are carefully put away for the balance of the year, and the grotesque Spanish spoken in the streets during the fiesta is heard no more. This particular attempt to revive the Mexican *Fiesta de la Primavera*, like most similar attempts in Southern California, was first launched in the mid-twenties, its immediate motivation in Santa Barbara being the popularly sensed need to inject a note of good cheer in the Santa Barbarans after the earthquake of 1924. The Santa Barbara fiesta is often highlighted by some extraordinary antic. Some years ago, for example, Cedric Gibbons and Dolores del Rio of the motion-picture colony, dressed in fiesta costumes and astride their handsome palominos, were the first couple to be married on horse-back, a type of marriage ceremony now a regular feature of the fiesta.

About the most incongruous ceremonial revival of this sort in Southern California is the annual ride of the *rancheros visitadores*. This particular re-vival is based on the alleged practice of the rancheros, in former years, of making the round of the ranchos in the area, paying a visit to each in turn. "In May 1930," to quote from the *Santa Barbara Guide,* "some sixty-five riders assembled for the first cavalcade. Golden palominos and proud Arabian thor-oughbreds, carrying silver-mounted tack, brushed stirrups with shaggy mus-tangs from the range. Emerging from the heavy gray mist of a reluctant day, they cantered with casual grace down the old familiar trails of the Santa Ynez, to converge in Santa Barbara....Here, amid the tolling of bells, the tinkling of trappings, and the whinnying of horses, the brown-robed friars blessed them and bade them *"Vayan con dios!*...This was the start of the first revival of the annual ride of the *rancheros visitadores."*

Since this auspicious beginning, the affair has steadily increased in pomp and circumstance. Nowadays it is invariably reported in the Southern Cali-fornia press as a major social event of the year. A careful scrutiny of the names of these fancily dressed *visitadores*—these gaily costumed Rotarians—reveals that Leo Carrillo is about the only rider whose name carries a faint echo of the past and he is about as Mexican as the ceremony is Spanish. Osten-sibly a gay affair, the annual ride represents a rather grim and desperate effort to escape from the bonds of a culture that neither satisfies nor pleases. Actu-ally, there is something rather pathetic about the spectacle of these frustrated businessmen cantering forth in search of ersatz weekend romance, evoking a past that never existed to cast some glamour on an equally unreal today.

All attempted revivals of Spanish folkways in Southern California are similarly ceremonial and ritualistic, a part of the sacred—rather than the pro-fane—life of the region. The 3,279 Mexicans who live in Santa Barbara are doubtless more bewildered by these annual Spanish hijinks than any other group in the community. For here is a community that generously and lav-ishly supports the "Old Spanish Fiesta"—and the wealth of the *rancheros visitadores* is apparent for all to see—but which consistently rejects proposals to establish a low-cost housing project for its Mexican residents. However, there is really nothing inconsistent about this attitude, for it merely reflects the manner in which the sacred aspects of the romantic past have been completely divorced from their secular connotations. The residents of Santa

Barbara firmly believe, of course, that the Spanish past is dead, extinct, vanished. In their thinking, the Mexicans living in Santa Barbara have no connection with this past. They just happen to be living in Santa Barbara. To be sure, many of them have names, such as Cota or Gutierrez, that should stir memories of the *dolce far niente* period. But these names are no longer important. They belong to the profane, and happily forgotten, side of the tradition. The sacred side of this tradition, as represented in the beautifully restored Mission, is worshipped by all alike without regard to caste, class, or religious affiliation. The restored Mission is a much better, a less embarrassing, symbol of the past than the Mexican field worker or the ragamuffin *pachucos* of Los Angeles.

Mecca of the Miraculous

1947

CALIFORNIA PROPHETS, like its geraniums, grow large, rank, and garish. In this state where imported llamas browse on the hillsides near San Simeon, where oranges are sold in Chinese pagodas, and bootblacks, such as the Duke of Hollywood, wear top hats and crimson capes, eccentrics flourish in abundance. Strange influences, occult and psychic, esoteric and mundane, undeniably are at work. What are these cults that to many are the state's most amazing characteristic? What forms and shapes emerge from the smoke of dreams, the cloudy occultism of California?

None quite compares, in charm and wonder, with Mighty "I AM." A weird brew of Theosophy, Rosicrucianism, New Thought, Buck Rogers, and Superman, the "I AM" ideology—the quotes must *always* be placed around the title—was dreamed up by Guy W. Ballard and his wife, Edna. After a career as a paper hanger, stock salesman, and mine promoter, Ballard came to Los Angeles around 1932. Two years later he published, under the nom de plume of Godfré Ray King, a work entitled *Unveiled Mysteries*.

The deity of the cult is the Ascended Master, Saint Germain. As Ballard tells the story, he first met Saint Germain (the "Saint" must *never* be abbreviated) on the slopes of Mount Shasta. Appearing out of the void, Saint Germain offered Ballard a cup of "pure electronic essence." On drinking the essence and chewing a tiny wafer of "concentrated energy," Ballard was enveloped by a "white flame which formed a circle about fifty feet in diameter." Lifted into the stratosphere, Ballard and Saint Germain were whizzed through time and space, visiting, among other places, the buried cities of the Amazon, France, Egypt, Karnak, Luxor, the fabled Inca cities,

17

the Royal Tetons, and Yellowstone National Park. Wherever they journeyed, they found an abundance of treasure that, as a mine promoter, Ballard had never succeeded in discovering: jewels, Spanish pirate gold, rubies, pearls, diamonds, gold bullion, casks of silver—the plunder of antiquity. Unbelievable as it may sound, this revelation, at $2.50 a copy, sold by the thousands in Southern California. The Ballards were soon ensconced in a great barnlike tabernacle where a blazing neon light flashed word of the Mighty "I AM" presence.

Then the Ballards added to their merchandise: a monthly magazine; books; photographs of Ballard, The Messenger; phonograph recordings of the "music of the spheres," composed by Ballard; lectures; charts of the "Magic Presence" for twelve dollars; a steel engraving of the "Cosmic Being, Orion, better known as the Old Man of the Hills," for two dollars; special "I AM" decree binders; "I AM" signet rings (twelve dollars); a special electrical device equipped with colored lights called "Flame in Action," which sold, in varying sizes, for fifty dollars and two hundred dollars. Finally, there appeared a "New Age Cold Cream."

After the death of Ballard, his wife was indicted and convicted in the federal courts of using the mails to defraud (the case is now on appeal). A federal audit revealed that over $3 million had been collected in sales, contributions, and "love offerings." From its beginning in Los Angeles, the movement spread to Chicago, New York, Salt Lake City, Fort Worth, and Dallas, with an estimated 350,000 converts.

WISHING MAKES IT SO

At the trial it was testified that Mrs. Ballard's late husband, with the aid of K-17, one of the Ascended Masters, had providentially sunk three submarines which Adolf Hitler had dispatched to blow up the Panama Canal. Well groomed, heavily veiled ladies took the stand and confessed their breathless belief in the doctrine of "precipitation"—meaning that if you concentrate hard enough on anything you want, a jewel, an automobile, or an orchid, you can precipitate it.

For months before his death, Ballard had warned his followers that Los Angeles would be destroyed on February 29, 1936. Veteran victims of California earthquakes shuddered and besought The Messenger to intervene with Saint Germain, who, at the zero hour, obligingly averted the catastrophe. A bulletin of the cult contained this terse communique: "The inner work of

Mr. Ballard's Ascension was completed in Honolulu in 1936, but his Etheric Body did not withdraw until December 29, 1939." Apparently Ballard had been a zombie for three years.

One might think that conviction in the federal courts would have worked some diminution in Southern California's powerful will to believe, but the movement actually gained strength by the "crucifixion" of Mrs. Ballard, known in the cult as Joan of Arc, Chanera, Jesus, and Saint Germain. A recent visit to the "I AM" Sanctuary at 1320 South Hope Street, Los Angeles, convinced me that the Ascendant Master is still doing all right. Classes are conducted from 7 A.M. to midnight every day. One must first have read and approved Volume I of the volumes dictated to Ballard by Saint Germain before one can be enrolled in the freshman course.

In the Sanctuary's Temple of Music, recordings of "the music of the spheres" have been played without interruption for twenty-four hours a day since June 30, 1945. No word has ever been spoken in the Temple, to which only initiates are admitted. During my interview with a representative of The Messenger, the walls vibrated to the chant of a class in a nearby room. For the "adorations," "affirmations" and "decrees" of the cult are chanted in unison, repeated over and over again, rising to an almost intolerable shrillness and vehemence as the initiates demand radios, automobiles, perfumes, and pressure-cookers of Saint Germain.

Great stress is placed in the "I AM" cult on color vibrations. Followers will not wear red or black, or have these colors in their homes, for black is symbolic of Night, Darkness, and Death; while red signifies Blood, Danger (as witness the red "stop signs" in traffic), and Destruction. Science has even proved, I was informed, that the color has been known to drive people crazy. The only red tolerated in the cult is that of the American flag.

Like so many other California cults, the "I AM" folk are strict vegetarians. Sex, except for procreation, is rigidly prohibited. Explaining this taboo, my informant pointed to the increasing divorce rate and blithely stated: "Everyone knows that ninety percent of the divorces are due to the indulgence of sex as a pleasure." Essential to their ideology is the concept of a layer of atmosphere above the earth charged with the evil emanations of mankind. This layer must be "blasted," "exorcised," "lifted" by the magic "I AM" presence. Great stress is placed on words such as "riches," "power," and "jewels"—symbols of wealth and energy. "Blasted" is a key word. Obstructions to the will of the individual must be blasted by the dynamic energy of Saint

Germain's "magic Purple ray" and the "atomic accelerator." Almost pure Buck Rogers, "I AM" is, perhaps, the first cult of the atomic age.

En route from San Francisco to Los Angeles, the curious traveler can make the acquaintance of any number of bizarre wayside prophets and hot-dog-stand savants. On the highway between Santa Cruz and San Jose is Holy City, where "Father" W. E. Riker, perennial candidate for governor, "The Wise Man of the West," presides over "the world's most perfect government." Holy City itself consists of a restaurant, a post office, a print shop, and Riker's headquarters, over which appears the sign: HOLY CITY—INFORMATION BOOTH—ALL MYSTERIES ANSWERED. Along the highway, Holy City is advertised by signs reading: "If you are contemplating marriage, suicide, or crime see us first" and "Dispel the idea that you are different from God or the other fellow when sifted down."

The magnum opus of "Father" Riker, a former showman and circus barker from the Middle West, is a book called *The Perfect Government,* written in question-and-answer form. Thus:

> QUESTION: When was this philosophy established?
> ANSWER: In 1908, prior to the great Halley's Comet.
> QUESTION: Are any of your people married?
> ANSWER: They are all married to Wisdom.

Riker is a typical California prophet in at least three respects: his lack of modesty, his vigorous self-esteem, and his violent rhetoric. As Conrad Aitken once observed, there is about the state "that somewhat specious and stagy largeness which California so impartially visits upon trees, fruits, and prophets alike.

Down the coast, in Atascadero, lives William Kullgren, publisher of *The Beacon Light,* food faddist and astrologer.

Kullgren, who bitterly opposes sex, smoking, and drinking, asserts that individuals can attain real insight into the mysteries of the Cosmos only by the regular intake of his specially prepared foods: the dry herb Kamba; Papaya Tablets; Kelp-Carbon tablets; Vegex; Alfalfa; Lemon Juice Powder; Kol-N-Zyme; Beet Root Powder; and above all, raw kelp.

From various "lunations" which he has worked out, Kullgren is convinced that Southern California awaits destruction. Kullgrenites are advised to purchase trailers and stake out possible retreats, which should be located at elevations of not less than two thousand nor more than three thousand feet. "You may think I am crazy," warns the prophet of Atascadero, "but my responsibility ends when I warn you of what I know will come. The religion of the old Piscean Age is crumbling." In a land haunted by fear of earthquakes, such Jeremiahs of the highway can't fail to attract a following.

WHERE STARS ARE SHY

It is one of the paradoxes of Los Angeles that here, where it is almost as difficult to see the stars as it is to see the sun in Pittsburgh, should be located the international headquarters of astrology. For most of the year, the stars are lost in the soft mist of the night skies. Yet crystal-ball gazers, horoscope readers, and other magicians specializing in predicting the future have long flourished. Perhaps the at-times-uncertain future of Southern California has contributed to their prevalence. To be assured that Southern California did have a future—even by an astrologer—must have been comforting. The practice reached such peaks of extravagance that, some years ago, the City of Los Angeles adopted an ordinance making the prediction of the future for a fee a misdemeanor.

Astrology, one of the oldest of the arts, was thus compelled to go underground. But the itch to know the message of the stars did not abate; it became more prevalent. In December 1945, Mrs. Colby Griffin, formerly secretary of the American Federation of Astrologers, was arrested in Los Angeles, convicted, and fined $100. At her trial, the courtroom was packed with anxious astrologers. Hope ran high that Judge James Pope would hold the ordinance unconstitutional, but it was dashed when word spread that Judge Pope was a Virgo. The three appellate judges who heard the appeal must also have been born under the sign of Virgo, for, in July 1946, the conviction was sustained and the ordinance upheld.

For practicing astrologers in Los Angeles, the motion-picture colony, as one investigator has pointed out, offers "richer diggings than the forty-niners ever found in the Mother Lode." Actors are notoriously superstitious folk, forever jittery about the future. Such stars as Maria Montez and Alan Hale have no hesitancy in expressing their reliance upon astrology. Miss Montez refuses to appear at the studios on days when the signs are not propitious, while Mr. Hale ascribes the success of his marriage of thirty-three years largely to astrological forecasts. It is not at all uncommon for an actor to pay $500 for a single "delineation." Some have contracts with astrologers for the preparation of regular monthly forecasts. One such horoscope that I saw gave the following intimations for a Thursday: "Good for publicity, advertising, business matters, dealings with relatives, especially brothers and sisters, and for all Arien types of interest. Make Hay while the Sun Shines these Beautiful May Days."

Among the favorite teachers of astrology in Hollywood is Mrs. Blanca Gabriella Holmes, wife of Stuart Holmes, star of the silent films. The Holmeses live in a house that once served as headquarters for the Theosophy Society, indicating the curious overlapping of cultic influences in Southern California. Another Hollywood wizard is Carroll R. B. Righter, who calls people by their birthday instead of their name. "Hello, June 18," he will cheerily greet a friend.

Los Angeles is also the headquarters of Llewellyn George, "the dean of American astrologers," who publishes the *Astrological Bulletina*. George plants flowers and vegetables in his garden in accordance with a horoscopic schedule: "Vegetables bearing below the ground when the moon is tipped downwards, those bearing above the ground when the crescent of the moon is slanted upwards."

HIGH PRIESTESS OF ASTROLOGY

The First Temple and College of Astrology, at 736 South Burlington Street, Los Angeles, founded by James Keifer, an osteopath, has been in operation for thirty-nine years. Presided over by Mrs. Harriet K. Banes and a faculty of eight ebullient ladies, the First Temple offers courses in Ancient and Modern Astrologers, Scientific Embryology Applied to Pre-Natal Astrology, Mundane Astrology, and Horary Astrology.

Californians show chronic interest in cults based upon some phase of sun worship. The oldest is the Mazdaznan cult, which has its international headquarters at 1159 South Norton Street, Los Angeles. Based upon the "ancient Parsee Sun-Worship teachings of Mazda," or Zend-Avesta, this cult was brought to California some thirty years ago by Dr. Otoman Zar-Adusht Ha'nish. When I first made the acquaintance of Dr. Ha'nish, he was leading the followers in a chant which went something as follows:

> I am all in One individually and one in All collectively;
> I am present individually and omnipresent collectively;
> I am knowing individually and omniscient collectively;
> I am potent individually and omnipotent collectively;

> I am Mazdaznan and recognize the Eternal Designs of
> Humata, Hubata, Hu-varashta A-shem, Vo-hu, A-shem
> Vo-hu, A-shem Vo-hu.

Doctor Ha'nish passed away in 1936, and was succeeded in the role of high priest by Gloria Maude Gasque. Mother Gloria, as she is known in Mazdaznan circles, appears at meetings in a priestly, cream-colored silk gown with knotted girdle. Strict vegetarians, the Mazdaznans are in revolt against Angro Mainyus, or the spirit of Evil. Flesh eating destroys the purity of the blood; smoking pollutes the Breath of God; while alcohol interferes with "the Glandular activity upon which the Infinite Intelligence depends." Man is possessed of extra senses: Transmission, Telepathy, Spiritual Discernment, Clearsight, and Realization. The elaborate declaration of principles requires an intensity of concentration which, frankly, I have never been able to devote to it. One runs across such passages as the following: "Keeping abreast with the Spirit of the Times, Mazdaznan remains conscious of its monism, unitism, dualism, trinitism, panism, and polyism, as revealed in the macrocosm and microcosm of the Infinite and Finite, completedly over blending but never ending."

Rosicrucianism has always been a fountainhead of the esoteric. The Rosicrucian dispensation, which numbered such occultists as Marie Corelli and Bulwer-Lytton among its European adherents, was brought to California around October 1911, when its prophet, Max Heindel, established the colony at Oceanside, between Los Angeles and San Diego. It is a beautiful, fifty-acre tract, with a vegetarian cafeteria, a temple of healing with murals of the zodiac, a chapel, and a dozen or so cottages for the residents. This branch of the Order of the Rose Cross is devoutly vegetarian, astrological, and esoteric. It believes with Goethe's Mephisto that "blood is a juice of a very special kind." Its magazine, *Rays from the Rose Cross*, offers horoscopes, articles on diet, and learned treatises on the curative power of precious gems. Thus the emerald is a laxative; amber, being highly magnetic, is good for asthma; and red coral, if worn about the body, will eliminate stomach disorders.

This group, which calls itself a fraternal order rather than a cult, claims to have anticipated the atomic bomb in its teachings. When the Sun, by reason of the procession of the equinoxes, shall have entered the Sign of Aquarius, the Slavic race will become dominant; but the seventh and final race of the Aryan Epoch will arise in the United States, presumably in Southern California. Many of the newer cults have borrowed heavily from Rosicrucian teachings.

THE CULTS BRANCH OUT

The Rosicrucians, like most Californian cults and fraternal orders, are divided into northern and southern branches. The Heindelian set is highly concentrated in the south, while the Amorc sect has its headquarters in San Jose—AMORC being Ancient and Mystical Order Rosae Crucis. The Amorcs are strictly Egyptian in ritual and symbolism; the Heindelians more on the Anglo-American pattern. Visitors who have traveled along the famous El Camino Real (Highway 101) have doubtless been inspired at the sight of the AMORC headquarters, an impressive upsurge of pure Egyptian architecture in the mocking sunlight of California.

All manner of esoteric outcroppings may be found in the great white sand dunes of Pismo Beach and Oceano—long a favorite hideaway for mystics, occultists, new religionists, poets, and vegetarians. In Pismo Beach is published *The American Vegetarian*, which contains the highly diverting advertisements of the Carey-Perry School of the Chemistry of Life (Hollywood); the Essene School of Life, which sponsors an annual Biochemical Grape-Cure at Tecate; and the Lemurian Ambassador. Never be surprised at what you find in the dunes of Oceano.

Beautiful, sun-drenched Ojai Valley, near Santa Barbara, is the center of Theosophical speculation. Driven from Hollywood by the encroachment of motion pictures and big business, Albert Powell Warrington brought the remnants of his Krotona Colony to Ojai in 1920. It is also the home of Edgar Holloway, termed the Man from Lemuria, who declares that he flew into the valley some years ago in a great flying fish. The beginning of Ojai, however, dates from the publication of an article in the early twenties by Dr. Ales Hrdickla, the anthropologist, predicting the evolution of a new sixth subrace in California. Prompted by this revelation, Annie Besant came to California and purchased a 465-acre tract in Ojai Valley as a home for Jiddu Krishnamurti, "the vehicle of the New World Teacher, the Lord Maitreya," whose last incarnation, so we are informed, was in the person of Jesus Christ.

In 1929 he renounced the messiahship in a great meeting in Hollywood Bowl. But prior to this renunciation, the annual encampments of the faithful brought thousands of visitors. One can't be in Ojai Valley for ten minutes

without becoming conscious that the whole region is alive with cultic vibrations. Robust ladies in flat-heeled shoes scurry about with an air of deep
metaphysical involvement; while young men with lilac manners hold high
discourse on things unseen.

Currently Vedanta is making the greatest stir in Southern California.
While it is, perhaps, unfair to call Vedanta a cult, there are cultic implications
against the background of present-day Hollywood. An outgrowth of the
Ramakrishna Mission founded by Sri Ramakrishna (1836–1886), Vedanta is
based upon the Veda scrolls, the oldest religious teachings. The first swami
or monk of the Ramakrishna Mission to reach America was Swami Viveka-
nanda, who in 1893 attended a religious conference at the Chicago World's
Fair. The present high priest of Vedanta, Swami Prabhavananda, followed
him to California in 1923. With unerring insight, he concluded that Hollywood should be the center of Vedanta in America and established it there
in 1929.

At first the Vedanta Society made its headquarters in the home of Mrs.
C. M. Wyckoff, now eighty-six, a woman of considerable wealth, but the meetings are now held in a $12,000 alabaster replica of the Taj Mahal at 1946 Ivar
Street. Lectures are given every Sunday morning and a class is held every
Thursday evening. The interior walls are painted a dull gray green and are
adorned with pictures of Krishna, Jesus, Buddha, and Confucius. The services open with Swami Prabhavananda slowly walking into the temple in a
long, bright yellow robe—the robe of renunciation. Sitting cross-legged on a
raised portion of the temple floor near a shrine brought from India, with a
gray shawl over his shoulders, the swami meditates in silence for ten or fifteen minutes. Then he chants an invocation in Sanskrit, concluding on the
words "Peace, peace, peace," gives a lecture on some phase of Vedanta, takes
questions from the audience.

Extremely interesting philosophically, the Vedanta creed has won a number of famous disciples. In 1938 Gerald Heard, the British Diogenes, author
of such works as *Pain, Sex and Time* and *The Ascent of Humanity*, came to live
in Los Angeles after a period of tutelage in Quaker mysticism in Pennsylvania. He had heard of Swami Prabhavananda in London. After a year of tutor-
ing with the swami, Heard became a disciple of Vedanta and, in turn, induced
Aldous Huxley to take up residence in Southern California. Mr. Huxley's
initial impressions are to be found in his novel *After Many a Summer Dies the
Swan* (1939), in which Heard appears as the character Propter. Soon Huxley

was a bona fide disciple. Their presence then attracted the brilliant young English writer Christopher Isherwood, author of *Prater Violet, The Last of Mr. Morris,* and *Berlin Stories.*

Near the strange temple on Ivar Street is a monastery in which Swami Prabhavananda resides with four or five male disciples. For some time, Isherwood lived here; in fact, it was only recently that he decided not to become a Vedanta swami. He has conducted services in the temple, participated in its ritual, and writes regularly for its magazine. "I cannot imagine living without Vedanta," he is quoted as having said. The society has issued a book called *Vedanta for the Western World,* with contributions by Heard, Huxley, Isherwood, and John van Druren, the playwright. Naturally, the conversion of such sophisticates has given Vedanta a special fillip among the cults of California.

For a time, a main item of gossip in Hollywood was whether Isherwood was the original for the central character in Somerset Maugham's novel *The Razor's Edge.* Maugham did come to Hollywood to consult Swami Prabhavananda before writing it.

Membership in the Vedanta Society is highly heterogeneous. There are about 115 members at present, including two doctors, a restaurant owner, an architect, four college professors, a banker, and, curiously enough, two Protestant clergymen: a Presbyterian and a Congregationalist. In Mrs. Wyckoff's home the society maintains a school for novitiates who hope to become nuns (present enrollment five). They lead a semicommunal existence, sharing income, eschewing beef in deference to the Sacred Cow of India, and following a severe regimen of meditation, prayer, and study.

The income for this establishment is largely derived from an orange grove near Whittier, which, together with a $250,000 trust fund, was bequeathed the society by the late Spencer Kellogg, Jr., a manufacturer of linseed oil. Swami Prabhavananda himself has an income left by Kellogg. The swami frankly states that "it is, indeed, a goodly sum."

It is to be doubted that Vedanta will ever kindle fires in the angry eyes of Los Angeles's spiritually dispossessed. Its creed is essentially too civilized and urbane for the restive hordes, raised in the belief that some must necessarily be damned; that without the damned there could be no elect....

COSMIC RAYS

Following the destruction of Hiroshima by an atomic bomb, Southern California experienced a remarkable outcropping of cosmic-ray cults. In the autumn of 1945, thousands of invalids flocked to the Cosmic Research Laboratories in Long Beach operated by Roy Beebe. Several thousand Southern Californians claim to have been cured of a wide variety of ailments, pains, wheezes, and sniffles by Beebe's controlled cosmic ray. During the height of the hegira, the Pacific Electric lines had to add more buses. Each day hundreds of pilgrims sat in the backyard of Beebe's establishment, exposing themselves to the ray which emanated from a "cosmic box" he had rigged up in his laboratory or consuming slight portions of wheat meal hopped up with cosmic rays.

Mr. Beebe first discovered "the cosmic" while doing research on Halley's Comet in the Arkansas Ozarks back in 1902. "In 1912," he says, "I succeeded in getting it under control where I could emit it out to the good of humanity. I been usin' it ever since."

NOT HERE TO STAY?

Something about Southern California certainly seems to lend an air of verity to its prophets of doom. Perhaps it is the quality, noted by J. B. Priestley, of a "sinister suggestion of transience," of impermanence. In the folklore of the region, this seems to be linked with theories of oil-well depletion and water supply exhaustion; and, of course, with earthquakes. In no other area are visions of doom so quickly seized upon, so rapidly and fearfully accepted.

Various Southern California cultists in recent years have proclaimed themselves the Messiah. The most flamboyant is unquestionably Dr. Joe Jeffers. A guest of the Nazis in Berlin in 1938, Jeffers is a violent anti-Semite and Catholic-baiter. Right now Jeffers is whipping audiences of two thousand people into a lather of excitement over the impending total destruction of Los Angeles by the greatest earthquake of all time. Shouting at them to fast, to prepare for the end, he urges them to sell their earthly belongings and to give him the proceeds so that a Zion may be established while there is still time. The only hope of salvation seems to lie in a great floating land mass which is rising off the coast.

It was on December 25, 1875, according to prophet Arthur Bell, that a group of men held a secret meeting at which Mankind United was formed. From 1875 to 1919, these men spent exactly $60 million on research into the causes of war and poverty, disease and crime. And by 1934, Bell, known also as "The Voice," was able to publish a remarkable book outlining the nature of the plan of salvation. The program is revealed in the cryptic slogan 4–4–8–3–4—four hours work a day, four days a week, eight months a year, for an annual wage of not less than $30,000 for each adult, with four months annual vacation. When precisely 200,000 people have subscribed to this formula, the plan will be put into effect. Then the Universal Service Corporation will be able to provide an annual income of $30,000 for every member, and a $25,000 home with radio-automatic vocal-type correspondence equipment; automatic news and telephone recording service; airconditioning; fruit trees; vegetable gardens; hothouses; athletic courts; swimming pools; and sundry other appurtenances. Members will speak an international language and travel free to every part of the globe. In one year alone, Bell received $97,500 from the sale of this new bible of Mankind United.

On May 6, 1943, "The Voice" and some of his associates were convicted of sedition in the federal courts. While the case was on appeal, Bell formed Christ's Church of the Golden Rule to carry on the program of Mankind United. According to the Attorney General of California, Robert W. Kenny, Bell had collected by March 1, 1944, in love offerings, sales, and donations, a sum in excess of $2.5 million. When Kenny brought suit to revoke the church's charter, he discovered it owned and operated several office buildings, stores, large hotels, and a beautiful estate near Burlingame, equipped with sliding panels, secret doors, and other paraphernalia of a house of mystery. Numbers of people had been induced to surrender their worldly belongings to the Church and work on its properties for a nonutopian wage. No one knows how many people joined Mankind United between 1934 and 1946, but the Attorney General, in his complaint, estimates 250,000.

I don't know what it is about California that stimulates this desperate quest of Utopia. Emma Harding, who wrote a history of spiritualism, concluded that cults thrive on the Pacific Coast because of the wonderful transparency of the air, the heavy charges of mineral magnetism from the gold mines, which set up favorable vibrations, and the still-living passions of the forty-niners, which create "emanations."

Sociologically they are to be explained as phenomena of migration. Two out of every three citizens of California were born outside the state. Migration severs old ties, undermines ancient allegiances. It creates the social fluidity out of which new cultic movements arise. But migration does not provide the complete answer.

In part the cults of California, with their emphasis on sun worship, vegetarianism, and apocalyptic visions of an ever-impending doom, are an oblique response to the physical environment. Social panaceas flourish in this empire of prodigious crops, Brobdingnagian vegetables, and rose bushes with 200,000 blossoms, because here natural abundance stimulates dreams of plenty. Since 1875, when the mystic Thomas Lake Harris established the Brotherhood of the New Light colony at Santa Rosa, California has pulsed with vibrations of the otherworldly and trembled under prophecies of doom. It is a land of Visions, Dreams, Exaltations, and New Harmonies, this beautiful, sensuous Land of Mu by the Western Sea.

Sister Aimee

1946

THE EXISTENCE OF a large number of transients here always stimulated the cult-making tendency. It should be rememberd that, for the last twenty-five years, Los Angeles had, on an average, about two hundred thousand temporary residents. In such an environment, it was, of course, foreordained that a Messiah would someday emerge. The first local Messiah was a poor, uneducated, desperately ambitious widow by the name of Aimee Semple McPherson.

Aimee, who was "not so much a woman as a scintillant assault," first appeared in California at San Diego in 1918. There she began to attract attention by scattering religious tracts from an airplane and holding revival meetings in a boxing arena. That Mrs. McPherson's first appearance should have been in San Diego is, in itself, highly significant. In San Diego she unquestionably heard of Katherine Tingley, from whom she probably got the idea of founding a new religious movement on the Coast and from whom she certainly got many of her ideas about uniforms, pageantry, and showmanship.

From San Diego Mrs. McPherson came to Los Angeles in 1922 with her Four Square Gospel: conversion, physical healing, the second coming, and redemption. She arrived in Los Angeles with two minor children, an old, battered automobile, and $100 in cash. By the end of 1925 she had collected more than $1 million and owned property worth $250,000. In the early twenties, as Nancy Barr Mavity has pointed out in an excellent biography of Mrs. McPherson,* "Los Angeles was the happy hunting ground for the physically

---

* *Sister Aimee,* by Nancy Barr Mavity (Doubleday, 1931).

disabled and the mentally unexacting….No other large city contains so many transplanted villagers who retain the stamp of their indigenous soil….Most cities absorb the disparate elements that gravitate to them, but Los Angeles remains a city of migrants," a mixture, not a compound.

Here she built Angelus Temple at a reputed cost of $1.5 million. The Temple has an auditorium with five thousand seats; a $75,000 broadcasting station; the classrooms of a university which once graduated five hundred young evangelists a year; and, as Morrow Mayo pointed out, "a brass band bigger and louder than Sousa's, an organ worthy of any movie cathedral, a female choir bigger and more beautiful than the Metropolitan chorus, and a costume wardrobe comparable to Ziegfeld's."

Mrs. McPherson founded a magazine, *The Bridal Call,* and established two hundred and forty "lighthouses," or local churches, affiliated with Angelus Temple. By 1929 she had a following of twelve thousand devoted members in Los Angeles and thirty thousand in the outlying communities. From the platform of Angelus Temple, sister Aimee gave the *Angelenos* the fanciest theological entertainment they have ever enjoyed. I have seen her drive an ugly Devil around the platform with a pitchfork, enact the drama of Valley Forge in George Washington's uniform, and take the lead in a dramatized sermon called "Sodom and Gomorrah."

Adjutants have been praying, night and day, for thirteen years in the Temple. One group has been praying for 118,260 hours. While Mrs. McPherson never contended that she could heal the sick, she was always willing to pray for them, and she was widely known as a faith-healer. A magnificent sense of showmanship enabled her to give the Angelus Temple throngs a sense of drama and a feeling of release that probably did have some therapeutic value. On state occasions, she always appeared in the costume of an admiral of the fleet, while the lay members of her entourage wore natty nautical uniforms.

On May 18, 1926, Sister Aimee disappeared. Last seen in a bathing suit on the beach near Ocean Park, she had apparently drowned in the Pacific. While Los Angeles went wild with excitement, thousands of her followers gathered on the beach to pray for her deliverance and return. A specially chartered airplane flew over the beach and dropped flowers on the waters. On May 23, an overenthusiastic disciple drowned in the Pacific while attempting to find her body. A few days later, a great memorial meeting was held for Sister at Angelus Temple, at which $35,000 was collected.

Aimee reappeared at Agua Prieta in Mexico, across the border from Douglas, Arizona.

Her entrance into Los Angeles was a major triumph. Flooded with requests from all over the world, the local newspaper and wire services filed ninety-five thousand words of copy in a single day. Airplanes showered thousands of blossoms upon the coach that brought Sister back to Los Angeles. Stepping from the train, she walked out of the station on a carpet of roses. A hundred thousand people cheered while she paraded through the streets of the city, accompanied by a white-robed silver band, an escort of twenty cowboys, and squads of policemen.

The jubilation, however, did not last long. Working hard on the case, the newspapers soon proved that the kidnapping story which she had told on her return was highly fictitious. In sensational stories, they proceeded to trace her movements from the time she disappeared, through a "love cottage" interlude at Carmel with a former radio operator of the Temple, to her reappearance in Mexico. Following these disclosures, she was arrested, charged with having given false information designed to interfere with the orderly processes of the law, and placed on trial. Later the charges against her were dropped.

No one bothered to inquire what crime, if any, she had committed. It was the fabulous ability with which she carried off the kidnapping hoax that infuriated the respectable middle-class residents of Los Angeles. Although I heard her speak many times, I never heard her attack any individual or any group, and I am thoroughly convinced that her followers felt that they had received full value in exchange for their liberal donations. She made migrants feel at home in Los Angeles; she gave them a chance to meet other people; and she exorcised the nameless fears which so many of them had acquired from the fire-and-brimstone theology of the Middle West.

Although she managed to maintain a fairly constant following until her death from an overdose of sleeping powder in 1944, she never recovered from the vicious campaign that had been directed against her in 1926. The old enthusiasm was gone; the old fervor had vanished. She was no longer "Sister McPherson" in Los Angeles, but merely "Aimee." In many respects, her career parallels that of Katherine Tingley: both were highly gifted women with a great talent for showmanship; both had lived in poverty and obscurity until middle age; both founded cults; and both were ruined by scandal.

"God Will Slap You Cockeyed"

1950

C. (FOR "CASH") THOMAS PATTEN and his wife, Bebe, who had been trained in the Four Square Gospel preached by Aimee Semple McPherson, bounced into Oakland, California, in a broken-down jalopy in 1943, at the mid-point of the war. The Patten show started slowly but soon shifted into high. The debonair, thirty-seven-year-old Patten was full of plans: his revivalists were going to build a hospital, a refuge for orphans and retired ministers, a radio station, and a theological seminary—projects that required a great deal of money. War-rich Oakland was generous and gullible. Between 1944 and 1948 Patten deposited $1,354,706.75 in personal bank accounts. Over $250,000 was contributed just for the purchase of the Oakland City Women's Club. "This building," said Patten, "is going to be Gawd's house until the hinges rust off the door." Three years later the building was sold for $450,000, and Patten promptly stashed the money away.

Love offerings for Bebe Patten—special collections taken for her support—ranged from $3,000 to $5,000 a month, while the regular monthly church collections averaged about $40,000. Over a period of five years, $50,000 was collected in tuition and registration fees at the Pattens' Bible school. When Patten wanted anything, he simply took up a collection: $269.70 for the purchase of Bozo, an English bulldog; $150 for Peter, a Boston bull. If extraordinary expenses had to be met, as when Mrs. Patten gave birth to twin daughters, a special collection was taken. When "Cash" had to pick up $3,000 worth of IOUs from a Reno gambling casino, he simply borrowed the money from members of his congregation. All this, and more, came out during the record-breaking eighty-four-day trial in which the complaints of disgruntled ex-converts finally resulted, on June 29, in Patten's conviction on five counts of grand theft. He received a five-to-fifty-year jail sentence and is appealing.

The chunky "Cash" is an extraordinary showman. With his hamhock-and-turnip-greens accent, his penchant for flashy clothes, and his Western drawl, "Cash" was just the man to kid the folks into loosening their purse strings. Bouncing around the stage in a tight-fitting tuxedo and cowboy boots, he would shout: "There'll be a hot time in the old town tonight!" His collection spiels often lasted twice as long as his wife's "sermons." The Pattens went in for college yells and brass bands. Platter passing was assigned to teen-age Bible-school students dolled up in fancy block *P*—for Patten—sweaters.

"Cash" didn't always coax and kid; he knew when and how to be tough. On one occasion when he had been able to raise only $1,250 of $3,514.60 needed for a special project, he suddenly shouted at the congregation: "God is going to slap you cockeyed in about two minutes!" Later in the meeting he thundered: "This is where the fireworks start. God has been talking to one man here for five minutes. I don't know whether he is going to knock him off his seat or not. God is going to…" And with that, according to the trial transcript, he broke off with "Bless you, Jesus," and the people said "Amen." Evidently, the sinner had reached for his wallet.

During Patten's trial, the corridors were lined almost daily with Bible-bearing, hymn-singing, *P*-sweatered students who cheered when "Cash," in one of two dozen different suits but always in cowboy boots, strolled into the courtroom. One day his wife—clad in a blue pleated skirt, a blue sweater with a gold-colored *P* embroidered above gold crosses, and a gold-colored blouse—drove up to the courthouse in her Cadillac limousine and was escorted to the courtroom by a "guard of honor" of a hundred students. In the nineteenth week of the trial, "Cash" had a heart attack, and the last sessions were held in a hospital auditorium, with the defendant, wearing pale champagne-colored pajamas, rolled in on a metal wheelchair.

The theory of the prosecution was that the Pattens had exerted a "hypnotic spell" over their "emotionally sincere" and "intensely religious" followers, but certain occurrences cast doubt on the validity of this theory. Toward the close of the trial, Bebe Patten delivered a "sermon"—with eighteen Bible students in attendance—over a pink rose that had been taken from the funeral casket of a woman who had quit the movement. At the cemetery, a student had snatched the rose as the casket passed by. "This is just one of the many flowers that will come from the graves of those opposing us," said the evangelist; "it came from the casket of that woman....Now she has no power to change God's word; she is praying in Hell tonight." As she predicted that retribution would fall upon other "enemies," Bebe's listeners rocked back and forth, clapping their hands and calling out "Amen!" and "Hallelujah!" Those who oppose Bebe Patten, they were told, are "sinful and ungodly" followers of Cain. "God has chosen to reveal his power to those who are with him. Those who are against him shall go to a premature death." After "Cash" had been convicted, one of the prosecution witnesses received another rose—tied to a rock that had crashed through the window of his home.

The suggestion of violence occurs in many of Bebe's sermons. She once told a follower that she preferred the doctrine of an eye for an eye and a tooth for a tooth to the Christian belief in turning the other cheek. "I have always regretted," she said, "that I did not live in the Old Testament days, because you could take your weapons and go to war....In this battle we are having right now [the trial], my prayer is that the Lord will rise up and smite someone." Then she told of a minister who had opposed a Patten revival meeting in Decatur, Alabama, only to drop dead the next day. "And this outfit in Oakland has touched the spirit of God. I'm looking for some people to drop dead. My prayer is: Lord, smite just one, to encourage us—just anyone to show us You are on our side. The Lord knows that if He had left it to us we would have done it already. I think fifty would include them all. There's nothing so encouraging as to see the Lord walk into battle and slay someone. Lord, knock someone cold, no matter how unimportant, just to show us You're on our side."

Here is a voice which speaks eloquently to the social outcast, the urban misfit; to those lost and forsaken, guilt-ridden people who like to be abused and imposed upon and frightened "half out of their wits." It is the voice of authority speaking with sternness and fire to less articulate warped personalities, commanding them to obey, demanding the surrender of their souls and wills. If the Pattens imposed on their congregation, the congregation invited the imposition. To be sure, a few finally broke away, but most of them stayed and are still loyal. Bebe is still conducting services. Even if Patten's conviction should be upheld, there will be other Boris Karloff evangelists in the big tent, preaching the ideology of psychic fascism and threatening that God will knock you cockeyed if you don't contribute.

The Folklore of Earthquakes

1933

ON THE BASIS OF their reaction to the word "earthquake," Californians can be divided into three classes: first, the innocent late arrivals who have never felt an earthquake, but who go about avowing to all and sundry that "it must be fun"; next, those who have experienced a slight quake and should know better, but who nonetheless persist in propagating the fable that the San Francisco quake of 1906 was the only major upheaval the state has ever suffered; and last, the victims of a real earthquake—for example, the residents of San Francisco, Santa Barbara, or more recently, Long Beach.* To these last, the world is full of terror. They are supersensitive to the slightest rattles and jars and move uneasily whenever a heavy truck passes along the highway.

This diversity, based on dissimilar experience, is probably responsible for the amazing earthquake folklore that thrives in California. Fresh outpourings of popular fancy appear whenever the region feels another twister. Science is not as sure about earthquakes as it ought to be, and so the Californians make out a fairly plausible case for the superiority of their own lore to the so-called scientific pronouncements elicited by the press from the staffs of the local universities whenever a quake gives another blow to the tourist trade.

This popular fancy about earthquakes has crystallized into a trinity of superstitions. They are as follows: that tall buildings in a quake area are peculiarly perilous structures; that quakes are caused by the drainage of oil from the bowels of the earth, and that they are invariably preceded by periods of what is known as "earthquake weather." Los Angeles, under the influence of

---

* The Long Beach earthquake in this article (magnitude 6.4) took place March 10, 1933.

a widespread belief in the first of these superstitions, adopted an ordinance limiting the height of buildings years ago. As a consequence of this ordinance (which is also said to have been favored by local realtors animated by ulterior motives), the city has become annoyingly decentralized. In fact, if its tendency to decentralization is not corrected, it will soon become a collection of widely dispersed shopping districts connected by boulevards of racing traffic.

The belief in earthquake weather is persistent and unshakable. I have heard old residents quarrel endlessly among themselves over the exact definition of it, but they all agree that it exists and that it invariably presages the coming of a quake. Despite the fact that it is common knowledge that earthquakes have occurred in summer and in winter, in spring and fall, and at every hour of the day or night, regardless of temperature, the belief in this earthquake weather survives. In the popular sense, the phrase seems to designate a close, stifling, sunless, muggy atmosphere. One might be ready to believe that such weather does presage the coming of quakes if it were not for the fact that the description obviously refers to an atmospheric condition that, in California, is the subject of universal detestation. The conclusion is almost irresistible that the residents have merely made the loathsome "close days" responsible for calamities that could not, in loyalty, be imputed to any other kind of weather.

The belief in the oil-drainage superstition is of equal antiquity and tenacity. There is, as a matter of fact, a slightly melodramatic quality about oil fields. The great shining storage tanks glisten in the sun; the forest of derricks assume fantastic shapes in mist and cloud, light and darkness; and the ceaseless thumping of the pumps makes for an atmosphere of doubt and misgiving. Oil drillers themselves are a notoriously superstitious breed of men.

But the range of popular fancy is not limited to any particular set of superstitions. After the recent temblor that caused such heavy damage at Long Beach and the surrounding towns, I was able to cull the following yarns from the local press and from conversations overheard during the next few days. It seems that a hen laid three eggs a few moments after the first shock was felt; that a woman who had been suffering from paralysis for years was cured by the vibrations of the quake and walked forth from an invalid's room without assistance; that the quake was predicted by the "scientists" weeks before it occurred, but that the information was suppressed by certain sinister interests variously known as the big men, the bankers, and the university presidents; that a woman was taking a bath in Long Beach when the first shock came, causing a section of the wall to fall in and block the doorway, so that she was forced to remain in the bathroom without clothes for three days and nights until she was rescued by some Legionnaire; that sixteen boys were caught in the plunge of the Polytechnic High School in Long Beach, but that they have never been reported missing, and that their parents have been hushed up; that while standing in a neighboring building gazing out at the new Los Angeles City Hall (twenty floors and a tower), a group of people saw the hall sway out of sight, come back into sight, sway out of sight in the opposite direction, and then come to rest "with an awful jar"; that a worker in a chemical plant near Long Beach was thrown thirty feet in the air after the first shock, and that, on hitting the ground, he bounced skyward and was thus tossed up and down three times "in rapid succession"; that the earthquake was caused by the moving mountain near Durango, Colorado; that an automobile, while being driven along a boulevard in Long Beach, shook so hard that it lost all four tires; that the undertakers in Long Beach didn't charge a penny for the sixty or more interments following the quake; that the quake was the first manifestation of the awful curse placed on Southern California by the Rev. Robert P. Shuler after its residents failed to elect him United States Senator; that sailors on vessels a mile or more off shore from Palos Verdes saw the hills (quite high) disappear from sight; that the bootleggers of Long Beach saved hundreds of lives by their public-spirited donation of large quantities of alcohol to the medical authorities; that women showed the most courage during the quake and that men can't stand up under earthquakes; that the shock of the quake caused dozens of miscarriages in Long Beach, and that an earthquake will often cause permanent, and annoying, irregularities among women; that every building in Southern California that was not damaged by the quake is "earthquake proof"; that another earthquake will be experienced within three months "at the other end of the fault"; that a cross on a Long Beach church was not damaged, though the rest of the building was destroyed; that the quake will disturb the production of oil by causing it to flow from one underground reservoir to another; that every life lost during the quake was due solely to the obdurate willfulness of the dead in not doing what the speaker would have brilliantly done under the same circumstances; that an earthquake is much more terrifying than a cyclone, but not quite so frightening as a tornado, and just slightly less ghastly than a hurricane; that Californians should construct earthquake cellars, just as Middle

Westerners build cyclone cellars; that the "first quake is always the hardest," and that, in reality, there is only one quake, the subsequent temblors being regarded as merely "echoes" or "repercussions" of the first; that the safest place to be when an earthquake occurs is indoors, outdoors, in a doorway, standing next to an interior partition, lying relaxed on the floor; that the outdoor camping and enforced communalization of life after the quake in Long Beach produced widespread immorality; that it is extremely dangerous to rush out of doors during an earthquake, for the reason that "great cracks" are likely to occur in the paving, or one may be struck by a runaway vehicle; that the last quake occurred in California in Santa Barbara in 1926, and the first in San Francisco in 1906, and that, between these dates, California did not experience an earthquake; that every community in Southern California which escaped serious damage in the last quake "is not in the path of the fault," and is, therefore, immune from peril; that the earthquake, followed by the appearance of a mighty meteor on March 24, presages the beginning of the end.

The Politics of Utopia

1946

ODD—AND UTOPIAN

This, in a way, would be exceeding odd
And almost justify man's ways to God—
If, by the healing of these hills, the blind
Receive an inner sight, and leave behind
Their narrow greed, their numbing fears, and fare
Forth with new souls to breathe the honest air;

If rich man, poor man, lawyer, merchant, thief
Declare with one accord that they'd as lief
Laugh and forget, and make a gracious truce
With sea and mountain; learn again the use
Of Earth and sky and ocean-ranging breeze,
And dance, and dance, beneath the pepper trees.
         —James Rorty

SINCE THE ABUSE OF LOS ANGELES has become a national pastime, no phase of its social life has attracted more attention than its utopian politics, its flair for the new and the untried—a tendency dismissed by all observers as "crackpotism," still another vagary of the climate, a by-product of the eternal sunshine. With so much attention being focused upon the socio-political phenomena of the region, it is amazing that the roots of this tendency should have been so consistently ignored. In the bulky writing about political crackpotism in Los Angeles, for example, I find not a single reference to the Julian debacle and all that this debacle implied to the residents of the region.* Judging from articles in the national press, it would appear that the impression is widespread that, about 1934, Southern California became politically insane. Westbrook Pegler even suggested that a guardian should be appointed and the region declared incompetent. Here, again, the lack of continuity in the traditions of the region is strikingly apparent. For the Utopian Society and the Epic Movement did not spring miraculously into being overnight; both movements had their roots in the past; they were growths, not immaculate conceptions.

ECONOMICS OF THE OPEN SHOP

Following the collapse of the "great real-estate boom of 1886," the population of Los Angeles declined at the rate of nearly one thousand a month during 1888 and 1889. The construction industry was brought to a standstill, business declined, many houses were vacant, and the railroads ran empty cars. "A critical moment," in the words of Charles Dwight Willard, "had arrived in the history of Los Angeles." At this juncture a group of men, all newcomers to the region, decided that they would take over, that they would create an agricultural-industrial empire out of the wreckage of the boom. The famous "new beginning" was launched at a meeting called on October 15, 1888, when Colonel Harrison Gray Otis presented the motion which resulted in the formation of the Los Angeles Chamber of Commerce.

Born in Marietta, Ohio, February 10, 1837, Otis had come to Santa Barbara in 1876, a veteran of the Civil War, a man without resources, a typical drifter of the period. For a number of years, he edited the *Santa Barbara Press,* but with the failure of this venture, he received an appointment as special agent for the Treasury Department in Alaska, where he served from 1879 to 1881. Returning to Los Angeles, he became editor of the *Times* in 1882, on the eve of the boom. The paper made a great deal of money during the boom, enabling Otis to acquire full control by 1886. Belligerent, choleric, opinionated, the Colonel quickly developed the fixed idea that he owned Los Angeles, in fee simple, and that he alone was destined to lead it to greatness. In retrospect, it is easy to understand how this notion came to dominate his

---

* This refers to the Julian Petroleum Company ("Julian Pete"), founded by C. C. Julian and financed by unorthodox stock trading; by the time it was shut down, 3614% of the company had been sold to investors. Julian Pete's collapse in the late 1920s drew lurid press coverage, discredited several politicians and businessmen, and ruined many small investors as well as several banks and brokerage houses.

thinking. For here was a unique situation: a small group of men, under the leadership of Otis, had not merely "grown up with" a community, in the usual American pattern, they had conjured that community into existence. Having taken over at a moment of great crisis, when the older residents had suffered a failure of nerve, they felt that not only had they "saved" Los Angeles, but that it belonged to them as a matter of right. Over the years, this notion became a major obsession with General Otis (he was breveted Major-General for "meritorious conduct in action at Calocan" during the campaign in the Philippines).

The hatred that Otis came to inspire in those who did not share his fixation is epitomized, for all time, in Hiram Johnson's characterization of the man (delivered in a speech in Los Angeles). "In the City of San Francisco," said Johnson, "we have drunk to the very dregs of infamy; we have had vile officials; we have had rotten newspapers. But we have nothing so vile, nothing so low, nothing so debased, nothing so infamous in San Francisco as Harrison Gray Otis. He sits there in senile dementia with gangrene heart and rotting brain, grimacing at every reform, chattering impotently at all things that are decent, frothing, fuming, violently gibbering, going down to his grave in snarling infamy. He is one thing that all California looks at when, in looking at Southern California, they see anything that is disgraceful, depraved, corrupt, crooked and putrescent—that is Harrison Gray Otis."

During the "hard times" which followed the collapse of the boom, the *Times* announced a 20 percent reduction in wages. Prior to this announcement, most of the employees in the mechanical department were union members; Otis himself carried a card in the union. When the *Times* refused to negotiate or to discuss the reduction with the union, a strike was called on August 3, 1890, which, in effect, was to continue until October 1, 1910. The calling of this strike really marks the beginning of social and industrial conflict in Southern California. While the other newspapers quickly adjusted their differences with the union, the *Times* remained adamant and began to import strikebreakers from the Printers' Protective Fraternity of Kansas City. As the union continued to seek a settlement, primarily by the use of the boycott, Otis began to organize the community in defense of the open shop. "Thus by the decision of this one man," writes Irving Stone, "Los Angeles became immersed in a half century of bloodshed, violence, hatred, class war, oppression, injustice, and a destruction of civil liberties which was to turn it into the low spot of American culture and democracy."

To personalize the issue in this manner, however, is to overlook a basic consideration. Long the center of wealth and population in the state, San Francisco by 1890 had a forty-year handicap on Los Angeles. Not only had San Francisco acquired undisputed industrial leadership as a result of this headstart, but, unlike Los Angeles, it possessed conspicuous natural advantages: one of the finest harbors in the world, a rich agricultural and mining hinterland, superb river communications, and the accumulated wealth of the bonanza period. Otis and his colleagues were quick to realize that the only chance to establish Los Angeles as an industrial center was to undercut the high wage structure of San Francisco, long a strongly unionized town, and, at the same time, and by the same process, to attract needed capital to the region.

The major asset of Los Angeles in 1890 consisted in the annual winter influx of tourists and homeseekers. It should be noted that this annual influx embraced two distinct currents, people of means, or "tourists," and workers, or "homeseekers." Both currents were of equal importance, the tourists to provide the capital and revenue, the homeseekers to provide a pool of cheap labor. They were, in fact, the heads and the tails of a single coin. Just as the tourist influx was artificially stimulated by various devices, so the flow of homeseekers was encouraged. During the winter months, special "home-seekers' excursion trains" brought thousands of workers to the region at cut rates. Having land to burn, the Southland dangled the bait of "cheap homes" before the eyes of the prospective homeseekers. "While wages are low," the argument went, "homes are cheap."

At first, as Dr. Ira Cross has pointed out, "the mild climate attracted invalids, many of whom were able to work at light jobs. Others who had small incomes or small savings and who were therefore willing to sell their services for almost any wage also arrived in great numbers. Husbands and fathers, wives and mothers, came with their sick ones and made their contributions to the local labor supply." The homeseeker element, as one observer said, did not belong to the "limited class who came here to die"; on the contrary, they came to Southern California to work.

From early beginnings around 1900, the homeseeker influx was gradually increased by systematic recruitment and advertising. By 1910 the annual winter influx of homeseekers was estimated at thirty thousand, and the excursion trains, starting in October, arrived at the rate of one a week. So great was the influx that, by Christmas of each season, an acute relief problem had developed. On numerous occasions, the City Council of Los Angeles protested against the practice of inserting "homeseeker excursion" ads in the Eastern and Middle Western newspapers, but the protests were ignored.

Naturally such a situation created a highly competitive labor market in Los Angeles, a market characterized by an extraordinarily high turnover. From 1890 to 1910, wages were from 20 to 30, and in some categories, even 40 percent lower than in San Francisco. It was precisely this margin that enabled Los Angeles to grow as an industrial center. Thus the maintenance of a cheap labor pool became an indispensable cog in the curious economics of the region. For the system to work, however, the labor market had to remain unorganized; otherwise it would become impossible to exploit the homeseeker element. The system required—it absolutely demanded—a non-union open-shop setup. It was this basic requirement, rather than the ferocity of General Otis, that really created the open-shop movement in Los Angeles.

Once lured to the region and saddled with an equity in a cheap home, most of the homeseekers had no means of escape. Just as the open-shop principle was essential to the functioning of the cheap labor market, so the continued influx of homeseekers made possible the retention of the open shop. If the influx had ever stopped, the workers stranded in the region might have organized, but they could never organize so long as the surplus existed. In effect, the system was self-generating and self-perpetuating; once started, it could not be abandoned. Like a narcotic addict, the system required increasingly large shots of the same poison. Needless to say, this hopping-up process was inherently dangerous to the civic health of the community, nor was it long before some symptoms of the acuteness of the malady became apparent.

OTISTOWN: THE BLOODY ARENA

> It is somehow absurd but nevertheless true that for forty
> years the smiling, booming sunshine City of the Angels has
> been the bloodiest arena in the Western World!
>
> —Morrow Mayo

The depression of 1893, coming so shortly after "the new beginning" had been inaugurated, had serious repercussions in Southern California. Low prices for farm products ruined scores of farmers, and their failure, in turn, resulted in a run on the local banks. In June 1893, six banks closed their doors. Then the mechanics on the Santa Fe line went on strike. Hundreds of unemployed workers were enrolled in pick-and-shovel brigades, while others joined the Southern California contingent of Coxey's Army.* Those who enlisted in Coxey's Army, however, did not get farther east than Colton, California, where two hundred of the marchers were arrested for disturbing the peace and sentenced to four months in jail.

When the employees of the Pullman Company walked out on May 11, 1894, the American Railway Union tied up eleven rail lines running out of Chicago. By June 27, California was completely cut off from the rest of the country. With large shipments of perishable fruit accumulating in Los Angeles, the strike quickly assumed major proportions. Since the *Times* represented the spearhead of the antiunion movement, the railroad workers directed most of their activities against this bastion of reaction. "Daily a cordon of strikers," reported the *Times*, in a retrospective account, "would gather about the Times Building, forcibly take the bundles of papers from the emerging route men and carriers, and litter the surrounding streets for blocks with tattered fragments of newsprint." Large demonstrations in support of the railroad strikers were held throughout the city. A sweeping injunction against picketing was promptly obtained from Judge Erskine M. Ross of the Federal District Court. When the injunction failed to break the strike, two companies of the First Regiment, United States Infantry, were ordered into Los Angeles. By July 15 the rail lines were able to resume service and the strike was broken. As part of the aftermath of the strike, the Los Angeles leaders of the American Railway Union were indicted, tried before Judge Ross, convicted, and given long prison sentences which were later upheld by the United States Supreme Court.

Known in local annals as the Debs Rebellion, the railroad strike marshaled the fruit growers, who had suffered substantial losses, and the local merchants, who shared the same losses, in support of the *Times*'s anti-union campaign. A Merchants' Association had been formed in 1894, the year of the strike, to promote La Fiesta de Los Angeles, a gaudy tourist ballyhoo. The following year a Manufacturers' Association was formed, and in 1896 the

---

* Jacob Coxey led a group of five hundred men on a march to Washington, D.C., in 1894 to protest the U.S. government's failure to relieve the impact of the depression of 1893.

two groups merged under the leadership of the *Times* as the Merchants and Manufacturers Association, which quickly became, in the words of Peter Clark MacFarlane, "the greatest closed-shop organization this country has ever known."

One of the first acts of the newly formed M & M was to raise $25,000 by subscription for the purpose of "rounding up the large army of idle men in the city and putting them to work." Emboldened by a number of similarly easy victories, the M & M and the *Times* decided to make Los Angeles an open-shop town and to spread the fight on a nation-wide basis. Up to this time, the labor movement in San Francisco had largely ignored Los Angeles, but with the issue being so sharply drawn, a campaign was finally launched to organize the City of the Angels. At the request of the International Typographical Union, the American Federation of Labor decided in 1907 that the Otistown threat must be met. For by 1907 it had become apparent that, at the rate industry was growing in Los Angeles, it was only a question of time until the city would be in a position to challenge the industrial supremacy of San Francisco, thereby endangering organized labor's great Western stronghold. A local newspaper, the *News*, was purchased, its name was changed to the *Citizen*, and the great battle was on.

From 1907 to 1910, a state of war existed in Los Angeles, with the community being torn apart by industrial strife. Realizing that the outcome of the fight might be decisive, not only of local, but of regional and national phases of the same issue, both sides poured thousands of dollars into Los Angeles. With the eyes of the nation riveted on Los Angeles, neither side could afford to call a truce. It is altogether likely that the *Times* might have succumbed, during this period, had it not been for the continuing support it received from sources outside the state and from the incoming tide of Middle Western farmers who were strongly inclined toward the anti-labor position. The culmination of this bitter three-year struggle—vividly described in an excellent chapter in Morrow Mayo's book about Los Angeles*—occurred on the fateful night of October 1, 1910, when the plant of the *Los Angeles Times* was dynamited.

In the spring of 1910, a series of strikes had occurred in Los Angeles, first of brewery workers, later of metal workers. Called after a general lockout had been ordered, the metal-workers' strike was the issue that led directly to

---

* *Los Angeles* by Morrow Mayo (A.A. Knopf, 1933)

the dynamiting of the *Times*. As soon as the strike was called, the various companies involved obtained injunctions which prohibited all types of picketing. Instead of breaking the strike, the injunctions only further infuriated the workers and the picket lines became increasingly militant. Sensing that a real crisis existed, the M & M proceeded to draft and to dictate the adoption on July 16, 1910, of an anti-picketing ordinance. One of the most sweeping ordinances of the kind ever enacted in this country, the Los Angeles ordinance is famous in labor history as the original anti-picketing ordinance later used as a model by various employer groups across the nation. Within a few weeks after its adoption, 470 workers had been arrested in Los Angeles.

So far as the workers of Los Angeles were concerned, the enactment of this ordinance was the straw that broke the camel's back. Smarting under the accumulated resentments and humiliations of two decades of industrial conflict, they decided to smash the coalition of open-shop forces in the community. The strike had been regarded as another industrial dispute, but the ordinance raised a major political issue. Juries began to release defendants charged with violating the ordinance almost as fast as they were arrested. Over twenty thousand copies of Clarence Darrow's pamphlet "The Open Shop" were distributed in Los Angeles; the circulation of the Socialist publication, *The Appeal to Reason,* jumped to forty thousand a week; and membership in the Socialist Party doubled overnight. A Union Labor Political Club was formed, delegates from which sat on the county central committee of the Socialist Party, and the headquarters of the party were transferred to the Labor Temple.

Long before this crisis, the people of Los Angeles had given indication of a tendency to depart from traditional norms of political behavior. Charlotte Perkins Gilman, in her autobiography, has given an interesting account of the social enthusiasm rife in Southern California in the eighties. "California," she wrote, "is a state peculiarly addicted to swift enthusiasms. It is a seed-bed of all manner of cults and theories, taken up, and dropped with equal speed." A major enthusiasm of the eighties had been Edward Bellamy.* For several years Mrs. Gilman had managed to earn a living by lecturing on everything from "Human Nature" to "Social Economics" to the various Nationalist or Bellamy clubs with which Southern California was honeycombed. Under the

* Author of *Looking Backward,* the essential utopian novel, published in 1888.

leadership of the brilliant trade-union lawyer Job Harriman, the Socialist Party had succeeded in capturing much of this early social enthusiasm. But it was the anti-picketing ordinance that suddenly converted a movement of social idealism into a fighting political force.

Still another development led up to, and was a factor in precipitating, the crisis of 1910. This development was largely a result of the work of the pioneer liberal and reformer Dr. John R. Haynes. Settling in Los Angeles in 1887, Dr. Haynes had made a large fortune in real estate. Just where he derived his reforming social impulses I do not know, but he became one of the earliest advocates of the initiative, referendum, and recall in the United States. Almost entirely due to his efforts, the City of Los Angeles was one of the first cities in the nation to adopt these measures as part of its charter in 1902. The recall measure was first used in 1904, to recall a councilman who had voted to give the city's legal advertising to the *Los Angeles Times* despite the fact that its bid was $15,000 higher than the lowest bid. In the years of 1900 to 1910, a strong Good Government movement had developed in Los Angeles around men like Dr. Haynes, a movement which was, needless to say, anathema to General Otis and associates. Not long prior to the dynamiting of the *Times*, the Good Government League had recalled a corrupt mayor, one of the earliest uses of the recall to oust a mayor in American political history. At the recall election, the league had elected George Alexander as mayor against the vigorous opposition of the *Times*. Thus at the time the metal-workers' strike occurred, the conservative elements of the community were divided.

With the conservative forces divided, the Socialist Party, functioning as the political arm of the trade-union movement, began to record striking gains. In a series of parades organized by the party, as many as ten and twenty thousand workers marched through the streets of Los Angeles singing, shouting, and chanting the slogans of the early Socialist movement. Against this background, the labor fight assumed the character, as Mr. MacFarlane pointed out in *Collier's*, "of the most desperate battle against the incoming or upgrowing of labor unions that any American city has ever witnessed." In effect, this tense situation existed in Los Angeles for seventeen months prior to the dynamiting of the *Times*. With the dreadful explosion of October 1, 1910, in which twenty men lost their lives, a reign of unmitigated political terror was unleashed in Los Angeles. Importing scores of thugs, professional gunmen, and private detectives, the M & M sought to use the prosecution of the

McNamaras—active in the organization of the metal workers—as a means of braking the popular rebellion that had developed.

While the case was pending in the courts, Los Angeles began to prepare for a city election. At the primary, Job Harriman, running on the Socialist ticket, polled fifty-eight thousand votes for the office of mayor, a plurality of several thousand votes over the other candidates. Both the Otismen and the "goo-goos" (supporters of Good Government) were filled with fear and trembling by this amazing vote, which, be it remembered, was recorded after the dynamiting of the *Times*. The outcome of the final election involved more than the fate of the McNamaras (it was currently assumed that if Harriman won, they would probably be acquitted) and the control of the city government; it involved the very future of Los Angeles. For it happened that the city faced a serious financial crisis at the time. Of $23 million in bonds which the city had authorized for the Owens Valley aqueduct, only $17 million had been sold in 1911. In the meantime, the city had authorized still another bond issue of $3 million for the construction of a hydroelectric plant, and no portion of this issue had been sold. Furthermore, a bond issue of $10 million had been proposed for harbor improvements at San Pedro, of which $3 million had been authorized but not sold. Thus the interesting question arose: could this largely non-industrial city of three hundred thousand population sell $17 million in bonds if it proceeded to elect a Socialist as mayor?

To give this question added poignancy, Harriman had been campaigning on a platform which called for graduated taxes, complete ownership of all public utilities, including ice and laundry companies, and other major social reforms. That he stood a good chance of being elected was generally conceded. The "goo-goos" were backing Mayor Alexander for re-election; the *Times*, whose candidate had "failed badly in the primaries," loathed and detested Alexander; and both the *Express* and the *Examiner* had their own candidates for the office. When Harriman led the ticket at the primaries, all these elements finally decided to back Mayor Alexander. General Otis announced that he would support Alexander whether the so-and-so liked the idea or not. Seemingly assured of victory, Harriman had closed the campaign with a series of parades, demonstrations, and meetings of such magnitude that even the *Times* was moved to express its sense of "awe" and "wonder."

In the meantime, Lincoln Steffens had succeeded in negotiating a deal with General Otis, the essence of which was that the McNamaras would plead guilty on the eve of the election and receive prison sentences. These negotiations were handled with the utmost secrecy; for example, Harriman, I am convinced, did not know that a deal was pending. On December 1, 1911, four days before the final election, the McNamaras entered a plea of guilty to the charge. The news that such a plea had been entered came as a stunning, paralyzing blow to the labor movement, not only in Los Angeles, but throughout the nation (see, for example, Louis Adamic's vivid account of the aftermath of the case in *Dynamite*). The next day the streets of Los Angeles, which had been echoing with Socialist battle-cries, were littered with Harriman buttons and badges. Clarence Darrow, en route to his headquarters, was hissed and booed by a crowd of erstwhile supporters. Needless to say, Harriman was defeated.

The dynamiting of the *Times*, and more particularly, the plea of guilty entered by the McNamaras, aborted the labor movement in Los Angeles. It set back by twenty years a movement which, even in 1911, was dangerously retarded in relation to the growth of the community. The serious consequences of this abortion largely account for the subsequent political pathology of Los Angeles. Areas such as Los Angeles, where opposition to trade unions has assumed, in the words of a report of the LaFollette Committee,* "a conspiratorial pattern of malfeasance," become "a haven of would-be exploiters and those who would preach radical political and economic doctrines. They are breeding grounds for strange nostrums. They are subject to a continuing unhealthy unbalance of economic power and position, often accompanied by occasional outbursts of class violence and a constant undercurrent of class hostility. They frequently provide a reason for the location of industry at sub-standard levels and thereby stimulate counteraction in other urban areas where real estate, banking, and service business are drawn into a circle of vicious competition. Where there are large tributary areas, a whole state or section of the state may be dominated by the attitudes of industrial autocracy that prevail in the urban center....Such areas are likely to be vulnerable to the economic, social, and political evils that democracy must meet and vanquish if it is to survive. Our society has judged them not the 'white spots' but the cancer areas."

---

* Subcommittee of the Senate Committee on Education and Labor, headed by Senator Robert LaFollette, charged with investigating corporate violations of free speech and labor rights.

"BREAD AND HYACINTHS"

Job Harriman, the key figure in the fight to unionize Los Angeles, was an interesting person. Like General Otis and Dr. John R. Haynes, he had come to Southern California in the eighties (1886 to be exact), and like them he had been attracted by the tourist ballyhoo. Opening a law office, he practiced some years in Los Angeles, left for a short period, and finally returned in 1903. A prominent figure in the early Socialist movement, he was once the nominee of the party for the vice-presidency. After the McNamara debacle, Harriman came to the conclusion that a Socialist movement could never be based directly on trade-union organization implemented by political action. "I was so impressed," he wrote in *Communities of the Past and Present* (1924), "with the fact that the movement must have an economic foundation that I turned my attention to the study of means by which we could lay some such foundation, even though it be a small one as well as an experimental one. After two or three years, I decided to try to establish a co-operative colony."

Much as General Otis and his colleagues had decided to make a "new beginning" out of the wreckage of the land boom, so Harriman decided to launch a brave new world out of the wreckage of the labor-Socialist movement in Los Angeles. If Otis could build a city out of almost nothing, it did not seem too far-fetched to believe that another, and very different, kind of community might be established in this strange land in which so many things that seemed impossible of achievement had actually been realized. It is significant that the motivation of Harriman's utopianism stemmed directly from the defeat of the trade-union movement, a defeat which he rationalized, not in terms of the economics of the region, but as the outgrowth of a basic ideological weakness. In essence the idea of the project— "a retreat to the desert"—represented Harriman's violent reaction to the tragic events in which he had been involved.

In the name of the Llano del Rio Company (formed under the laws of Nevada with a capitalization of $2 million), Harriman acquired a tract of land in Antelope Valley, ninety miles by road from Los Angeles, located near the mouth of Big Rock Canyon, which had been known to the Spanish as *Rio del Llano*. The tract had originally been laid out as a temperance colony by the Mescal Land & Water Company. There the temperance advocates had formed an irrigation improvement district, issued bonds, and constructed a mile-long tunnel for water. Later the project had been abandoned when the company defaulted under the bond issue. Buying up these bonds for a nominal sum, Harriman was able to secure control of the entire tract for the Llano del Rio Company. In May 1914, the first group of five families moved to the project.

Harriman's conception of the structure of this utopian community is of considerable historical interest and importance. He had decided to use the private corporation as the legal instrument by which the colony was to be established. Although a private corporation, the Llano del Rio Company was, in effect, a collective farm, a workers' soviet. Colonists purchased stock in the company and received back an agreement from the corporation to employ them at wages of four dollars a day payable out of the net earnings. Since only settlers were permitted to purchase stock, it followed that they would also own all the assets of the company. While settlers were eventually drawn from many different localities, the original colonists were persons who had long been associated with Harriman in the Socialist-labor movement in Los Angeles. Among these pioneer colonists were Frank E. Wolfe, editor of a labor paper (he made a motion picture about the Tom Mooney case in 1916 entitled "From Dusk to Dawn" in which Harriman and Clarence Darrow appeared); W. A. Engle, chairman of the Central Labor Council of Los Angeles; and Frank P. McMahon, who had formerly been an official of the Brick Layers' Union.

Today Antelope Valley is a prosperous farming community in which alfalfa is raised for the dairy farms of Los Angeles, but in 1914 it was a desert. On this desert, the Llano colonists labored with incredible tenacity to demonstrate the workability of the socialist ideal. On the project, they constructed barns and silos, an office building, a community of homes, a cannery, two hotels, and many other structures. Completing the tunnel for water, they removed the Joshua trees, sagebrush, and greasewood of the desert and planted 240 acres to alfalfa, 200 acres to orchard crops, and 100 acres to garden produce. They lined the irrigation ditches with cobblestone, drew up plans for the construction of a sawmill, and took out a permit to cut timber in the mountains. Functioning as part of the project were a print shop, a shoe-repair shop, a laundry, a clothes-cleaning establishment, a warehouse, a rug-making shop, a swimming pool, an art studio, a library, and a rabbit farm. Here, at Llano, was established one of the first Montessori schools in California. In 1917 the cannery produced two carloads of canned tomatoes.

During the time the project was in existence, over two thousand people visited Llano annually. One of these visitors reported that the social life of the colony "possessed a charm which held its members when the hardships of subjugating the desert nearly overwhelmed them." While Southern California has long been noted for the number of privately controlled co-operative enterprises, Llano represented the first real production co-operative in the region, and as such, it attracted intense local interest and widespread national comment. On May Day the colonists, dressed in their best clothes, marched through the streets of the settlement with their own band and a red flag flying at the head of the parade. "If you have two loaves of bread," they said, "sell one and buy a hyacinth to feed your soul."

Considering the background of the project, Harriman's insistence on proving the feasibility of socialism cannot be dismissed as quixotic. The Soviet Union was not in existence in 1914. Here on the desert of Southern California, on the eve of the First World War, he had determined to build an island of socialism, not only to establish the soundness of the socialist ideal, but to wipe out the memory of a disastrous defeat. The significance of the experiment was quickly recognized by its opponents. From the beginning, the Llano project was invested with an army of stool pigeons, informers, and agents provocateurs. Every difference of opinion which arose among the colonists was fanned into a flame by these internal enemies. Sensational news stories in the Los Angeles press heralded each squabble in the project as certain proof of the unsoundness of this utopia-on-the-desert. With colonists being encouraged by outside elements to file lawsuits against the company, the court records were soon littered with litigation. Harriman, the guiding intelligence of the project, was forced to spend most of his time in court defending one or another of the dozens of trumped-up lawsuits filed against the company.

Despite these difficulties, however, the project would probably have survived had it not been for the fact that a survey made in 1917 indicated that the water supply, when fully developed, would not be sufficient to meet the growing requirements of the colony. In 1917 Harriman made a trip to Louisiana, secured an option on twenty thousand acres of cut-over timber land, and determined to move the entire colony to New Llano. In December 1917, Llano del Rio was abandoned, and in a special train, the remaining colonists left for their new home in Louisiana. From 1917 to date, they have struggled to maintain themselves in their new location, where with characteristic energy they have built still another community, with stores, hotels, homes, and a lumber mill. While a receiver was appointed for the project some years ago, some of the original colonists are still living on the property. The story of these colonists who, for over a quarter of a century, have struggled to establish the feasibility of the socialist ideal is one of the moving episodes in the history of social movements in America. Over the years, I have come to know some of the colonists who eventually abandoned New Llano and returned to Los Angeles. Although a few of them are rather disillusioned, the enthusiasm of most of them has not abated. They still speak of those early days at Llano-on-the-desert with an elation which has survived through the years. Certain of these colonists have been active leaders in the self-help co-operative movement in Southern California. A former Llano colonist, Walter Millsap, founded the United Cooperative Industries in Los Angeles in 1923....

"THE WHITE SPOT"

Some years after the armistice, three thousand longshoremen went on strike at San Pedro. The rebirth of the labor movement in Los Angeles, after the great disaster of 1910, really dates from the call for this strike. As soon as the strike was called, the M & M promptly intervened. "Black Jack" Jerome, a notorious strikebreaker of the period, and scores of professional gunmen were sent into the harbor district to smash the strike. Not only were strikers arrested for the offense of merely being on strike, but anyone who showed the slightest sympathy for the strike was likely to be arrested. An Episcopalian clergyman was arrested in the streets of San Pedro when he asked a policeman to direct him to the strike headquarters. The owner of a restaurant was jailed for the offense of having fed some of the strikers. Employed at the time by the *Los Angeles Times,* I used to watch the screaming Black Marias of Police Chief Louis Oaks roll up to the First Street Station loaded with strikers. At the height of the strike, over six hundred strikers were in jail in Los Angeles.

In 1915 Upton Sinclair, then at the pinnacle of his fame, had come to live in Pasadena. Learning of the disturbances at San Pedro, Mr. Sinclair announced that he intended to speak at Liberty Hill, on a small tract of privately owned land which had been rented for the occasion. On the night of the meeting, Liberty Hill was black with the massed figures of the strikers. Mounting a platform illuminated by a lantern, Mr. Sinclair proceeded to read

Article One of the Constitution of the United States and was promptly arrested. Hunter Kimbrough then mounted the platform and started to read the Declaration of Independence and was promptly arrested. Prince Hopkins then stepped on the platform and stated, "We have not come here to incite to violence" and was immediately arrested. Hugh Hardyman then followed Hopkins and cheerfully announced, "This is a most delightful climate" and was promptly arrested. For eighteen hours these four men were held incommunicado while their lawyer, John Beardsley, now a judge of the Superior Court of Los Angeles County, tried frantically to discover where they were being held. He finally succeeded in serving a writ of habeas corpus, and the next day they were all released. A few days later, all but twenty-eight of the six hundred strikers in jail were released, and, in effect, the strike had been won.

Disturbed by this resurgence of protest, the *Times*, the M & M, and their allies determined to make Los Angeles "the white spot" of the nation. From 1920 to 1934, they ruled Southern California with an iron hand. From its enactment in 1919 to 1924, 531 men were indicted in California for violation of the Criminal Syndicalism Act. Of those arrested, 264 were tried, 164 convicted, and 128 were sentenced to San Quentin Prison for terms of from one to fourteen years. A large part of these prosecutions arose in Southern California. In 1920 the Better America Federation was formed in Los Angeles with funds largely provided by the various private utilities. The wages and expenses of three professional informers who were used in virtually all of the criminal syndicalism prosecutions were paid by this organization. In response to its demand, *The Nation* and *The New Republic* were removed from reading lists in the Los Angeles schools. Teachers who advocated public ownership of utilities were denounced as bolsheviks. It was the Better America Federation that forced the City of Los Angeles to establish a "Red Squad" under the leadership of the well-known Captain William ("Red") Hynes. For fifteen years, this squad made a mockery of the right of free speech in Los Angeles. Conducting a perennial witch-hunt for "reds" and "pinks" in all walks of life, the Red Squad drove numberless teachers and clergymen from their posts and presided, like an S.S. Elite Guard, over the City of Los Angeles. I have watched the members of this squad break up meetings in halls and public parks with a generous use of tear-gas bombs and clubs. Throughout these years, as the reports of the LaFollette Committee abundantly demonstrate, the City of

Los Angeles, the Better America Federation, and the M & M employed a host of spies, stool pigeons, and informers to disrupt trade unions, to provoke violence, and to ferret out the "reds." Strikes of agricultural workers were broken in the very backyard of Los Angeles with a brutality and violence remarkable even in California.

For twenty years, a well-known clubwoman of Los Angeles was paid by these employer organizations to spy upon the activities of various liberal and progressive groups. Even her dues in these organizations were paid by her employers. She sat on the board of directors of virtually every liberal organization in the city and regularly reported to the police and to her employers. During the years when Los Angeles was being advertised as "the white spot" of the nation, the entire civic life of the community was honeycombed with these informers. Typical of these years is a little boxed story that appeared in the Los Angeles press: "This will be 'shove Tuesday' for the Los Angeles police. The communists plan to stage another demonstration today, according to Capt. Wm. Hynes, which means that 500 police will be held in readiness. If the communists demonstrate, the policemen will shove and keep on shoving until the parade is disrupted." The "shove days" were of regular occurrence in Los Angeles.

"Unemployment is a crime in Sunny California," wrote Louis Adamic of the decade 1920 to 1930. "The state is advertised as a paradise, and when 'come-ons' come and fail to get work they are jailed. Shabby-looking men are stopped in the streets, dragged out of flophouses, asked if they have work; and if they answer in the negative, are arrested for vagrancy....Few persons in Los Angeles know about these things. The press of course is mum on the subject; for the tourists must not get the idea that anything is wrong with Los Angeles. Then, too, who cares about a lot of bums and reds? Folks are so busy enjoying themselves that a good-natured banker in town recently seriously announced a new 'service' his institution had just started, to relieve his clients of the 'hardship' of clipping their coupons!" The police statistics of the city amply substantiated this statement; in 1927 to 1928, 12,202 arrests were made in Los Angeles for "vagrancy."

"Is California civilized?" asked Robert Whitaker in *The Nation* (April 1931). "Yes, California is civilized. That is what is the matter with it; its civilization, economically considered, is the legal, political, and disciplinary ascendancy of a ruling class which lives by the exploitation of labor, and especially of unskilled labor....It will be forty-three years in August of this year since I first saw California, after a long ride through the desert....For more than four decades I have been privileged to live in one of the fairest and kindliest of all the regions of the earth. California is, indeed, a marvelous land; beyond anything the passing tourist can ever know, and many of its people are among the choicest fruits of human evolution. All of this only accentuates the bewilderment and bitter disappointment which must be felt by any thinking man at the social barbarism of California, provided he has any knowledge beyond what the pitiful public press gives of our ignorance, our intolerance, and above all our complacent social inertia."

It is this long background of terrorism and police brutality that the latter-day commentators on Los Angeles crackpotism so completely ignore. It was not the climate or the sunshine of Southern California that developed a strong undercurrent of liberal-radical thought in the community, but rather the extraordinarily shortsighted and stupid activities of the power-drunk tycoons who ruled the city. "Red" Hynes made a dozen radicals in Los Angeles for every arrest he ever made. Studying the "Cossackism" of the Los Angeles police in 1931, Ernest Jerome Hopkins correctly reported that radicalism had flourished under the lash of persecution which, for twenty-five years, had been so consistently applied in the community. The sensational mass political movements that developed in Southern California in the thirties did not "just happen." To a great extent, they represented the inevitable expression of political aspirations that had been maturing for a quarter of a century and which, during this period, had been brutally and systematically suppressed.

It should be emphasized that the trade-union movement did not begin to develop real strength in Southern California until 1937. Throughout the period from 1890 to 1937, Los Angeles was the "last citadel of the open shop," "the white spot" of the nation, the paradise of the professional patriot and the red-baiter. The mass political movements of the thirties were not inspired by the trade-union movement. They were popular, largely spontaneous, political movements, based upon the prior political experience of the community, the inevitable reaction to twenty-five years of irresponsible boosterism. When the depression swelled the ranks of the dispossessed with the numberless victims of land-swindles and business frauds, the situation was ripe for demagogic political movements. Just as the physical peculiarities of the region had compelled early settlers to devise new social forms to cope with their problems, so this novel combination of circumstances prompted the creation of new and untried political techniques. Unanchored to a strong trade-union movement, having few roots in the community, the dispossessed masses of Los Angeles were quick to invent new forms of action and new forms for the expression of social discontent. Much as the region had been built by boosterism and propaganda, so the mass movements, many of which were led by ex-realtors and ex-promoters and ex-clergymen, began to use the techniques of business to foster new political promotions.

Los Angeles itself is a kind of utopia: a vast metropolitan community built in a semi-arid region, a city based upon improvisation, words, propaganda, boosterism. If a city could be created by such methods, it did not seem incredible to these hordes of the dispossessed that a new society might be evoked, by a process of incantation—a society in which the benefits of the machine age would be shared by all alike, old and young, rich and poor. However naive the expression of this belief may have been, and the following sections will show that it was very naive indeed, it cannot be dismissed as mere crackpotism. The real crackpots of Los Angeles in the thirties were the individuals who ordered tons of oranges and vegetables dumped in the bed of the Los Angeles River while thousands of people were unemployed, hungry, and homeless.

PLENTY-FOR-ALL

> Utopias are often only premature truths.—Lamartine

Technocracy was the first major social enthusiasm, the initial manifestation of utopianism, to find expression in Southern California after the stock-market crash of 1929. While the movement was not spawned in Los Angeles, it is significant that no other community in the nation responded so quickly or so enthusiastically to the new dispensation. In part, the feverish interest which Technocracy aroused in Los Angeles was due to the energetic promotion given the new movement by Mr. Manchester Boddy, publisher of the *Daily News*.

In December 1937, the *Daily News* ran a sensational series of front-page stories about Technocracy, based on a series of articles which Wayne Parrish had contributed to the *New Outlook*. "While this series of daily articles was appearing," write Whiteman and Lewis in their study of Southern California mass movements (*Glory Roads*, 1936), "crowds congregated around the door of the pressroom as publication hour approached. When the first copies, ink scarcely dry, were off the press, the excitement rose to fever pitch. Men fought and scrambled. Dollar bills in the rear were often waved over the heads of those in front. Edition after edition would be sold out." Plenty-for-All clubs began to mushroom into existence throughout Los Angeles and, up in the lonely sand dunes of Pismo Beach (a section that has long nourished various mysticisms), E. L. Pratt founded a Technocratic newspaper. For approximately three months, Technocracy was a universal topic of conversation and discussion south of Tehachapi.

Although Technocracy proved to be a "flash in the pan" (interest in the movement collapsed almost as suddenly as it arose), the quickness with which the idea of Plenty-for-All caught on in Southern California was a harbinger of things to come. It was unquestionably the fountainhead from which flowed most of the ideas that were embodied in subsequent mass movements in the region. The mentality that embraced these ideas so avidly was essentially utopian as distinguished from ideological. "A state of mind is utopian," writes Karl Mannheim, "where it is incongruous with the state of reality within which it occurs." Ideologies, on the other hand, while they may "transcend the situation," in Mannheimian terms, are nevertheless a reflection of reality. In terms of existing social realities in Southern California, nothing could have been more utopian, in this sense, than the social order envisaged by the Technocrats. Torn apart by internal dissension, the Technocrats failed to organize the enthusiasm which their ideas had evoked, but it was not long before the new vision of abundance began to be systematically organized.

Although formally incorporated on February 20, 1934, the Utopian Society came into existence in the summer of 1933. The society was founded by Eugene J. Reed, a former bond salesman; W. G. Rousseau, a former promoter; and Merritt Kennedy, a former stock salesman for the Julian Petroleum Company. As a social movement, the Utopian Society had two novel features: it utilized the chain-letter technique of business to recruit members, and, both in ritual and in structure, the organization was patterned after the American secret society, or fraternal group. So effective was its secret fraternal character that the organization had acquired a membership running into the thousands before the press of Los Angeles even knew of its existence. By midsummer 1934, the society had a membership of at least five hundred thousand, with as many as 250 meetings being held every night in

Los Angeles. In fact, the Better America Federation estimated that a maximum of 1,063 neighborhood meetings were held one evening during the summer. The first public meeting of the society, held in Hollywood Bowl on June 23, was attended by twenty-five thousand people.

The essence of the movement's appeal consisted in its secret ritual designed to give the uninitiated a glimpse of "the new economic order" and to acquaint them with the arithmetic of plenty. Not only did the secrecy of the movement enable it to gain considerable headway in Southern California before the big guns of reaction were leveled against it, but its rituals fascinated thousands of ex-middle-class Americans for whom the secret fraternity was, perhaps, the social form with which they were most thoroughly familiar. In a community made up overwhelmingly of outsiders or newcomers, it had the great merit of bringing people together in small groups, in particular neighborhoods or localities, and of uniting them by a mystic bond. A significant feature of the society was its marked emphasis upon purely social activities. In this sense, it was a kind of colossal "Lonesome Club."

I wrote the first article to appear in the national press about the society (*The New Republic*, July 18, 1934), and watched its meteoric rise and fall at close range. The membership of the society was made up overwhelmingly of white-collar, lower middle-class elements. At one of the initiation meetings which I was permitted to attend, although I was not a member of the society, the neophytes consisted of a woman physician, an employee of a public-utility company, the owner of a small business, the manager of a lumber yard, a marine engineer, a garage mechanic, two city employees, a carpenter, and a barber. Politically inhibited and organizationally frustrated by the despotic dominance of reaction in Southern California, these elements saw, in the secret character of the Utopian Society, a means by which they might articulate their unrest and discontent. At the fourth-cycle initiations of the society, which were usually held at the Shrine Auditorium, the seven thousand seats would be filled hours before the ritual began, and literally thousands of people would be milling about in the streets seeking to gain admission. The promoters of the society were completely surprised by its success and never did seem to know just what to do with, or how to direct, the phenomenal enthusiasm they had aroused. Once all the neophytes had been taken through the four cycles of the ritual, there didn't seem to be anything else to do with them, and early in 1935, the movement fell apart. Between 1933 and 1935, however, it furnished the reactionaries of the community with the biggest fright of their lives.

Unnoticed by the press, Upton Sinclair had, in September of 1933, changed his political registration from the Socialist to the Democratic Party. A few months later, he announced that he would be a candidate for the Democratic nomination for Governor of California in the 1934 election. The announcement was greeted with mild ridicule. In explaining how he happened to become a candidate, Sinclair later said: "I saw old people dying of slow starvation, and children by the tens of thousand growing up stunted by the diseases of malnutrition—the very schoolteachers dipping into their slender purses to provide milk for pupils who came to school without breakfast. I saw hundreds of thousands of persons driven from their homes; the sweep of an economic process which had turned most of California over to money-lenders and banks. I saw one colossal swindle after another perpetrated upon the public; and for every official who was sent to jail I knew that a thousand were hiding with their loot." Launching his campaign with a pamphlet on how to End Poverty in California, Mr. Sinclair was soon speaking from one end of the state to another. Months before the August 1934 primaries, it was clearly apparent that he would win the Democratic nomination, for, as Charles W. Van Devander has pointed out, "the desperation of the times had coalesced all the dissident elements of the state into one great surging political movement."

Los Angeles County was the center, the home, of the Epic movement. By June 1934, three hundred thousand people were unemployed in Los Angeles. Commenting on the situation in the county, the monthly bulletin of the State Relief Administration for June 1934 pointed out: "Unemployment due to depressions is distorted and prolonged in Los Angeles by the deficiency of productive industries....It is believed that the oil boom of the early 1920s, the motion pictures and real-estate booms, the stimulations of tourist trade and migrations by the local chambers of commerce, have overpopulated the county with white-collar workers. Permanent jobs do not exist for them within the basic industries of the county. The population is over 85 percent urban, concentrated in twenty-nine cities, most of which cluster around Los Angeles. Since 1920, the population has more than doubled. The proportion of white-collar workers to all gainfully employed workers has become almost double that of the United States as a whole....The productive industries do not appear large enough to justify the size of the white- collar class....Less than one out of twenty gainful workers is employed normally in agriculture, against one out of five for the United States." Since the groups most severely affected by the depression in Los Angeles were white-collar, lower middle-class elements, it is not surprising that the expression of their discontent assumed novel forms. Essentially, Technocracy, the Utopian Society, and the Epic movement represented, therefore, an upsurge of lower middle-class, white-collar elements.

Nothing quite like the Epic campaign of 1934 had ever occurred in American politics. It was distinctly a grass-roots affair, organized, directed, and financed by "the little people" under the extraordinarily skillful leadership of Mr. Sinclair. By the close of the campaign, over eight hundred Epic clubs had been formed in the state, with most of them being located, however, south of Tehachapi. Close to a million copies of Mr. Sinclair's original Epic pamphlet and his book, *I, Governor of California,* were sold to raise funds for the campaign. When the reactionary elements of the state realized that not only had Sinclair won the Democratic nomination but that he stood an excellent chance of being elected governor, they unleashed a campaign of unparalleled vilification, misrepresentation, slander, and abuse. According to Mr. Van Devander, over $10 million was spent to defeat Sinclair. The motion-picture companies, drawing upon their prize collection of villainous types, made fake newsreel interviews with "bums en route to California" which were shown in every motion-picture theater in the state. Intimidating notes were inserted in payroll envelopes, employees were directly threatened by their employers with discharge if they voted for Sinclair, and the best advertising brains in California were put to work culling scare-quotes from Mr. Sinclair's voluminous writings. In the final election, the ex-Iowan Frank Merriam was elected, the vote being Merriam, 1,138,000; Sinclair, 879,000; and Haight, 302,000. If the fight had been directly between Merriam and Sinclair, it is altogether probable that Sinclair would have been elected. As a matter of fact, it is altogether possible, as Mr. Van Devander explains, that Sinclair actually was elected governor, for there were many circumstantial indications that the count at the polls was fraudulent.

Although Mr. Sinclair was defeated, the Epic campaign was one of the most successful experiments in mass education ever performed in this country. Throughout the campaign, Mr. Sinclair expounded the economics of capitalism from one end of the state to the other with matchless skill, lucidity, and brilliance. While not a great orator, he is the peerless expositor, the great popularizer, the unexcelled pamphleteer. Years after the campaign was over, I used to see, in my travels about the state as Commissioner of Housing and Immigration, New Economy barber shops, Epic cafes, and Plenty-for-All stores in the most remote and inaccessible communities in California. I have seen the slogans of the Epic campaign painted on rocks in the desert, carved on trees in the forests, and scrawled on the walls of labor camps in the San Joaquin Valley. So swiftly had the depression engulfed thousands upon thousands of middle-class elements in California that people thought nothing of enlisting in the campaign of an internationally famous Socialist, selling his pamphlets and books, and preaching the doctrine of "production for use." Five years previously, these same people, as Walter Davenport pointed out, would no more have voted for Sinclair than they would have voted for Satan himself. While the movement was widespread throughout the state, its greatest strength was recorded in the areas of heaviest migration, notably in Los Angeles County and the East Bay district of Northern California....

HAM AND EGGS

During periods of great social stress in industrial communities, the dispossessed are likely to smash factory windows, or to conduct hunger marches, or to dramatize their desperation in some concrete manner. But in an area without smokestacks where the sale of real estate has been the major industry, there are no visible symbols upon which the distressed masses can vent their fury. To the extent that their discontent can personalize a victim, it is likely to be the "moneylender" or the "big banker." Their hatred is inclined to be expressed in abstract form; their dreams to be dominated by abstract symbols, "money," "riches," "jewels," "wealth." Consequently, when they dream of Utopia, it is not of a well-planned, perfectly governed garden city, but of a perfect scheme or get-rich-quick system. Their archangel is not Sir Thomas More or Patrick Geddes, but the promoter who promises to deliver, the salesman with enticing phrases, the business magician.

The early mass political movements in Southern California, characterized by marked social inventiveness, were a healthy manifestation of a people's impulse to do something for themselves. Continued frustration of this impulse, however, soon began to produce rank and unhealthy social growths. Of all these latter-day growths, the Ham and Eggs movement is, by all odds, the most fantastic, incredible, and dangerous. The story of this movement, which follows, is largely based upon an interesting document by Winston and Marian Moore, entitled *Out of the Frying Pan,* published in Los Angeles in 1939. Incredible as they may sound, the facts set forth in this document, which I have summarized, have never been disputed or denied.

The story starts with the arrival in Los Angeles of Robert Noble, a neurotic but plausible rabble-rouser, young in years, attractive in appearance, dynamic in manner. He first appeared as a platform and radio speaker in the Epic campaign of 1934. Shortly after the Epic campaign, he began to make a name for himself as a radio commentator on Station KMTR, attracting a large following by his attacks on an unpopular city administration. Observing the rapidity with which the Townsend Plan* had spread throughout the region, he decided to conjure up a pension plan of his own based upon an article which he had read by Professor Irving Fisher on "stamp" money. Without bothering to prepare a plan, he simply began to speak on the air about a scheme that would pay the oldsters $25-Every-Monday. The slogan was excellent, the promise attractive, and soon the flow of nickels, dimes, and quarters began to increase in volume.

In the Hollywood building where Noble made his headquarters was also located the office of the Cinema Advertising Agency, operated by two brothers, Willis and Lawrence Allen, both talented promoters. Shortly before they had formed the Cinema Advertising Agency, Willis Allen had been involved in some promotional fancywork in connection with Grey Gone, a hair tonic. In need of assistance, Noble induced the Cinema Advertising Agency to manage his program and to negotiate, in the name of the agency, a contract for radio time on Station KMTR. As Noble's attacks on the city administration became increasingly violent and vitriolic, Captain Earl Kynette was assigned the task of devising ways and means to take him off the air. After making a cursory inspection of the situation, Kynette decided to kill two birds with one stone: to get Noble off the air and to get in on the pension scheme himself. Suggesting that Noble was not the man to head the movement, Kynette made a cash loan to the Allen brothers which enabled them to carry off a clever *putsch.*

A "rump" meeting of the pensionites was accordingly held in September

---

* A forerunner of Social Security: in 1933, Dr. Francis E. Townsend, a doctor from California, proposed a monthly federal pension of $200 for Americans age sixty and older, to be funded by a 2 percent national sales tax. The idea was widely popular, and Townsend Clubs sprang up across the nation to push for its implementation.

1937 in Clifton's Cafeteria, where many plots of the sort have been staged, and where many movements have been born. The meeting adopted articles of incorporation prepared by the Allens and then proceeded to elect an Allen-controlled board of directors. When Noble next appeared at Station KMTR, he found Willis Allen seated behind the microphone. And, when he called a meeting of the faithful to discuss this shrewdly executed maneuver, the meeting was disrupted by policemen making excellent use of stench bombs and tear gas. In desperation, Noble then attempted to throw a picket line around Station KMTR, but Capt. Kynette was again on hand with the "boys," and the picket line melted away like snow in the sun. In a final effort to regain control of the movement, Noble filed papers with the Secretary of State in which he sought to protect the slogan $25-Every-Monday. Not the kind of operators to be thwarted by such a ruse, the Allens immediately adopted the slogan $30-Every-Thursday, which was more pleasing to the ear and more attractive to the purse. Noble was out. And soon the interesting Captain Kynette was also "out"; for, shortly after the Noble *putsch* was effected, he clumsily planted a time-bomb in the automobile of an investigator who was probing the city administration and was caught, tried, and sentenced to San Quentin Prison.

Left in undisputed control of $30-Every-Thursday, the Allen brothers did not know quite what to do with the movement. They needed, first of all, an effective spellbinder. The orator was soon discovered in the person of Sherman Bainbridge, whose voice has long echoed in the cafeteria meeting rooms of Los Angeles. It was Bainbridge who coined the invaluable slogan "Ham and Eggs," which the pensionites shout with the frenzy of storm-troopers yelling *sieg heil*! All meetings of the Payroll Guarantee Association are opened with the shouted salutation "Ham and Eggs," and each speaker who appears on the platform must preface his remarks with the salutation. If he neglects to do so, the crowd will shout "Ham and Eggs" until he does. The Allens also needed a plan. Incredible as it may sound, they had been in control of the movement for eighteen months, conducting an intensive campaign by radio, newspaper, and open meetings, before so much as a line or a sentence had been placed on paper. They got the "plan" from Roy Owens, who for years had been an enthusiastic disciple of Father Divine.* The plan

---

* Father Divine's Peace Mission movement is premised on a belief in race neutrality and faith in Father Divine as the second coming of Christ. He was best known for his ability to feed thousands of people every day at free, fifty-course banquets during the depression.

contemplates the establishment of a state bank and the issuance of phony money to finance pension payments. They also needed "a situation," a springboard, from which they could really take off, and fate soon provided an occasion.

In San Diego—it would be San Diego—64-year-old Archie Price walked into a newspaper office one day and announced that, since he was too old to work and not old enough to qualify for a pension, he intended to commit suicide. The editor of the newspaper, a veteran in Southern California, scoffed at the suggestion. The next day Price committed suicide and was buried in a pauper's grave. Recognizing that Providence had provided them with the occasion for a spectacular mass demonstration, the Allens organized a march on San Diego. "Less than a month after the death of Archie Price," write the Moores, "Sherman Bainbridge led a funeral cortege of thousands of cars from Los Angeles to San Diego, where Archie Price was exhumed and re-interred amid an avalanche of gorgeous bloom, to the sound of lovely music and surrounded by a multitude of mourners which would have done justice to a monarch. Sheridan Downey, later United States Senator from California, assisted Bainbridge in speaking at the ceremony, and everything was very beautiful and impressive—and a little pitiful, because poor lonely Archie Price was so very dead." Poor lonely Archie Price became the Horst Wessel of the Ham and Eggs movement.*

So rapidly did the Ham and Eggs movement grow after this incident that, in 1938, its sponsors presented the Secretary of State with a petition signed by more than 750,000 residents of California asking that the $30-Every-Thursday proposal be submitted to the voters as an initiative measure. If enacted, the proposal would have involved the issuance of $30 million in warrants a week, or an annual turnover of $1.56 billion in warrant money. As soon as the politicians were informed of the number of signatures on the petition (789,000 to be exact: 25 percent of the registered voters of the state), they all began to shout "Ham and Eggs" in a deafening chorus, one notable exception being Robert Walker Kenny. So effectively had the Allens tended to the organizational details that, by simply sending out a call for letters, they could inundate any state official

---

* Horst Wessel, author of the poem that became the official song of Germany's Nazi Party, was murdered in 1930. Nazi propaganda claiming he had been murdered by a Communist accompanied a lavish funeral and made him a martyr in the Nazis' struggle against the Communists for power in Germany.

with from twenty-five thousand to thirty thousand letters in forty-eight hours. Whatever they asked their followers to do was promptly done. If they were asked to give money, they gave money; if asked to write letters, they wrote letters; if asked to march, they marched; if asked to demonstrate, they demonstrated. From the beginning of the movement to the present time, it has been characterized by the conspicuous absence of rank-and-file democratic controls. On the eve of the 1938 election, the organization thus dictatorially controlled by the Allen brothers had a regular dues-paying membership of two hundred thousand, and the organization itself was collecting an estimated $2,000 a day in contributions. All of the advertising and radio material of the Ham and Eggs movement has, of course, always been handled through the Cinema Advertising Agency, owned by Willis and Lawrence Allen.

This fantastic proposal came within an ace of being adopted in November 1938, being defeated by a vote of 1,398,000 opposed to 1,143,000 in favor of the proposal. Shortly after Culbert L. Olson took office in 1938, he was presented with a petition signed by 1,103,000 residents of California calling for a special election on the Ham and Eggs proposal. Once again the proposal received a staggering vote, but not enough to win. After the 1939 election, the movement began to decline, as the increasing prosperity of the defense program began to develop in California. When Governor Olson came up for re-election in 1942, he was defeated by his Republican opponent, Earl Warren, who was mysteriously in possession of the pension vote.

Today the movement languishes. In an effort to inject some new life into the movement, the Allen brothers have been collaborating with Gerald L. K. Smith, who was introduced at a meeting of the Payroll Guarantee Association by Willis Allen as "one of the greatest citizens of the United States."* This venture is not surprising, for there has always been an undercurrent of anti-Semitism in the Ham and Eggs movement. It should be emphasized that $30-Every-Thursday, unlike the Utopian Society, the self-help co-operatives, and the Epic movement, is not a product of the depression. It really dates from 1938.

---

* Gerald L. K. Smith (called "the greatest orator of them all" by H. L. Mencken) was a radical minister of the Disciples of Christ Church who proselytized for Huey Long's "Share Our Wealth" movement and tried to keep it going after Long was assassinated in 1935. A renowned anti-Semite, he proved to be too controversial to gain public favor and eventually ran into trouble for his alleged Fascist sympathies.

THE MESSIANIC NOTE

In a confused, distorted, half-crazy manner, these mass political movements represent a dim foreshadowing of the future. Certainly one cannot but be impressed by the recurrent Messianic note which echoes in these movements and in the various cult movements with which they are closely related. Several of the cultists, such as Guy Ballard, Arthur Bell, and Joe Jeffers, have actually proclaimed themselves Messiahs. The framed picture of Dr. Francis E. Townsend is to be found enshrined, like that of a patron saint, in many Southern California households. During the Epic campaign, Upton Sinclair was a Messiah, a Leader, a Prophet. In an effort to alienate his following, the opposition drafted the Rev. Martin Luther Thomas, leader of the Christian American Crusade, to attack Mr. Sinclair for his "anti-religious" tracts. Roy Anstey replied to these attacks with a poem:

> The people have awakened,
> And agree with one accord,
> That he who standeth for the POOR
> Is fighting for the LORD.
> The evil forces grew alarmed,
> The devil heard their prayer,
> And sent them spouting THOMAS
> To rant against SINCLAIR.

> Oh, God! that he should fall so low
> As to use YOUR HOLY HOUSE
> To crucify the leader
> Of a cause we all espouse.
> When SINCLAIR writes his final book,
> And his soul floats to the skies,
> We'll still hear spouting Thomases
> As they spew their Judas lies.

No man is more dangerous than the man who has caught a glimpse of a great idea, who has feverishly seized upon a fragment of truth and gone forth to battle chanting the slogans of a Messiah. I know of no one who has caught this undercurrent of crazy fury in Southern California quite as well as did the late Nathanael West in his novel *The Day of the Locust*:

It was a mistake to think them harmless curiosity seekers. They were savage and bitter, especially the middle-aged and the old, and had been made so by boredom and disappointment. All their lives they had slaved at some kind of dull, heavy labor, behind desks and counters, in the fields and at tedious machines of all sorts, saving their pennies and dreaming of the leisure that would be theirs when they had enough. Finally that day came. They could draw a weekly income of ten or fifteen dollars. Where else should they go but California, the land of sunshine and oranges?

Once there, they discovered that sunshine isn't enough. They get tired of oranges, even of avocado pears and passion fruit. Nothing happens. They don't know what to do with their time. They haven't the mental equipment for pleasure. Did they slave so long just to go to an occasional Iowa picnic? What else is there? They watch the waves come in at Venice. There wasn't any ocean where most of them came from, but after you've seen one wave, you've seen them all. The same is true of the airplanes at Glendale. If only a plane would crash once in a while so they could watch the passengers being consumed in a "holocaust of flame," as the newspapers put it. But the planes never crash.

Their boredom became more and more terrible. They realize that they've been tricked and burn with resentment. Every day of their lives they read the newspapers and went to the movies. Both fed them on lynchings, murder, sex crimes, explosions, wrecks, love nests, fires, miracles, revolutions, wars. This daily diet made sophisticates of them. The sun is a joke. Oranges can't titillate their jaded palates. Nothing can ever be violent enough to make taut their slack minds and bodies. They have been cheated and betrayed. They have slaved and saved for nothing.

In a final passage of this remarkable novel appears a scene in which all these people, armed with clubs and baseball bats, following lighted torches, decide they will march. "All those poor devils who can only be stirred by the promise of miracles and then only to violence…a super 'Dr. Know-All-Pierce-All' had made the necessary promise and they were marching behind his banner in a great united front of screwballs and screwboxes to purify the land. No longer bored, they sang and danced joyously in the red light of the flames." Frankly, it is a vision that has sometimes worried me, for I have seen the light that blazes in their eyes, I have heard the deafening "Ham and Eggs" chant, and I have listened to the anti-Semites addressing large crowds in the Embassy Auditorium.

Of course, the state of mind, the utopian mentality so vividly described by West is a national, not a local phenomenon. "We have developed a going understanding," writes Max Lerner in *PM* (June 1945), "that the advertisers don't have to be truthful and we don't have to believe them. It is all a sort of play in which it is one man's role to lie and the other's to be skeptical. Ours is a culture in which salesmanship continues to have a throbbing life of its own even when cut off from substance and truth, like the legs of a frog still quivering after being severed from the body...a curious combination of qualities: Nineveh and Sparta, luxury and violence....The reason is that we are a frontier nation that has moved, more swiftly than any in history, from hardihood to wealth, from timberlands to the big money. Our living standards are higher than in any other country in the world, but there is also a greater gap between lowest and highest than anywhere else. Ours is the land of success, but for every successful man there are hundreds unsuccessful. We have deep psychic hungers, all of us—hungers for money or power or dazzling beauty or acclaim."

As an embodiment of all these frustrations and fantasies, Southern California has become one of the most interesting and important regions of the nation. For here the swiftness of transition from rural to urban, from hardihood to wealth, has been most pronounced, here the social neuroticism produced by such a transition is most widespread, and here the extremes between "lowest" and "highest" are most patent and glaring. Here the movie-rich and the oil-rich are newcomers, lacking the sense of stability and the occasional sense of responsibility that wealth long possessed sometimes confers. Social discontent in Los Angeles has been fanned to a white heat by sensational newspaper stories of elaborate Hollywood parties, of oil tycoons giving $5,000 cocktail parties,* of banquet halls banked with roses and gardenias. Such anti-Semitic clichés as international bankers and moneylenders take on a horrible reality in the minds of the forty thousand people who purchased

---

* Adjusted for inflation, that's over $46,000.

forged Julian stock certificates with the hard-earned savings of a lifetime of work and effort, stock certificates which fluttered throughout Southern California like the torn fragments of telephone books in a city parade. Here the defeat of the American Dream has been most recent in point of time, most widely sensed, most sharply experienced. It was to this region that F. Scott Fitzgerald came to write *The Last Tycoon*. "If ever there was anything resembling communism or fascism in America," a Californian told R. L. Duffus in June 1945, "California would be the first to have it," and it would probably originate in the region south of Tehachapi.

It should be observed that the ferment of the depression years in Southern California, and the various movements which came out of this ferment, had a profound influence on the course of events not only in California but throughout the nation. Although Mr. Sinclair was defeated, some twenty-nine Epic-sponsored candidates were elected to the state legislature; the Epic movement sent Culbert L. Olson to the state Senate in 1934 on his way to the governorship in 1938; it elected Ben Lindsey to public office in Los Angeles; it sent Sheridan Downey to the United States Senate; and it sent such a hard-working public servant as Jerry Voorhis to Congress. The spectacular pension-plan movements of Southern California certainly played a part in securing the early adoption of the social-security program. Out of the ferment of these years has emerged a strong liberal and progressive movement in Southern California which, today, is allied with a powerful trade-union movement. Los Angeles ceased to be "the white spot" of the open shop in 1940, and in recent years the voters have repeatedly demonstrated that the hold of the old-guard reactionaries, the Better America Federation tycoons, has been broken. Today the "Red Squad" is no more, and democratic currents of thought and expression can, at long last, find free expression. With the trade-union and political-organization vacuum being filled, at long last, it is unlikely that demagogic movements could sweep the field as they did in years past. Above all, Los Angeles today has a real industrial foundation to support its inflated population.

Retiring from political life in 1934, Upton Sinclair now lives the life of a recluse in Monrovia, perennially engaged in writing the Lanny Budd novels. A remarkable man, this Upton Sinclair. During the Epic campaign, I interviewed him one insufferably hot August afternoon with a brush fire burning furiously in the hills back of Pasadena. We sat in a darkened room, the blinds pulled, our eyes smarting with smoke from the fires. While he failed to convince me that the Epic plan was feasible, he thoroughly convinced me that poverty and want could be banished from the earth. On another occasion, in 1927, I had lunch with him in Long Beach, on the day Sacco and Vanzetti were executed. I well remember what he had to say about the Sacco-Vanzetti case, the light that it shed on our culture and what it portended for the future. Looking back on that occasion today, I can only say that his prophecy of the horrors and chaos to come grossly underestimated the reality....

2

THE POLITICS OF EXCLUSION

The fact that an opinion has been widely held is no evidence
whatever that it is not utterly absurd; indeed in view of the
silliness of the majority of mankind, a widespread belief is
more likely to be foolish than sensible.

—Bertrand Russell

The Lynching of Juanita

1948

IN THE SOUTHWEST, Anglos have always been "gringos" to the Hispanos, while Hispanos have been "greasers" to the Anglos. The two terms pretty accurately reflect the measure of mutual esteem which has prevailed. For many years the origin of the word "gringo" was traced to a song—"Green Grow the Rushes, 0!"—which the Yankees sang in 1846 when they marched into Mexico. Actually "gringo" is to be found in all Spanish dictionaries. Defined as a corruption of *griego,* or "Greek," it is said to be a nickname applied to foreigners. *Hablar en gringo* is to talk gibberish, much as Americans would say, "It's all Greek to me." In popular Southwestern usage prior to the conquest, "gringo" referred to any foreigner who spoke Spanish with an accent and was first recorded in the *New English Dictionary* in 1884.[1] It should be noted that the term, as used by Mexicans, is less insulting in its implications than "greaser."

The origin of "greaser" has been variously explained. It is said that a Mexican once maintained a small shop at the crest of Raton Pass where the ox-carts and wagons of the Santa Fe Trail were greased before they made the descent to the New Mexico plateau; hence a Mexican was literally a "greaser." In California the term has been traced to the days of the hide-and-tallow trade and is said to have first been applied by American sailors to the Indians and Mexicans who loaded the greasy, tick-ridden hides on the clipper ships. It is also said to have had some relation to sheep-shearing. The term was certainly well known in early California, for Harris Newmark tells of the lynching of an Anglo in Los Angeles in 1854 who objected most strenuously to being shuffled off "by a lot of greasers."[2] The term is defined by Vizetelly as

"Mexican; an opprobrious term," and a note states that it is "California slang for a mixed race of Mexicans and Indians," with Bret Harte's "Carquinez Wood" being cited as authority for this usage. The definition to be found in the *Century Dictionary* is: "a *native* Mexican or *native* Spanish-American, originally applied contemptuously by the Americans of the Southwestern United States to Mexicans" (emphasis added). In any case, gringo and greaser it has always been and it is in reference to the hostility and opposition which these terms imply that the pattern of Anglo-Hispano relations outside Texas will be discussed in this chapter....

MEXICAN MINERS from Sonora were among the first emigrants to arrive in California after the discovery of gold. Staking out important claims in the "southern" mines—those in Calaveras, Tuolumne, Mariposa, and Stanislaus counties—they had made remarkable progress before the stream of Anglo-American migration had reached California. Even before the arrival of the Sonorans, several hundred Chilean and Peruvian miners had reached the goldfields by the summer of 1848. Settled by Spanish-speaking miners, the towns of Sonora and Hornitos quickly became populous, world-famous mining camps. The first Anglo-American mining settlements were in the "central" and "northern" districts, along the American, Feather, Bear, and Yuba Rivers. It was not long, however, before the Anglo-Americans began to invade the southern mines.

"The Mexicans," writes Walter Noble Burns, "who poured into California during the Gold Rush, were still inflamed with the anti-American prejudices engendered during the Mexican War. Their attitude towards Americans was hostile from the first, and in return, the Americans regarded them as secret enemies and treated them with frank contempt." One of the first acts of the California legislature was the adoption of a foreign-miners' license tax, which was aimed specifically at eliminating the competition of Mexican miners. Shortly after this act was passed, a mob of two thousand American miners descended on Sonora, "firing at every Mexican in sight." The camp was burned to the ground and a hundred or more Mexicans were rounded up and driven into a corral or stockade. During the week that the rioting lasted, scores of Mexicans were lynched and murdered. In the wake of the riots, most of the Mexicans abandoned their claims and fled to the Spanish-speaking counties in the southern part of the state. One of these former miners, Joaquín Murieta, became the leader of a famous band of Mexican outlaws.

A year later, on July 5, 1851, a mob of American miners in Downieville lynched a Mexican woman who was three months pregnant. During the excitement of the previous day's Fourth of July celebration, a drunken miner had broken into a shack in which the Mexican woman, whose name was Juanita, was living with a man who may or may not have been her husband. "In keeping with the characteristics of her race [sic]," writes Owen Cochran Coy,[3] "Juanita had a quick passion." When the miner returned the next day, some say to apologize, a dispute arose which ended with the fatal stabbing of the miner. Stephen J. Field, later a justice of the United States Supreme Court, made an eloquent plea to the miners to spare the life of Juanita. The miners heard him out and then proceeded with the lynching. With incomparable courage, Juanita adjusted the rope with her own hands, smilingly bade the miners *"adiós,"* and swung from the scaffold.

The first person to be lynched in California was a Mexican and vast research would be required to arrive at an estimate of the number of Mexican lynchings between 1849 and 1890. In the mining camps, every crime or reported crime was promptly blamed on some Mexican, and lynching was the accepted penalty for crimes in which Mexicans were involved. "We can see only indirectly," wrote Josiah Royce, "through the furious and confused reports of the Americans themselves, how much of organized and coarse brutality these Mexicans suffered from the miners' meetings." As violence mounted throughout the mining camps, the Mexicans took refuge in the "cow counties" of Southern California, where, in canyon and foothill hideouts, they licked their wounds and plotted their revenge.

The *gente de razón* enjoyed, of course, immunity from the violence which raged in the mining districts.* Ties of marriage and bonds of commerce brought them quickly into the American camp. During the first years of the conquest, the Americans were at some pains to distinguish between "native Californians," meaning *gente de razón,* and "Mexicans," meaning "greasers" and *cholos.*† For it was generally recognized that the *gente de razón,* if properly cultivated, could be of major importance in consolidating American rule in

---

* *Gente de razón* ("people of reason," as distinguished from *gente sin razón,* "people without reason") was the Spanish term for the Spanish newcomers born in Spain and believed to be at the top of the New World social order.

† Literally "half-breed" and used in Latin America for people of Spanish and Indian ancestry, *cholo* now also refers to "member[s] of U.S. Southwest anti-social, counter-prestige culture" (*University of Chicago Spanish Dictionary,* fourth edition).

California. When the first constitutional convention was called, seven out of forty-eight delegates were "native Californians." Needless to say, the *cholos* were not represented. But by 1876 Walter M. Fisher, the English journalist, could report that "the meanest runaway English sailor, escaped Sydney convict, or American rowdy despised without distinction the bluest blood of Castile and the half-breeds descended from the Mexican garrison soldiers, habitually designating all who spoke Spanish by the offensive name 'greasers,' for whom remains only the rust and the dust of a lost power."[4]

The ease and swiftness of the victory over Mexico and the conquest of California had bred in the Americans a measureless contempt for all things Mexican. This feeling naturally found violent expression in California, for there was really no government in the state from 1846 to 1850. The miners who made up the major element in the Anglo-American population were a tough and hard-bitten lot. Indeed, the circumstances were unique, for here a large body of restless, adventuresome, single men had been suddenly catapulted into a foreign land, with the excitement of gold in the air, and with no government of any sort to curb their predilection for violence and direct action. "Nowhere else," wrote Josiah Royce, "were Americans more affected than here, in our lives and conduct, by the feeling that we stood in the position of conquerors in a new land...nowhere else were we driven so hastily to improvise a government for a large body of strangers." It is not surprising, therefore, that the manners and actions of the first Anglo-American immigrants to reach the state after 1848 produced a silent bitterness among the Californians which was to last for many years.

Crimes of violence had been almost unknown in California prior to the conquest. "Perfect security for the person prevailed in California," wrote the South American, Don José Arnaz of his stay in the province in the years from 1840 to 1843. But, after the conquest, the lower classes became extremely disaffected and their unrest often assumed a covert or "criminal" design. It was after 1846, wrote the historian J. M. Guinn, "that a strange metamorphosis took place in the character of the lower classes of the native Californians....Before the conquest by the Americans they were a peaceful and contented people. There were no organized bands of outlaws among them....The Americans not only took possession of their country and its government, but in many cases despoiled them of their ancestral acres and their personal property. Injustice rankles, and they were often treated by the rougher American elements as aliens and intruders, who had no right in the land of their birth."

Such, in general, is the origin of the much discussed "Mexican banditry" of the period. In the 1850s, the country between Los Angeles and Fort Miller in the San Joaquin Valley was infested with "Californian and Mexican outlaws" who raided the herds of cattle being driven north to the mines and looted the mining settlements. Two companies of rangers were recruited in Southern California to fight off the raids. Typical of the attitudes of the bandits was the statement of Tiburcio Vásquez, a native Californian who was executed in 1852. "A spirit of hatred and revenge," he said, "took possession of me. I had numerous fights in defense of what I believed to be my rights and those of my countrymen. I believed we were being unjustly deprived of the social rights that belonged to us."

The local county histories contain many references to the activities of these bold and daring outlaws: Vásquez, Joaquín Murieta, Louis Bulvia, Antonio Moreno, Procopio, Soto, Manuel García, Juan Flores, Pancho Daniel, and many others. Not a few of these men had fought on the side of Mexico in the war of 1846. Called *El Patrio*—"The Native"—by the Mexicans, Joaquín Murieta boasted that he could muster two thousand men. Many of the outlaw bands, in fact, contained a hundred or more men and were well organized for guerrilla fighting. "The racial loyalty of the Californians," to quote from one local history, "not to mention the entanglements of family relationships with the outlaws, plus a tacit policy of non-interference among the old American population, resulted in a negligent tolerance of these evils which within five years after 1849 swept the local situation entirely out of hand."

Mexican banditry gave a color of justification to the practice of lynching Mexicans, which soon degenerated from a form of vigilante punishment for crime to an outdoor sport in Southern California. In 1857, four Mexicans were lynched in El Monte; eleven in Los Angeles. Throughout the 1860s, the lynching of Mexicans was such a common occurrence in Los Angeles that the newspapers scarcely bothered to report the details. Horace Bell, who was himself once indicted for killing a Mexican, describes any number of murders and lynchings in which the victims were Mexicans in his memoirs, *Reminiscences of a Ranger* and *On the Old West Coast*. The last reported lynching of a Mexican occurred in August 1892, when one Francisco Torres was lynched in Santa Ana. A homicide a day was reported in Los Angeles in 1854, with most of the victims being Mexicans and Indians. The previous year California had more murders than the rest of the states combined, and Los Angeles had more than occurred elsewhere in California. The subordination of Mexicans in the social structure of California cannot be understood apart from this early-day pattern of violence and intimidation.

ENDNOTES
1. *New Mexico Guide*, p. 14
2. *Sixty Years in Southern California*, p. 140
3. See the article by Arthur E. Hyde, *Century*, March 1902, vol. 63, p. 690.
4. *Recollections of a Western Ranchman* (1884).

The Long-Suffering Chinese

1943

THE FABLE reads that mysterious and inscrutable China, determined to live in isolation from the world, built an enormous wall to protect its empire from invaders. The Great Wall had its counterpart, however, in the vast hemispheric wall built by the Occidental world—comprised of legal statutes rather than bricks and stones—against the Chinese. The creation of this invisible hemispheric wall dates from the period when America, in its feverish rush to the West, reached the Pacific. Not until we had reached the Pacific did we make a sharp break with the American tradition of free migration and enact the first restrictive immigration measures. Here a new frontier was established: Europe, through American eyes, looked across the Pacific toward Asia. As Dr. Robert E. Park once observed: "It is as if we had said: Europe, of which after all America is a mere western projection, ends here. The Pacific Coast is our racial frontier."

The great wall against the Orient dates from 1882, with the passage of the Chinese Exclusion Act. Today, however, there is no land under either the British or the American flag where Chinese labor is admitted. Following the American or California precedent, Australia, Canada, and New Zealand legislated, at an early date, against Oriental immigration. Later the wall was extended from Tijuana to Cape Horn, as Mexico, Guatemala, El Salvador, Nicaragua, Colombia, Ecuador, and Peru put up barriers against Chinese immigration. "European peoples around the Pacific," wrote Mr. Chester Rowell in 1926, "regard their borders as a racial frontier, which they are determined to maintain inviolate."

Throughout the whole Pacific area, the immigration dykes were built, sometimes only against the Chinese, but in other instances against all Oriental people. The United States, for example, first barred immigration from China, Japan, and the Philippine Islands and then extended the same prohibition to peoples from India, Siam, Indochina, Java, Sumatra, Ceylon, Borneo, New Guinea, and the Celebes. These dykes, moreover, have taken the form of rigid legal prohibitions setting the people of Asia sharply apart from those of Europe and America. In each instance, also, the prohibition has been based directly, emphatically, and explicitly on so-called racial considerations, thereby creating a situation which was certain to provoke, sooner or later, strenuous counter measures. In the Atlantic, the symbol of our policy was the Open Door; in the Pacific, the Yellow Peril. Now, in the middle of the twentieth century, we find ourselves excluded from a large section of Asia!

For years the movement of immigrants across the Atlantic was kept in a separate compartment from the similar movement across the Pacific. In the public mind, our "immigration problem," as such, was associated almost exclusively with the transatlantic migration, with Ellis Island, the Statue of Liberty, and the Melting Pot. Conversely, the transpacific movement was associated with an entirely different set of symbols: the Yellow Peril, the Chinese Must Go!, and Japanese Picture Brides. It was, as Dr. Edith Abbott pointed out, "an entirely different problem." Although the admission was not always made, the problem was "different" because the factor of race was involved. In time this difference in attitude crystallized into a dogmatic assumption that the yellow and brown races were "incapable of assimilation." Underlying the assumption, of course, was the unmistakable reality that we had refused to assimilate the Indian and the Negro.

The movement around the rim of the Pacific to set the European peoples apart from those of Asia had its origin in California. Here, in the words of Ching Chao Wu, "for the first time in the history of mankind, large numbers of Orientals and Occidentals, who had developed different racial characteristics and cultural traits during the long period of isolation, were thrown together to work out their destiny in the new land." Even today, a hundred years after the fact, it is impossible to appraise the full consequences of this fateful first meeting. Throughout the Pacific area and beginning in California, the exclusion movement has followed a definite course: from local agitation against a particular class or race of Asiatics to national movements directed against all Asiatics of every race and class; from economic arguments to cultural and biological arguments for restriction and exclusion. The pattern of the entire movement is implicit in the agitation against the Chinese in California. Just how, then, did the breach with our tradition of free migration occur? How was it possible for one state to force its views upon the nation and thereby to set in motion a chain of events of world-wide significance?

THE TECHNIQUE OF EXCLUSION

The year 1876 marked a definite turning point in the history of anti-Chinese agitation in California. Up to this point, most of the barbarous and obnoxious anti-Chinese legislation adopted in California had been declared unconstitutional as being in violation of treaty provisions, the Fourteenth Amendment, or the federal civil rights statutes. The federal courts, as a matter of fact, were constantly preoccupied with California's outrageous "Hottentot" or race legislation in the period from 1860 to 1876. For the Chinese in California had wisely decided to defend their rights along strictly legal and constitutional lines. Compact social organization made it possible for them to raise the large sums necessary for test cases in the courts. It was these "coolies" from Asia, not the Indians or the Negroes, who made the first great tests of the Civil War amendments and the legislation which came with these amendments. American constitutional history was made in such far-reaching decisions as *United States* v. *Wong Kim Ark* and *Yick Wo* v. *Hopkins*. Yet, years later, K. K. Kawakami, seeking to dissociate the Japanese from the Chinese, said that the early Chinese were "slavish, utterly callous to the Occidental environment, and content with the inhuman treatment meted out to them." The fact is, as the court reports eloquently attest, that the Chinese in California conducted a magnificent fight for the extension of human freedom in America.

By 1876 the Californians had reached an impasse in their agitation against the Chinese. Not only had the federal courts made effective use of the Fourteenth Amendment in striking down a series of discriminatory measures, but in 1875 Congress had adopted a general civil rights act. Although the act was primarily aimed at overriding the Black Codes, which the Southern states had adopted in an effort to circumvent the Fourteenth Amendment, it was also a blow at the attempt to Jim Crow the Chinese in California. It became necessary, therefore, to shift the campaign from the state to the national level; to move the debate, so to speak, from Sacramento to Washington. At the same time, the emphasis shifted from discriminatory legislation to immigration restriction, for the civil rights act barred the way to exclusion-by-harassment. Thus it was that a measure suspending Chinese immigration for ten years was finally forced through Congress in 1882 after both Presidents Hayes and Arthur had vetoed similar measures.

The enactment of this measure—the first restriction imposed by Congress on immigration—represented a change in American foreign policy as well as a sharp break with American tradition. In the early treaties with China (1844 and 1858) nothing was said about the rights of Chinese residing in the United States; presumably they had the same status as other aliens. But after the Central Pacific had started work on the transcontinental rail line in 1863, and after the Pacific Mail Steamship Company had established the first transpacific service in 1867, the United States became intensely interested in opening up trade and commerce with China. These developments were largely responsible for the negotiation of the Burlingame Treaty of 1868, which was hailed in this country as opening a new era in the Pacific.

The Burlingame Treaty also marked the dividing line between two distinct and contradictory policies on the part of the United States toward the Chinese. Up to this point our efforts had been directed toward *compelling* the Chinese to admit Americans to China for the purpose of trade and commerce. In this contention we asserted the broad principle of free migration and the duty of international intercourse. The Burlingame Treaty, which carried out this principle, was reciprocal in its provisions. Article VII conferred on American citizens in China the "same privileges, immunities, and exemptions" enjoyed by citizens of the most favored nation, and other provisions gave Chinese subjects here the same protection. The only exception was a proviso that "nothing herein contained shall be held to confer naturalization upon citizens of the United States in China, nor upon the subjects of China in the United States." The reason this provision was included was obvious: Negro suffrage was then being hotly debated in Congress and the clause was inserted to expedite ratification of the treaty. The ink was hardly dry on the signatures to the treaty, however, before political pressure from California forced the government to negotiate an amendment providing that the United States might regulate, limit, or suspend Chinese immigration but "may not absolutely prohibit it." This amendment paved the way for the legislation of 1882 suspending Chinese immigration for ten years.

In the debate on the bill, Senator Hawley had pointed out that we, as a nation, had bombarded China for precisely the same privilege—namely, free migration—which we now sought to deny her. "Make the conditions what you please for immigration and for attaining citizenship," he pleaded; "but make them such that a man may overcome them; do not base them on the accidents of humanity." As finally passed—by a combination of Southern and Western votes—the act not only suspended immigration but contained an express prohibition against the naturalization of the Chinese. Naturalization had been restricted to "free white persons" since 1790 but the limiting phrase had not been construed until 1878. In that year, in a case involving a Chinese, a Federal District Court judge in California had ruled that the word "white" referred to a person of the Caucasian race. Actually the phrase "free white persons" was used to exclude slaves, regardless of their color, and Indians living in tribal organizations. It will be noted, for example, that not all *white* persons were eligible; only those who were *free* could apply. But with the adoption of the 1882 act the United States was formally committed to a policy of racial discrimination at variance with its traditions and principles as well as its prior policies. The measure also sanctioned state discriminations, since it denied the Chinese the protection of citizenship and seriously undermined the philosophy upon which the federal civil rights legislation rested. Indeed, one year later, in 1883, the Supreme Court declared the general civil rights act unconstitutional.

With the passage of the exclusion measure in 1882 and the Supreme Court's decision in the civil rights cases in 1883, the agitation against the Chinese reached a new pitch of intensity and violence throughout the Far West. In September 1885, a riot occurred at Rock Springs, Wyoming, in which twenty-eight Chinese were murdered and property valued at $148,000 was destroyed. "Shortly afterward," writes Dr. E. C. Sandmeyer, "the entire West Coast became inflamed almost simultaneously. Tacoma burned its Chinese quarter, and Seattle, Olympia, and Portland might have done the same but for quick official action. In California developments ranged from new ordinances of regulation to the burning of Chinese quarters and the expulsion of the inhabitants. Among the localities where these actions occurred were Pasadena, Santa Barbara, Santa Cruz, San Jose, Oakland, Cloverdale, Healdsburg, Red Bluff, Hollister, Merced, Yuba City, Petaluma, Redding, Anderson, Truckee, Lincoln, Sacramento, San Buenaventura, Napa, Gold Run, Sonoma, Vallejo, Placerville, Santa Rosa, Chico, Wheatland, Carson, Auburn, Nevada City, Dixon, and Los Angeles."[1]

These pogroms were so humiliating that the Chinese government

promptly sought a modification of the treaty, and an amendment was negotiated suspending all immigration for twenty years and providing indemnity
for the loss of Chinese life and property. While this new treaty was being
ratified in China, Congress abruptly passed the Scott Act of 1888, which
slammed the doors to some twenty thousand Chinese who had temporarily
left the United States but who, at the time, had a perfect right of re-entry.
Over a period of years the Chinese government filed protest after protest
with the State Department against the enactment of this outrageously unfair measure without receiving even an acknowledgment of its notes. By this
time our attitude toward China, as reflected in this legislation, was so brutally overbearing that many foreign offices assumed that we were trying to
provoke a war.

Not content with this state of affairs, Congress then passed the notorious Geary Act of 1892 (again by a combination of Southern and Western
votes). Continuing the suspension of immigration for another ten years, the
bill denied bail to Chinese in habeas corpus proceedings and required certificates of residence from the Chinese in default of which they could be de-
ported. The effect of the Geary Act, which was denounced by the Chinese
Ambassador in Washington as being "in violation of every principle of justice, equity, reason, and fair-dealing between two friendly powers," was to
drive many Chinese from California and to terrify those who remained. In
1902 Congress indefinitely extended the prohibition against Chinese immigration and the denial to them of the privilege of naturalization. But further
indignities were still in order. Despite strenuous protests from the Chinese
government, Congress insisted on making the terms of the Immigration Act
of 1924 barring aliens ineligible to citizenship specifically applicable to the
Chinese, and at the same time made it impossible for American citizens of
Chinese ancestry to bring their alien wives to this country. In 1926, 1928, and
1930, resident Chinese groups sought to have this latter provision modified,
but to no purpose. At an even earlier date, also, we had projected our racially
discriminatory immigration laws into the Pacific by barring Chinese immigration to Hawaii and the Philippine Islands.

The process by which the Chinese were excluded in response to pressure
from California has been summarized by Mrs. Mary Roberts Coolidge as follows: "From suspension to restriction; from execution of treaty stipulations
to flat prohibition of treaty compact, the movement went on until it culmi-
nated in the Geary Act, which reiterated and legalized the severer features of

them all and added the requirement of registration. It was…progression from vinegar to vitriol."[2] It was also entirely in keeping with the history of our treaty dealings with the Indians. As a matter of fact, the exclusion of the Chinese squared perfectly with the policy of placing Indians on reservations and segregating Negroes by force of law. Modes of aggression which had been tried out against Indians and Negroes were easily transferred to the Chinese, and a Californian on the Supreme Court had little difficulty in convincing his colleagues that it was as easy to breach a treaty with China as with the Indian tribes. "Experts in violence," as Felix S. Cohen has noted, "do not usually retire when a war has been won."[3] They look for new victims.

While China was as powerless to retaliate as the Indian tribes or the former Negro slaves, she did voice her resentment on more than one occasion. Mrs. Coolidge states, for example, that the exclusion of the Chinese and the indignities perpetrated in this country "undoubtedly contributed to the accumulated resentment which found expression in the Boxer Rebellion." Mr. Wu has gone further and stated that the Boxer Rebellion was the expression of a spirit which, if China had been stronger, would have resulted in the exclusion of all Americans from China. History has since proved that Mr. Wu was engaging in prophecy, not speculation.

THE POLITICS OF EXCLUSION

In retrospect one is intrigued by the question: how was it possible for a single West Coast state to force its racial views upon the national government and to shape, in effect, the foreign policy of the country? The brief if somewhat cryptic answer would be that the views of California were in fact the views of the nation, since anti-Chinese prejudice can hardly be distinguished from the same prejudice against Indians and Negroes. But there is this difference: the measures which were adopted against the Chinese had international implications; they represented the first projection beyond the borders of this country of our domestic racism. Our dealings with Indians and Negroes had brought into being a set of conditioned reflexes which the Californians soon discovered were most responsive to racial propaganda. But the specific reasons for the success of California's agitation were these: the interrelations between the Negro and Chinese issues; the peculiar balance of political power within the nation; and the fact that both the Negro and the Chinese issue fused with a larger national capital-labor conflict.

"No small part of the persecution of the Chinaman," wrote Mrs.

Coolidge, "was due to the fact that it was his misfortune to arrive in the United States at a period when the attention of the whole country was focused on the question of slavery." Even so we started out to deal with the Chinese on a nondiscriminatory basis only to discover that this policy conflicted with our policy toward Indians and Negroes. Every issue affecting the Chinese cut across the whole complex of issues affecting the Negro. Without a single exception, the anti-Chinese measures were carried in Congress by a combination of Southern and Western votes. Southern Bourbons could not tolerate a policy in California that might have unsettling consequences in Alabama. Besides, the more California became committed to a Jim Crow policy in relation to the Chinese, the greater became its obligation to support Southern racial policies in Congress. At one time, too, the South had shown a lively interest in the possibility of substituting Chinese coolie labor for Negro labor; without the sanctions of slavery it was feared that the Negro might be unmanageable. The proposal was seriously discussed in Memphis in 1869, and on several occasions Southern plantation owners visited California with this proposal in mind. Indeed the project was only abandoned when it became clear, after 1876, that the nation did not intend to abolish Negro servitude. Once the federal government surrendered to the South on the Negro issue, it was logically compelled to appease California on the subject of "coolie" labor.

The Chinese were directly related to the slave question in still another way. The great outward movement of coolie labor from China, in the years from 1845 to 1877, was a direct consequence of the discontinuance of slavery in the British Empire. During these years a traffic developed in coolie labor that rivaled "the palmiest days of the Middle Passage." Over forty thousand coolies were imported to Cuba alone, of whom it has been said that at least 80 percent had been decoyed or kidnaped. By 1862 the movement had reached such proportions that the American government was forced to prohibit American ships from participating in the China–West Indies traffic. Wherever they were imported, the coolies were used to supplant Negro slaves in plantation areas, and they might have been used for the same purpose in the United States if we had really freed the slaves. Had this been the case, the Southern representatives in Congress would almost certainly have voted against exclusion of Chinese immigration. On the other hand, the way in which coolies were used as substitutes for slaves in the West Indies served to alarm white labor in California.

The debate on the Naturalization Act of 1870 points up the relation between the Chinese question and the Negro question. This act extended the
privilege of naturalization to "aliens of African nativity and persons of African descent"—an extension made unavoidable by the Emancipation Proclamation. During the debate, however, the question arose as to whether the
same privilege should also be extended to the Chinese. "The very men," said
Senator Carpenter, "who settled the question of Negro suffrage upon principle now hesitate to apply the principle…and interpose the very objections
to the enfranchisement of the Chinaman that the Democrats urged against
the enfranchisement of the Freedmen." Only in respect to nominal citizenship did we distinguish the two questions, and this we did because the specific issue had, so to speak, been settled by the Civil War.

As a matter of fact, the Chinese and Negro had been intimately related
in California long before 1876. "The anti-foreign feeling in California," writes
B. Schreike, "was unquestionably intensified by the presence of Southerners,
who comprised nearly one-third of the population in the first decade of
American rule."[4] A number of Southerners brought their slaves with them
to California, where Indian peonage was as old as the first settlements. California enacted a fugitive-slave statute, refused to accept the testimony of
Negroes in judicial proceedings until 1863, and rejected ratification of the
Fifteenth Amendment. An early statute read that "no Black, or Mulatto person, or Indian shall be allowed to give evidence in favor of, or against a white
man." Chief Justice Hugh C. Murray, a member of the American, or Know-
Nothing Party, described by the historian Bancroft as "immoral, venal, and
thoroughly corrupt," construed this statute to include Chinese! While he
may have been corrupt, he was certainly logical. "The same rule," he pointed
out, "that would admit them [the Chinese] to testify would admit them to all
the equal rights of citizenship, and we might soon see them at the polls, in
the jury box, upon the bench, and in our legislative halls."[5]

The national political situation in the post–Civil War decades was another factor which made it possible for California to blackmail the government on the Chinese question. During these decades, two Presidents were
elected by minorities in popular votes and two more by majorities of less
than twenty-five thousand. In these critical postwar decades, the control of
both the Presidency and the two houses of Congress frequently shifted between the two major parties. The two major parties were parties of the North
and the South; hence the Pacific Coast states came to be looked upon as

holding the balance of power.[6] In effect both parties were compelled to appeal to the anti-Chinese sentiment in California. In 1880, six of seven California electors cast their voices for the Democratic Presidential nominee despite the fact that the state legislature was overwhelmingly Republican. The Republicans in Congress had not accepted the California "line" on the Chinese. Four years later, California was back in the Republican column because the Democrats had not been sufficiently "anti-Chinese." The reason for this peculiar national political situation is quite clear: the post-bellum Solid South had a measure of political power out of all relation to the percentage of its citizens who were permitted to vote. Not only were the Negroes excluded, but, to ensure white supremacy, a one-party system had been established. Since it was useless for the South to campaign in the North, and vice versa, both regions campaigned in the West.

These same decades also marked an important period in the history of American labor. In the years from 1870 to 1890, a new industrial society was coming into being, and the social stratification that came with this new dispensation created great misgivings and fears among working people. From coast to coast, this feeling of fear and hostility tended to be vented against minority groups. Just as workers once rioted against the use of machines and destroyed the machines, so, in these decades, they tended to be hostile toward groups that *seemed* to threaten them with unfair competition; witness the attitude of the "poor white" toward the Negro. Hatred of the new social order fused with, and stimulated, a hatred of groups that could be identified as competitors.

In California the Chinese were mistakenly identified as the cause of the seemingly inexplicable economic distress which came at the end of the fabulous Gold Rush decades (1850–1870). Although the argument seemed plausible, there would have been a depression in California in the 1870s if the entire population had been made up of lineal descendants of George Washington. "White American" workingmen were pouring into the state: 59,000 in 1869; 150,000 in the period from 1873 to 1875. What with the completion of the Central Pacific, the decline in placer mining, and the generally undeveloped economy of the state, there were simply not enough jobs. The rapidity with which the argument against the Chinese shifted from the economic to the biological, from "unfair competitor" to "incapable of assimilation," exposed the delusion on which it rested.[7]

On the other hand it seemed plausible to say—although the argument

was equally fallacious—that the difficulty was purely racial and not economic. What Senator Morton had to say on this score made a great deal of
sense:

> If the Chinese in California were white people, *being in all*
> *other respects* what they are, I do not believe that the com-
> plaints and warfare against them would have existed to any
> considerable extent. Their difference in color, dress, man-
> ners, and religion have [sic], in my judgment, more to do
> with this hostility than their alleged vices *or any actual injury*
> to the white people of California....Looking at the ques-
> tion broadly, and at the effect which Chinese labor has ex-
> erted in California, running through a period of twenty-five
> years, I am strongly of the opinion that, *but for the presence*
> of the Chinese, California would not now have more than
> one-half or two-thirds of her present population; that Chi-
> nese labor has opened up many avenues and new industries
> for white labor, made many kinds of business possible, and
> laid the foundations of manufacturing interests that bid fair
> to rise to enormous proportions....[8]

The latter part of this argument was clearly sound. It is to be doubted, indeed, if the Chinese were ever in *direct* competition with white Americans,
their labor tended to complement rather than to supplant the labor of other
groups. Actually, there is good reason to believe that, by their presence, they
tended to bolster up rather than to depress the wage standard of the white
Americans, which had been greatly increased by the abnormal conditions
prevailing during the Gold Rush.[9]

To see the real source of conflict, one must cut back to the first contacts.
The Chinese were "looked upon as a veritable god-send" when they first appeared in California, as, indeed, they were.[10] The difference in color, dress,
manners, and religion to which Senator Morton referred was not then a source
of conflict. With few exceptions, California *employers* consistently regarded
the Chinese as a desirable, cheap, submissive, and efficient source of labor
and looked upon these *differences* as fortunate traits precisely because they
made assimilation difficult if not impossible.[11] In California the opposition to
the Chinese was overwhelmingly a working-class opposition; hence its political potency and social power. Where two laboring groups are both being

exploited, but one more than the other, it often happens that the exploitation will generate conflict between the two exploited groups either because they fail to see the real source of the trouble or because the more powerful labor group finds it expedient to attack not the exploiter, but the other victim. Out of this "false" conflict came the anti-Chinese agitation and out of this agitation came a racist ideology which survived in California for three generations.

The conflict was false, in economic terms, because it was extremely short-sighted and self-defeating. "The exclusion law," observes Mr. Wu, "which prevents aliens from coming in, cannot keep capital from going out.…If people are prevented from competing with one another in the same political region, their goods will still compete in the same world market." When the flow of Chinese labor was finally stopped, that of other groups, such as the Japanese and Filipino, was promptly stimulated. At the same time, American capital was seeking outlets throughout the Far East and in Central and South America, and in many instances was actually seeking out the so-called cheap labor areas. Had the California labor leaders elected to organize the Chinese, they could have worked out a strategy and policy which would have discouraged the importation of Oriental labor.

Today we are beginning to realize that the argument against "cheap coolie labor" is the counterpart of the argument that Western industrial technology should be monopolized by Western peoples. Both arguments are essentially isolationist. Having held back and sought to prevent the industrialization of the Far East, we now find ourselves in the position of sending, in dollar value, billions of industrial products to the Far East in the form of planes, and tanks, and guns. Today we complain that we have no spokesmen, no emissaries, to send to the Far East who understand the peoples and speak their languages and who could explain "our" point of view to "them." Nor have we yet seen the light on this score. For example, on December 17, 1943, we repealed the Chinese exclusion acts and made resident Chinese aliens eligible for citizenship. But we then established a quota permitting the entry of 105 Chinese per year! This quota can be catalogued as a sociological joke, for the number of Chinese leaving the United States each year will exceed the quota or, if not, the return of husbands marooned from their wives, and vice versa, will fill the quota easily. Of the quota figure, furthermore, 25 places must be reserved for resident Chinese who desire to leave the country and return under the quota. Repealing the exclusion laws was a good gesture but it was just that—a gesture.…

ENDNOTES

1. *The Anti-Chinese Movement in California,* by Elmer Clarence Sandmeyer, 1939, p. 97.

2. *Chinese Immigration,* by Mary Roberts Coolidge, 1909.

3. *Commentary,* August 1948, p. 137.

4. *Alien Americans,* by B. Schreike, 1936.

5. Sandmeyer, p. 45.

6. Ibid., p. 111. See also Chapter x, in my book *California: the Great Exception,* 1949.

7. See *Oriental Exclusion,* by R. D. McKenzie, 1927, p. 15.

8. Sandmeyer, p. 88. Emphasis added.

9. See, for example, Dr. Varden Fuller's study, to be found in Vol. 54, LaFollette Committee Transcript, p. 19, 823 et seq.

10. Sandmeyer, pp. 11, 14.

11. Ibid., p. 33. See also article by Dr. William S. Bernard on "The Law, the Mores, and the Oriental," *Rocky Mountain Law Review,* vol. x (1933), nos. 2 and 3.

The Joads at Home

1942

AS THE SEEMINGLY ENDLESS PROCESSION of Joads began to move westward, a common assumption took form. The plight of the migrants was characterized as a "natural catastrophe"—"a tragedy of the dust bowl"—and the migrants themselves became "refugees from drought." A variation was occasionally played upon the theme with "tractor" being used as the symbol of displacement and distress. The migrants, it was said, were either "dusted out or tractored out."

In the fall of 1940 I visited Oklahoma to discover, if possible, why thousands of American farm families had been uprooted from their homes and set adrift on the land. I had not been in Oklahoma long before I realized that "dust" and "tractors" accounted for only a small part of the migration. Sallisaw, the home of the Joad family in *The Grapes of Wrath,* is far from the dust bowl, and there were probably not more than ten tractors in all Sequoyah County in 1937. Mr. Steinbeck's slightly confused geography is merely indicative of a general failure to understand the deep-seated causes of poverty and unrest in Oklahoma's farm population.

The tragedy of the Joads is, most emphatically, not a natural disaster. The Joads are the victims of grab and greed as much as dust and tractors. Their distress is the end-product of a process of social disintegration set in motion as early as 1900. Their problem is distinctly a man-made problem. Their tragedy is part of a greater tragedy—the wasteful and senseless exploitation of a rich domain—the insane scramble of conflicting group interests which frustrated the promise of the frontier and (within a decade) converted a pioneer territory into a sink of poverty.

The impressions I formed of the Joads at home are necessarily some-what sketchy and tentative. It would take a volume to do full justice to the story in all its ramifications. In this chapter I merely attempt to touch upon one or two neglected phases of their problem at home, before they became migrants on the road.

WHEN THE GREAT tides of settlers moved westward across the Mississippi in quest of new lands to farm, Oklahoma was passed over. As one observer pointed out, it formed, in this tide of migration, a "red island in the West." It was neglected, not because it was inaccessible or undesirable, but largely because the national government had decided to round up the scattered In-dian tribes from Florida, Georgia, Illinois, and other states and settle them in Oklahoma. While the western part of the state was organized as a territorial government, under an organic act creating the Territory of Oklahoma (May 2, 1890), the eastern part of the state remained "Indian Territory"—a no man's land so far as settlement was concerned, a "region set aside as the perpetual home of the red man."[1] Through a series of involved treaties negotiated with various Indian tribes subsequent to the Civil War, a number of tribes were settled in the territory. While the terms of the treaties were not identical, a general pattern for the settlement of tribal lands was established. Land allot-ments, "nontaxable and inalienable during the lifetime of the allottee," were made to the members of the tribes. The balance of the Indian lands, over and above the allotments, were then purchased or acquired by the govern-ment and thrown open for settlement at intervals from 1889 to 1906. When the initial opening occurred on April 22, 1889, thousands of land-hungry American farm families "made the rush" for "the last frontier in America." "They had followed," writes Oscar Ameringer, "on the heels of the Chero-kees, Choctaws, Chickasaw, Creeks, and Seminoles, like the stragglers of routed armies. Always hoping that somewhere in their America there would be a piece of dirt for them."

This celebrated "last frontier," however, was somewhat of an illusion from the beginning. A considerable part of the excess or reserve land was sold in "strips and by runs and lotteries," making it difficult, if not impos-sible, for settlers to acquire tracts of sufficient size to constitute economi-cal farm units. The lands in the eastern part of the state were broken up into odd-sized fragments, and the region was soon dotted with tiny hold-ings of ten, fifteen, and twenty acres. Throughout this eastern part were

large Indian holdings, nontaxable and inalienable. From the outset, many
settlers discovered that they could only farm as tenants of Indian owners.
"Dead Indian lands" might, through a cumbersome process, be placed on
the market; the bulk of the land, however, was not subject to alienation during the lifetime of the allottee. The Indians had, moreover, large families,
and before many years had passed their original allotments (through inherit-
ance) began to break up into smaller and smaller parcels. Tenants and sharecroppers soon found themselves operating semi-subsistence tracts. Over a
period of years (generally subsequent to 1908), Indians were permitted to
sell land. But by the time title could be acquired, the units had become fragments and the soil was already badly overworked. "Thus the typical farms in
eastern Oklahoma," writes Mr. Clarence Roberts, "were too small to begin
with. Most of them should have been twice as large; some might have been
five times as large in order to create a unit of land with productive capacity
adequate to support a family."[2] The basis upon which Indian lands were operated led to various rackets and speculative devices. Land hawks, working
with Indian agents, leased large sections of the Indian lands and, in turn, sub-
leased them to settlers. At the time of the Walsh (Industrial Relations Commission) Hearings in 1915, one witness told of a firm of speculators who
controlled thirty thousand acres of land in the Indian Territory and leased it
to over fifteen hundred tenants. This was by no means an exceptional case; in
fact, it was quite typical of the time. The government, with no clearly formu-
lated policy on Indian affairs, was a party to this conspiracy in the sense that
it was quite willing, as Oscar Ameringer has pointed out, to let the "poor
white keep the Indians." Thus the novel spectacle was presented of "White,
native, Protestant Americans working as the land slaves, tenants, and sharecroppers of the aboriginal Indians." They were not so much the "slaves" of
the Indians, however, as they were of the land sharks, the crafty lawyers, the
"lease hounds" of the period.

This crazy pattern of land settlement resulted, from the outset, in deplorable social conditions. Since the Indian lands were nontaxable, it became
extremely difficult to support public schools. Illiteracy became the norm;
literacy the exception. Yet, to this day, critics of the Okies like to regard the
low educational level of migrants as still another indication of their inherent
shiftlessness. This celebrated shiftlessness was in itself merely a reflection of
a generally hopeless situation. Settlers soon became discouraged when, as
pioneers in quest of homes and farms, they found themselves tenants and

sharecroppers. Many of them abandoned all hope of eventual landowner-ship. By the time they could purchase a twenty-acre tract, the land itself was worn-out and exhausted. It was not long before they lost interest in improv-ing the land or in building substantial homes. The pattern of land settlement discouraged such ambitions. Nor were they actively interested in the com-munity—its churches, schools, or social life—for the next year they might be somewhere else. "Not knowing what the Indian Agent will do next year," as one witness said at the Walsh hearings in 1915, "the tenant just jogs along as best he can." As a footnote to this comment, it might be observed that Indian lands are still exempt from taxation in Oklahoma and that Indian agents still make only one-year leases.

Not only were these settlers uninterested in the community, but they were made to feel that they were excluded from it. On the one hand were the residents of the "electric light" towns—lawyers, merchants, usurers, and lease sharks—and on the other a dispossessed rural horde of quondam settlers. The rural masses had their own churches—the Holy Roller Tent-Tabernacle in the brush—and their own schools—a shack by the roadside open about four months in the winter and a few weeks in the summer, between cotton chopping and cotton picking. The one-crop system was at once riveted upon settlers, and its baneful limitations kept them in perpetual poverty. They needed operating capital badly—for equipment, supplies, homes, improve-ments. The giving or withholding of this capital was the exclusive preroga-tive of the landlords and merchants, or bankers. To what extent the people were literally enslaved by such a system may be variously illustrated. Interest rates on chattel mortgages ranged from 20 percent to 200 percent. Mr. E. J. Giddings, testifying at the Walsh hearings, said: "In the cities I have had usu-rious contracts for laborers that went as high as 230 percent." Even in the western part of the state, where landownership by homesteading was pos-sible, the equities soon shrank to the vanishing point. By 1915 it was esti-mated that 80 percent of the farms of the state were mortgaged for 40 percent of their value, and that 62 percent of the mortgaged farms had been lost through foreclosure. Considering that Oklahoma was our "last frontier," the following excerpt from a report on *Farm Tenancy in Oklahoma* (1939), issued by the Oklahoma Agricultural and Mechanical College, is illuminating:

> When the agricultural census of 1890 was taken, less than
> 1 percent of the farms of the state were operated by tenants.

It should be recalled that much of this territory was first opened for settlement in 1889, and therefore, the early home-steaders were still "proving up" their land. By 1900, over two-fifths of the farms of the state were tenant-operated. During the next decade, the number of tenant-operators more than doubled while the owner-operators increased approximately one-fifth. By 1910, 54.8 percent, or slightly over one-half of the farms, were operated by tenants.[3]

To understand how this shocking transformation of a frontier into a sump-hole of poverty was effected, it should be pointed out that during the critical, formative years of settlement, the people were in effect powerless to govern themselves. The western part of the state had been organized as a territory in 1890, but the state as such was not admitted to the Union until 1907. The absence of local self-government created the perfect milieu for social exploitation. It made, also, for a definite lag in institutional development. Surrounding Oklahoma were states such as Missouri, Arkansas, Texas, and Colorado which had been able, since 1861, to govern their own affairs. Oklahoma, as Mr. Milton Asfahl states, was retarded in its economic and social development for fifty or seventy-five years. The consequences of this retardation take on added significance in view of the fact that, while the other states were populated by the gradual extension of settlement, Oklahoma was settled overnight. Although admitted as a state as late as 1907, Oklahoma today has a population greater than that of Kansas, or Arkansas, or Iowa, or Nebraska, or Louisiana, or Mississippi. In a predominantly agricultural state, the constant pressure of population on resources soon became acute. As oil, mining, and lumbering activities began to decline, workers from these industries crowded into the already overpopulated areas in search of subsistence farms. The number of farms increased in precisely the poorest, therefore the cheapest, farming areas in the state. As farming units got smaller and smaller, soil erosion, already far advanced, began to claim the land. Dr. W. L. Thurman, testifying at the Walsh hearings, pointed out the desperate plight of farm families in 1915: "They are forced to live," he said, "in Indian huts. These Indian shacks are leaky and rotting down. It is in these hog pens and rawhide houses that thousands of our Oklahoma tenant families live. In the tenant quarters of the state, hundreds of thousands of acres have been ru-ined—through soil erosion—the soil has just washed away." The last frontier had become a rural slum, of the worst imaginable poverty, within a decade or less from the time it had been thrown open for settlement. "Instead of escaping industrialism and finance capitalism," writes Oscar Ameringer, "as they had hoped, the last frontiersmen had brought it with them, as they had cockleburs to their blue-jean breeches and flowing Mother Hubbards."

Ameringer came to Oklahoma in 1907. It would be difficult to imagine a more impressive summation of the degraded social conditions that even then prevailed in eastern Oklahoma than he has written. "I found," he writes, "toothless old women with sucking infants on their withered breasts. I found a hospitable old hostess, around thirty or less, her hands covered with rags and eczema, offering me a biscuit with those hands, apologizing that her biscuits were not as good as she used to make because with her sore hands she no longer could knead the dough as it ought to be. I saw youngsters emaciated by hookworms, malnutrition, and pellagra, who had lost their second teeth before they were twenty years old. I saw tottering old male wrecks with the infants of their fourteen-year-old wives on their laps. I saw a white man begging a Choctaw squaw to persuade the man who owned the only remaining spring in that neighborhood to let him have credit for a few buckets of water for his thirsty family. I saw humanity at its lowest possible level of degradation and decay. I saw smug, well-dressed, overly well-fed hypocrites march to church on Sabbath day, Bibles under their arms, praying for God's kingdom on earth while fattening like latter-day cannibals on the sharecroppers. I saw windjamming, hot-air-spouting politicians geysering Jeffersonian platitudes about equal rights to all and special privileges to none; about all men born equal with the rights to life, liberty, and the pursuit of happiness without even knowing, much less caring, that they were addressing as wretched a set of abject slaves as ever walked the face of the earth, anywhere or at any time. The things I saw on that trip are the things you never forget."[4]

But, unfortunately, these things are forgotten. By 1940 the Tolan Committee had to remind us of what the Walsh Committee had discovered—a quarter of a century ago. In 1915 there would have been mass migration from Oklahoma, if transportation facilities had been sufficiently developed. But still another generation had to grow to maturity on eroded acres before "escape" was possible for a few of them. Misery, as long as it can be localized, as long as it hides itself in sod huts in Oklahoma, can be ignored. It can be ignored, that is, until it explodes in violence, and even then it is soon forgotten. No one heeded Dr. Thurman when, in 1915, he said that there was "very deep-seated unrest" in eastern Oklahoma. By the time the Green Corn Rebellion occurred in 1917, people had already forgotten the warning of 1915.*

This rebellion had as its immediate cause the resentment of the tenants against the draft, registration for which was ordered for June 5 by President Wilson ("Big Slick" to the croppers). The war was undoubtedly very unpopular in the rural sections of Oklahoma, but a more fundamental cause of unrest was the appalling condition of the croppers. Their distress was fertile ground for the activities of organizations like the IWW, the Renters' Union, and the Working Class Union, and by 1917 these groups had made considerable headway—much of it at the expense of the more conservative Socialist Party. The Working Class Union seems to have had more to do than the others with the organization of the violence which flared up in several counties some weeks after the relatively uneventful Registration Day. From August 2 to August 6 insurrection raged throughout the area, but by the latter date the whole affair had fizzled out. Some locals failed to mobilize; the plans inevitably misfired. And the outbreak of the rebellion provoked a "veritable white terror" throughout Oklahoma, with thousands of people being arrested on the slimmest evidence.

The rebellion, of course, dealt a crushing blow to the progressive cause in Oklahoma. All of the patient, careful organizational work of the Socialist Party was snuffed out in four days as reaction smashed the last vestiges of progressive political leadership. The Socialist Party dissolved; the Renters' Union was crushed; soon even the rebellion was an episode in local history. Then came the postwar debacle and the rise of the Ku Klux Klan. Once again the old Socialist leadership, headed by men like Oscar Ameringer and Patrick Nagle, made a bid for power. In 1922 they formed the Farmer-Labor Reconstruction League and elected their candidate, J. C. ("Jack") Walton, as governor. No sooner had he been elected, however, than Walton began to go "sour." He turned up with a $40,000 mansion, and within a few weeks it was quite apparent that Oklahoma had been tricked. The Governor was soon impeached, and the farmer-labor crusade collapsed. One of Ameringer's associates committed suicide, so great was his disillusionment; as for Ameringer

* A 1917 armed rebellion in Oklahoma, in which farmers—blacks, poor whites, and Native Americans—refused to be drafted to fight in Europe in what they considered to be a rich man's war.

himself, he writes, rather sadly, that the Walton debacle "politically left me so limp that I have not voted for an Oklahoma Governor since."...

ENDNOTES

1. See *Oklahoma and Organized Labor,* by Milton Ernest Asfahl, 1930.
2. Part 5, hearing transcript of House Select Committee Investigating National Defense Migration, 77th Congress (Tolan Committee), p. 2129.
3. Incidentally, by 1935, farms operated by other than owners stood at 72.5 percent of all farms in the state. Part 5, Tolan Committee Transcript, p. 2179.
4. *If You Don't Weaken,* by Oscar Ameringer, 1940.

Exodus from the West Coast

1944

THERE EXISTED ON THE WEST COAST on December 7, 1941, a deep fault in the
social structure of the area. This fault or fissure separated the small Japanese
minority from the rest of the population. Like the earthquake faults that run
along the coastal area, this particular fault was deeper in some places than in
others; it had been dormant for years, but, in the language of the seismolo-
gists, it was still potentially active. While the fracture had begun to heal, the
fitting-together process was incomplete. Past history had shown that almost
any jar would disturb this fault. The attack on Pearl Harbor was more than a
jar; it was a thunderous blow, an earthquake, that sent tremors throughout
the entire Pacific area. The resident Japanese were the victims of this social
earthquake. This is the root fact, the basic social fact, which precipitated the
mass evacuation of the West Coast Japanese—"the largest single forced migration in American history," in the words of Dr. Paul S. Taylor.

Since this fault lay beneath the surface and had not been active for some
years, it had been generally ignored. The military, for example, had never
contemplated mass evacuation in the event of war. Only one group in the
population was fully aware of the existence of this social fault—namely, the
anti-Oriental diehards. Knowing of the existence of the fault, they not only
anticipated an earthquake, but had laid the foundation, in fear and in fantasy,
to capitalize upon the shock when it came. They had kept the old lies circulating; they had revived, from time to time, the old hatreds and the old fears.
In March of 1935 a California Congressman had told his colleagues that there
were 25,000 armed Japanese on the West Coast ready to take to the field in
case of war. The *San Francisco Chronicle*, at the same time, quoted a state

official to the effect that the "Japanese in California are training for war." In May 1936, Bernarr MacFadden published an open letter in *Liberty* addressed to the President in which he increased the number of Japanese "soldiers" in California to 250,000. Throughout these years, the "scare" stories continued to appear.[1]

On February 21, 1940, William Randolph Hearst had written an editorial in the *Los Angeles Examiner* in which he had said:

> Colonel Knox should come out to California and see the myriads of little Japs peacefully raising fruits and flowers and vegetables on California sunshine, and saying hopefully and wistfully: "Someday I come with Japanese army and take all this. Yes, sir, thank you." Then the Colonel should see the fleets of peaceful little Japanese fishing boats, plying up and down the California coast, catching fish and taking photographs.

The interests who inspired these and other stories knew what they would do the moment the earthquake struck: as early as 1939, Mr. Lail Kane, chairman of the National Defense Committee of American Legion Post No. 278, had stated, "In case of war, the first thing I would do would be to intern every one of them."[2]

Evacuation is over; it is past. No purpose would be served in discussing the matter at this time were it not for the fact that this social fault still exists on the West Coast. Formerly a local phenomenon, it now threatens to become nation-wide. Evacuation, moreover, is now being cited on the Coast as *proof* of the disloyal and untrustworthy character of this entire minority. It is a cloud that follows the evacuees wherever they go. For these reasons, it requires reconsideration, not for the purpose of reopening the issue itself, but of lifting, if possible, this cloud of suspicion. Just why was evacuation ordered and by whom? But, first, a brief statement of *how* it was effected, in order to clarify certain points in the explanation itself.

EVACUATION

On December 11, 1941, the Western Defense Command was established, the West Coast was declared a theater of war, and [Lieutenant] General J. L. DeWitt was designated as commander of the area. On December 7 and 8, the Department of Justice arrested, on Presidential warrants, all known "dangerous enemy aliens." Subsequently, by a series of orders, the first of which was issued on January 29, 1941, the Department ordered the removal of all "enemy aliens" from certain designated zones or so-called spot strategic installations, such as harbors, airports, and power lines.

Following the appearance of the Roberts Report on Pearl Harbor, January 25, "the public temper on the West Coast changed noticeably"[3] and "by the end of January, a considerable press demand appeared for the evacuation of all aliens, and especially of the Japanese from the West Coast." The moment this *press campaign* was launched, a highly significant meeting of the entire West Coast Congressional delegation took place in Washington under the chairmanship of Senator Hiram Johnson (a leader of the old anti-Oriental forces in California). On February 13, 1942, this delegation submitted a letter to the President recommending "the immediate evacuation of *all persons of Japanese lineage*" and suggesting that this might be accomplished without a declaration of martial law (martial law had been proclaimed in Hawaii on December 7). On February 14, 1942, General DeWitt submitted a memorandum to the War Department in which he recommended mass evacuation of the Japanese.[4] On February 19, 1942, President Roosevelt signed Executive Order No. 9066, authorizing the War Department to prescribe military areas and to exclude any or all persons from these areas. The next day Mr. Stimson delegated this responsibility to General DeWitt, who, on March 2, 1942, issued Proclamation No. 1, setting up certain military areas.

Subsequently the General, on March 27, prohibited all persons of Japanese ancestry from leaving these military areas, and by 108 separate orders, the first of which was issued on March 24, ordered all such persons to move from Military Areas No. 1 and 2 (embracing the states of Washington, Oregon, California, and a portion of Arizona). Congress, in effect, ratified this action on March 21, 1942, by the passage of Public Law No. 503, making it a criminal offense for a person or persons excluded from military areas to refuse to move. By June 5, 1942, all persons of Japanese ancestry had been removed from Military Area No. 1; by August 7, Military Area No. 2 had been cleared. This is a brief log of events in the evacuation procedure—the *how* of evacuation.

It can be seen from this brief chronology that it was General DeWitt who made the decision in favor of mass evacuation, and who, along with the West Coast Congressional delegation, had recommended it. The President and the Secretary of War were naturally preoccupied with more important matters at the time and relied upon the General's appraisal of the situation. In the last analysis, it was his responsibility; he had to make the decision. Now why did he order *mass* evacuation?

The explanation given at the time was "military necessity." The military necessity itself was not defined. But with the issuance of the General's final report on evacuation, dated July 19, 1943, but not released until January 1944, it now becomes possible to review the reasons prompting mass evacuation. The report clearly establishes the existence after December 7, 1941, of a grave and serious risk of an invasion of the West Coast. Guam was captured on December 13; Hong Kong fell on December 24; Manila on January 2; Singapore in February. Our fleet had been badly crippled at Pearl Harbor; for a time the disposition of the enemy's fleet was not known. On February 23, 1942, a Japanese submarine had shelled the California coast near Santa Barbara. The risk of imminent invasion was obvious and real, but it was as grave in Hawaii as on the mainland.

General DeWitt's responsibility was of the most serious character. He was a military commander, and military commanders have to make quick decisions; they have to act on the basis of possibilities as well as probabilities; they cannot weigh considerations with the nicety of a scientist working in a laboratory. The General must, also, have been haunted by the specters of Admiral Kimmel and General Short, who had been charged with dereliction of duty in Hawaii. Clearly, a serious military hazard existed on the West Coast; but what made the General relate the presence of the West Coast Japanese to this hazard?

In his report, two considerations, not strictly military in character perhaps, but certainly related to military security, are stressed: the danger of sabotage and the risk of espionage. The General knew, however, by February 14, that *no acts of sabotage* had occurred in Hawaii. If the Japanese population contained actual saboteurs, it is inconceivable that they would not have made their appearance during the attack on Pearl Harbor, which the Japanese government obviously intended to be a smashing, crippling blow. What is more disconcerting, however, is the fact that General DeWitt cites the absence of sabotage as "a disturbing and confirming indication that such action will be taken." In other words, the absence of proof (and no Japanese on the West Coast or in Hawaii have been convicted of sabotage) is taken as evidence of a fact. It is also disturbing to note that the General's suspicions were riveted on one minority and that he minimized the likelihood of sabotage on the part of German and Italian nationals, who were possibly in a better position to commit such acts by reason of the fact that their race did not identify them as enemy nationals.

There was strong evidence that espionage was being practiced on the West Coast. But the General notes that raids on Japanese communities failed to stop, for example, off-coast signaling. Who was engaged in this espionage? No answer is to be found in the report; but evidence of another character exists which throws some light on the problem. Prior to Pearl Harbor, two native-born white Americans had been convicted of being espionage agents for the Japanese government: John Farnsworth, a former naval officer, and Harry Thomas Thompson, a former seaman. Later, after the outbreak of war, an indictment was filed against Frederick Vincent Williams and David Warren Ryder, charging them with having been unregistered agents of the Japanese government. They were both convicted. David Warren Ryder had, for many years, been a well-known Pacific Coast journalist. Arthur Clifford Reed, another native-born white American, was indicted as an unregistered agent of Japan (he had been a corporal in the Army).[5] Heizer Wright, indicted for being an unregistered agent of Japan for ten years prior to Pearl Harbor, was a member of the editorial staff of the *New York Daily News*.[6] On June 14, 1943, the Office of War Information (OWI) revealed that the persons who did the actual signaling at Pearl Harbor on the eve of the Japanese attack were Nazi agents (not local resident Japanese). Joseph Hilton Smyth, purchaser of *The Living Age*, was certainly not a Japanese-American, any more than were his associates in this camouflaged Japanese propaganda scheme. Ralph Townsend, sentenced to jail for being an unregistered agent of Japan, was a leader in the America First movement. For some years prior to Pearl Harbor, a Los Angeles police captain had received money, from time to time, from the local Japanese consul for the ostensible purpose of spying on resident citizens of Japanese descent.[7] It has been pointed out that after the attack on Pearl Harbor, Tokyo relied almost entirely on non-Japanese agents and for obvious reasons.[8] This evidence is, of course, by no means conclusive, but it does indicate that the real betrayal was not "from the East," as suggested by Mr. Alan Hynd, but from sources much closer to home. No resident Japanese-American, either in Hawaii or on the mainland, has been convicted of being an unregistered agent or of having engaged in espionage activities. To focus attention on local residents of Japanese descent actually diverted attention from those who were busily engaged in espionage activity.

General DeWitt also states that the resident Japanese were in danger of mob violence and that he acted, in part, to protect them. He notes, however, that most of the reports of attacks against them were, upon investigation, "either unverified or were found to be cumulative."[9] What are the facts? With the war clouds becoming increasingly darker throughout 1941, public opinion on the West Coast remained surprisingly sympathetic toward the resident Japanese.[10] Even the shock of the attack on Pearl Harbor failed to produce popular hysteria; and public opinion remained quite unbiased.[11] "Every Japanese," wrote Chester Rowell, "good or bad, is visibly a Japanese; and if there comes a wave of hysteria, caused by the conduct of some Japanese, there are precedents in every country for the psychology that would visit anger on them all. *I am glad to report that, so far, there has been no evidence of any such feeling.*"[12] "Despite the nature of Japan's attack on Pearl Harbor," wrote Dr. Eric Bellquist of the University of California, "there was no immediate widespread reaction of suspicion of aliens and second-generation Japanese."[13] Dr. Bellquist notes that it was not until *after* the "commentators and columnists, 'professional patriots,' witch-hunters, alien-baiters, and varied groups and persons *with aims of their own*," began inflaming public opinion in January 1942 that hysteria began to develop. It was then, in his phrase, that "patterned patriotism on the loose" became apparent, and the "clamor for un-American restrictive measures became rife." There were no disturbances in the Northwest, reports Selden Menefee,[14] no disorders of any sort, but, on the contrary, "expressions of sympathy" toward the resident Japanese. (As to the remarkable calmness which prevailed throughout the Pacific Coast on December 7, 1941, see the hour-by-hour report prepared by the correspondents of *Time, Life,* and *Fortune,* entitled *The First Thirty Hours*.) I know of only two reported instances of violence in California: on December 27, 1941, a fight occurred between Filipinos and local Japanese in Stockton;[15] and on January 1, 1942, unknown persons fired at the home of a resident Japanese in Gilroy, California.[16] And if there was a danger—which the facts do not show—then it becomes pertinent to inquire, why did the authorities fail to take proper measures to allay *possible* hysteria (as they did, for example, in Hawaii); and why were no authoritative statements issued to negate the widespread and continuous rumors of sabotage in Hawaii?

It develops, also, that a number of nonmilitary considerations entered into General DeWitt's meditations. He began to engage in psychological speculation: were these people loyal? How would they act? "While it was *believed* that *some* were loyal, it was known that many were not."[17] He was not of the opinion, except hypothetically, that *any* were loyal. While much circumstantial proof is cited in support of this hypothesis, the report contains *not one word* of reference to the manner in which these people had tried to demonstrate their loyalty long before Pearl Harbor. Since it is an official report, this omission serves to fix a cloud of suspicion upon the entire group.

In the files of the *Congressional Record*, throughout 1940 and 1941 may be found numerous memorials and petitions from the West Coast Japanese attesting their undivided allegiance to the United States. On October 21, 1940, the entire Japanese population of Imperial Valley, Nisei and Issei alike,* assembled on the courthouse steps in El Centro and reaffirmed their loyalty to this country. On March 9, 1941, the Japanese-American Citizens League (JACL) met with the Los Angeles City Council, pledged their fullest support, and asked to be given a chance to demonstrate, in any manner suggested, their loyalty. A similar meeting was held on March 21, 1941, with officials of the Army and Navy intelligence services, at which plans were adopted to put all of the facilities of the JACL at the disposal of the authorities and at which the Nisei were complimented upon their patriotic action. These were merely sample demonstrations.

A local resident Japanese, Shuji Fujii, a Kibei, editor of the militant anti-fascist publication *Doho*, consistently denounced the fascist elements among the West Coast Japanese, and frequently by name.[18] The editor of the English section of *Rafu Shimpo* (a Japanese-American daily published in Los Angeles) protested against the drive for contributions for the relief of soldiers wounded in the Sino-Japanese War. Lieutenant Commander Ringle of Naval Intelligence has written[19] that many Nisei cooperated with him in his work as an intelligence officer and that, in his opinion, 85 percent of the entire resident Japanese population was unquestionably loyal. None of this evidence is mentioned in General DeWitt's report. Today these prewar acts of loyalty are actually referred to, by such persons as Mayor Fletcher Bowron of Los Angeles, as *suspicious* circumstances.

---

* "Issei" refers to the first immigrant generation from Japan. "Nisei" means second generation. "Kibei," found in the next paragraph, refers to Japanese Americans born in the United States and educated in Japan.

Undeniably there were dangerous individuals among the West Coast Japanese; undeniably there was a strong current of nationalistic feeling among certain Issei leaders. But the point is that these elements were well known to the authorities. They were promptly arrested on December 7 and 8, both on the mainland and in Hawaii. Writing in *Collier's* in October 1941, Jim Marshall observed that "for five years or more there has been a constant check on both Issei and Nisei—the consensus among intelligent people is that an overwhelming majority is loyal. The few who are suspect are carefully watched. In event of war, they would be behind bars at once. In case of war, there would be some demand in California for concentration camps into which Japanese and Japanese-Americans would be herded for the duration. Army, Navy, or FBI never have suggested officially that such a step would be necessary....Their opinion, based on intensive and continuous investigation, is that the situation is not dangerous and that, whatever happens, there is not likely to be any trouble. With this opinion West Coast newspapermen, in touch with the problem for years, agree most unanimously." Lieutenant Commander Ringle, who was as closely in touch with the entire problem as any official, did not think mass evacuation was necessary. That the authorities *had never contemplated* evacuation indicates that they had never regarded such a measure as being a matter of "military necessity."

It also develops that "military necessity" involved a judgment, by an Army official, on purely sociological problems. "The continued presence of a large, unassimilated, tightly knit racial group, bound to an enemy nation by strong ties of race, culture, custom, and religion," states General DeWitt, "constituted a menace which had to be dealt with.[20] Obviously there was a problem involved on this score; but it is interesting to note that West Coast sociologists who had studied the problem for years did not draw the same conclusion as the General, and needless to say, they were not consulted by him. No consideration whatever was given to the possibility of launching a special morale program or a campaign of so-called "preventive politics" in order to cope with the problem. No comparison was drawn between the manner in which these communities were organized and the manner in which German and Italian consuls had, in the most notorious fashion, conducted subversive activities on the West Coast. The problem of weighing these so-called "ethnic affiliations" was hardly one that, as a matter of proper function, should have been assigned to a military commander. Granted that a special problem was involved, it by no means follows that mass evacuation was the only method of coping with it.

And it further develops that racial considerations were also regarded as part of the "military necessity." "The Japanese race," states the General, "is an enemy race and while many second and third-generation Japanese born on United States soil, possessed of United States citizenship, have become 'Americanized,' the racial strains are undiluted....It therefore follows that along the vital Pacific Coast over 112,000 potential enemies, of Japanese extraction, are at large today."[21] (This was part of the General's initial report.) I can draw but one inference from such a statement, namely, that the General regarded the entire group as potential enemies because they were racially related to the enemy. I do not understand, furthermore, why General DeWitt felt compelled, in this instance, to put the word "Americanized" in quotation marks. Unfortunately, the General has since convicted himself of being deeply prejudiced on the score of race. Testifying on April 13, 1943, in San Francisco before the House Naval Affairs Subcommittee, he volunteered this statement:

> A Jap's a Jap. They are a dangerous element, whether loyal or not. There is no way to determine their loyalty....It makes no difference whether he is an American; theoretically he is still a Japanese and you can't change him....You can't change him by giving him a piece of paper.

This cynical appraisal of citizenship as "a piece of paper" and its brusque disregard of the factor of citizenship in general is rather disconcerting. It certainly demonstrates that it was the racial factor, rather than the so-called "ethnic affiliations," which really bothered the General.

Lastly, it now develops that political pressure was exerted on General DeWitt. This pressure was (a) exerted directly on him; and (b) indirectly brought to bear upon him through the technique of an organized campaign. Testifying before the Dies Committee* in Los Angeles, Mayor Fletcher Bowron made this interesting comment:

> I may say that I was quite active in getting the Japanese out of Los Angeles and its environs. I held various conferences with Tom Clark, now Assistant United States Attorney General, who was designated in charge of enemy alien activities

---

* The Special House Committee to Investigate Un-American Activities and Propaganda, 1938–1944, chaired by Martin Dies, an extremely conservative Democrat from Texas, was the forerunner of the well-known House Un-American Activities Committee.

on the Pacific Coast, and together with him and the then
Attorney General, now Governor Warren, we held a long
conference with General DeWitt relative to the situation,
*and I hope we were somewhat helpful in General DeWitt making
his decision.*[22]

After the Pacific Coast Congressional delegation had recommended mass
evacuation on February 13, and before the President had issued Executive
Order No. 9066, the delegation dispatched the Tolan Committee* to the West
Coast "so that local communities could voice their attitude toward the developing program." The committee came to the West Coast immediately (before the order was signed) and held hearings (February 21 to March 2, 1942).
If this were a matter of "military necessity" it is a little difficult to understand
why it was necessary to take "the pulse of opinion" on the West Coast. It also
develops that, at the time, the Attorney General of the United States was
opposed to mass evacuation, particularly in the absence of a declaration of
martial law, and that members of the West Coast delegation threatened to
lead an attack against the appropriation for the Department of Justice unless
some satisfactory solution could be reached.

Unlike their confreres in Hawaii, the dominant business interests on the
West Coast did not want to see martial law proclaimed.[23] These interests felt
that, if some means could be devised to get the Japanese excluded from the
West Coast without a declaration of martial law, then such a declaration
might be altogether avoided. The action of the West Coast delegation in
dispatching the Tolan Committee to the Coast before the President had acted
on their demand indicates an intention to exert public pressure on the administration. This was precisely what the Tolan hearings did. For, as so often
happens, the "pro" groups, those favoring evacuation, were prepared for the
occasion and dominated the hearings. Virtually no Issei testified; and the Nisei
were appearing under a severe handicap, for they were forced, in effect, to
agree in advance to whatever was proposed as a solution, since they were
asked to do so "as proof of their loyalty." Although it was claimed that possible Filipino-Japanese strife might be a factor in the developing situation, no
Filipinos were called to testify. In general, no minority groups were called.

---

* The House Select Committee Investigating National Defense Migration, chaired by John
  H. Tolan, charged, among other things, with investigating the problems of evacuating
  Japanese Americans during World War II.

The German and Italian groups, including the Jewish refugee groups, were at great pains to distinguish their case from that of the resident Japanese, including the Nisei.

Through these hearings, definite pressure for evacuation was carefully organized (not because the committee itself was unfair—it was eminently fair—but because the "pro" groups took possession of the hearings). Pressure for mass evacuation came from several different sources: from politicians and political units (all seeking to pass the buck to the government); from groups that had an obvious and readily acknowledged economic interest in evacuation; and from the traditionally anti-Oriental organizations, such as the American Legion, the California Joint Immigration Committee, and similar organizations. The mayors of Los Angeles, San Francisco, Portland, and Seattle all favored mass evacuation; various grand juries and city councils and boards of supervisors presented similar demands; and law-enforcement officials, in general, spoke in favor of the proposal. Few rank-and-file citizen groups appeared. The parade of witnesses in favor of evacuation certainly had the appearance of organization. Although the press had been conducting a steady campaign for evacuation since the latter part of January, there was little public interest, as such, in the problem. The hearings in Los Angeles were attended by a handful of witnesses and perhaps a dozen spectators.

In reviewing the testimony of these "pro" witnesses, two considerations become of paramount importance. In the first place, there was an almost unanimous assumption that Japanese should be placed in a separate category from German and Italian nationals; and, second, everyone assumed that sabotage had been practiced by resident Japanese in Hawaii. The Attorney General of California (now Governor Warren) was, perhaps, the most forceful advocate of mass evacuation. "We believe," he testified, "that when we are dealing with *the Caucasian race* we have methods that will test the loyalty of them.[24] He professed to believe, as though to emphasize the racial factor, that the Nisei constituted *a more likely danger* than the Issei. Not only did most of the witnesses assume that acts of sabotage had been committed in Hawaii, but the chairman of the committee consistently questioned witnesses on the assumption that such acts had been established. It is also worthy of note that virtually all of these witnesses testified that evacuation was required for the safety and protection of the Japanese themselves; that it was *primarily* for their protection. These same individuals are now strenuously contending that no Japanese should be permitted to return to the West Coast even in the postwar period. Since witnesses were encouraged to believe that sabotage had occurred in Hawaii, considerable credence was given to Mr. Warren's theory that the West Coast faced "an invisible deadline of sabotage." Thus old dormant fears were revived; old suspicions were renewed; and the same cliches that had been echoing on the Coast for fifty years or more were repeated—although awkwardly and in a manner that indicated lack of recent practice.

The point—of which so much was made at the hearing by the introduction of fancy maps—that it was "more than mere coincidence" that so many Japanese were located near "vital installations" requires a special word of comment. There could be no question, for example, that the Japanese fishing colony on Terminal Island, in the center of Los Angeles Harbor, did constitute a potential hazard. But how did the colony happen to be there? It had been established thirty years prior to the attack on Pearl Harbor and by American canning interests, not by the Japanese. Since fishing boats arrive at all hours of the day and night, it is essential, and has always been essential, that cannery workers live near the canneries. They traditionally report for work when the whistle blows at the cannery, announcing the arrival of the boats. The canneries *compelled* these workers to live in close proximity to the plants. Early in 1941, the colony had been attacked as a likely center of espionage activities, and the community itself had requested a full investigation. Such an investigation was actually conducted by the FBI and Naval Intelligence, but no arrests were made. It is certainly a safe assumption that Naval Intelligence officers knew all about the background and activities of every resident of the island, since the island residents had been under surveillance for years.

All of the Japanese fishermen were members of the Seine and Line Fisherman's Union, and long prior to December 7, they had repeatedly made declarations of their loyalty and support in case of war. The devotion of these fishermen to their homes, their children, and to the schoolteachers who taught at the all-Japanese school had been a favorite topic of local newspaper columnists for years.[25] Yet overnight this colony of fishermen, tied to their island community by the dictates of the canning industry, became sinister proof of the disloyal attitude of the resident Japanese.[26]

Mr. Warren, ruler in hand, also pointed to small Japanese truck gardens shown, by the map, to be located near factories, power lines, and refineries.

The Japanese specialized in the production of fresh vegetables for the urban West Coast markets. By reason of freight and transportation costs, these gardening units had to be placed near the markets themselves. Located around the periphery of the city, they were naturally intermeshed with sites used for industrial purposes. Only the Japanese could farm these small plots successfully, since they alone, by their intensive cultivation methods, could pay the high rental demanded for land which was essentially industrial, and not agricultural, in character. Most of this land lay between Los Angeles and the San Pedro–Long Beach harbor area. Inevitably the Japanese farmed, therefore, near oil refineries; near factories; near important strategic installations.

But some of these units were located beneath high-tension power lines, and certainly this was a suspicious circumstance. The answer was revealed by inadvertence at a subsequent hearing. When the power lines were built, the companies had to purchase a thousand-foot right-of-way or easement through the center of which ran the line. The property within the path of the power line could not be rented for residential purposes; nor was it desirable for industrial or commercial use. Concerns such as the Southern California Edison Company found that they could rent this easement land to Japanese at fifteen or twenty dollars an acre. That is how the Japanese happened to be beneath the power lines.

But some of them farmed on the heights at Palos Verdes, from which they could overlook Los Angeles Harbor and "flash signals" to boats at sea; they could even see, in the famous Los Angeles phrase, "Catalina Island on a clear day." Certainly this location was most suspicious. Later it developed that the reason the Japanese farmed on the Palos Verdes hills was because the land was high and free from frost; and because they needed one area near Los Angeles for dry-land farming so that early tomatoes and beans and peas might be placed on the tables of Los Angeles consumers. The Los Angeles County Farm Advisor later testified that there was no other area available which met these requirements. And that is why the Japanese happened to be where they "might see Catalina on a clear day." Italian "enemy alien" truck farmers and Italian "enemy alien" fishermen could have been indicted as suspicious characters by a similar unscrupulous use of circumstantial evidence by prejudiced observers. But no such indictment was made; and its omission is the best proof of the racial bias of the ruler pointers who appeared before the Tolan Committee and had its members gasping and panting over the menace of an "invisible deadline for sabotage."

ETHNIC TIES

While insisting that mass evacuation was primarily essential to protect the resident Japanese against mob violence—an argument that sounds strange indeed when advanced by high-ranking law enforcement officials—witnesses before the Tolan Committee advanced the usual stock arguments against the Japanese which had been repeated during all the previous agitations. Particular emphasis was placed on the language schools, the charge of dual citizenship, and the influence of Buddhism and Shintoism upon the resident Japanese.

A sense of ordinary common fairness should long ago have dictated a recognition of the peculiar language problem faced by Japanese residents on the West Coast. Immigrant parents felt the necessity of having their children instructed in the Japanese language in order to preserve family ties and to maintain some basis of communication with children who were speaking English in the schools, on the playgrounds, and in their everyday life. But from the outset there was a difficulty involved in securing competent instructors. The language school, supported by private funds, was devised to meet this clearly recognized need. Knowledge of their language was not only important from their parents' point of view, it was also important to those Nisei who, in later life, might seek employment in Japanese firms or in the export-import business.

It is indeed difficult to read anything subversive into the frankly expressed wish of Japanese parents that their children should know something about the history and culture of Japan. It is probably true, however, that some of these schools used text material that was objectionable. In Hawaii, the Japanese themselves sponsored legislation to bring the vernacular schools under state regulation. And many people have forgotten that in December 1920, the Japanese Association of America suggested that California should enact similar legislation. In fact, such a bill was enacted in California, only to be ruled unconstitutional in 1927. One of the reasons it was held unconstitutional was that the Catholic Church felt that such legislation might be extended to their parochial schools. And what has also been forgotten is that, in Oregon, the Japanese were finally successful in getting one public school to form a Japanese language class. Over a period of years, the vernacular schools were discussed at length in the Japanese-American press on the West Coast and many proposals were made, in the

States and in Canada, to integrate these language schools with the public school system. That this step was never taken is to be attributed not to the Japanese, but to our own failure to recognize the existence of a definite educational problem. As to the schools themselves, Mr. Vierling Kersey, Superintendent of Schools in Los Angeles, once said: "We have absolutely no objection to these schools."[27]

The fact of the matter is that these schools were never successful. As one observer has so well said, the Japanese youngster spent a "precious hour and one-half tossing spit balls at his classmates and calling his teacher names in American slang which she pretended not to understand. Physically he was in school; mentally he was making a run around left end for another touchdown. He was restless. He counted the minutes. At the gong, he dashed to freedom." Based on three years' experience as an instructor in one of these schools, Saikichi Chijiwa predicted in 1927 that they would soon pass out of existence. That they failed even in their primary purpose of language instruction is shown by the fact that the Army, scouring the relocation centers for Nisei who knew the language, found that only 15 percent of the Nisei could speak Japanese and that only about 5 percent could read or write Japanese. Furthermore, parochial schools have taught foreign languages to immigrant children in America for generations; and no serious complaint has ever been filed against them. Prior to December 7, 1941, the Italian consulates had distributed Fascist-inspired textbooks and other materials to Italian language schools in California. But at the Tolan Committee hearings, only the Japanese language schools were deemed subversive or otherwise suspect. Later a California legislative committee found that Italians had sponsored similar language schools in which official Fascist propaganda was taught and texts were used that were supplied by the Italian consuls.[28]

The "dual citizenship" charge was similarly unrealistic and unfair. The Japanese Nationality Code has always been predicated upon the doctrine of *jus sanguinis*—namely, that a child is Japanese if its father is a Japanese national at the time of its birth. Under the Fourteenth Amendment, we have always followed the doctrine of *jus soli*—except in the case of our own nationals abroad—that persons born in this country are citizens of the United States. That there are two such conflicting doctrines of nationality may be readily explained: countries having a heavy out-migration—the population exporting countries—almost uniformly follow the doctrine of *jus sanguinis*;

while countries of heavy in-migration—the population receiving countries—follow the doctrine of *jus soli*. There is nothing peculiar, therefore,
about the rule followed by Japan (it has been the rule of many European
nations).

What we have forgotten is that the Japanese on the West Coast themselves petitioned Japan in 1914 to modify its law. The law was, in fact, modified in March 1916, and again in December 1925, so as to make it possible for
Japanese born in this country to renounce any claim of dual citizenship. It is
a little difficult to see how such a claim could arise in actual practice, since we
have never recognized the principle of dual citizenship. In any case, after
1925 many Nisei did renounce Japanese citizenship (the Japanese-American
Citizens League carried on a ceaseless agitation to this end), and those born
after December 1, 1925, were automatically released from such a claim. It is,
however, true that many Nisei, largely through ignorance, or indifference,
neglected to renounce the claim. While stressing this matter of dual citizenship, the anti-Japanese forces have always failed to note the sharp and obvious cleavage between the first and second generation—a fact of far greater
significance.

Not being a theologian, I hesitate to discuss Buddhism or Shintoism as
possible factors making for strong currents of nationalism among the resident Japanese population. But it is difficult to believe that Buddhism, as practiced in America, is quite the same faith as Buddhism practiced in Japan. The
testimony of all observers is to the contrary. They point out that, as an imported cultural institution, Buddhism has undergone definite modifications
and that the Buddhist churches have tended to parallel the Christian churches,
adopting the same institutional paraphernalia, such as kindergarten schools,
Sunday schools, some of the same hymns, and most of the same societies.
Adherents of Buddhism have pointed out that an appreciation of its rites is
largely dependent upon some knowledge of Japanese; and that with the decline of a knowledge of the language there developed a loss of interest in the
faith. They also complained that children became involved in Christian practices merely as an incidence of their daily life. Generally speaking, Buddhism
seemed to have stronger roots in rural than in urban communities. It had
little interest for the Nisei. To them it was "odd" and "difficult" and the very
appearance of a ramshackle Buddhist temple was as incongruous to them as
it was to most other Americans.

I have examined any number of the proceedings of the Young Buddhist

Leagues—the so-called Bussei groups. They read almost exactly like the proceedings of a typical conference of young go-getting Methodists. There is certainly nothing esoteric about the proceedings: government officials appeared and discussed soil problems; social workers orated about the problems of the second generation; and civic leaders exhorted the faithful to take a more responsible part in the affairs of their communities. If there was a tendency on the part of these churches to undermine faith in American democracy, it is certainly not reflected in the proceedings themselves. It is, however, probably true that after 1937 some effort was made by Japan to use the vernacular schools and the Buddhist churches for propaganda purposes, both here and in Hawaii. For example, the *Literary Digest* of February 13, 1937, reported that some "forty young missionaries from the Buddhist University in Kyoto, Japan," had recently arrived in the United States. But to make religious faith a test of loyalty or to consider it as evidence affecting the question of loyalty was as unfair as to imply that race could be made a test of loyalty.

More serious than this age-old native-son gossip about language schools, dual citizenship, and Buddhism was the fact that the Japanese did have a tightly knit pattern of social organization and that most group activity was coordinated by the local Japanese Association, which, in turn, had close ties with the various consulates. The same type of co-ordination existed in the control which certain Japanese firms exercised over both Issei and Nisei and the relationship which existed between these firms and the consulates. What made this pattern particularly troublesome was the fact that in 1941 the leadership was still vested in the Issei. It is important to note, however, that the war had broken this pattern of relationships. The vernacular schools were closed; the consulates were closed; all aliens had been registered in 1940; the assets of the Japanese firms had been frozen in midsummer, 1941; and, immediately after December 7, the leaders of the various associations were in jail. Precisely the same relationship patterns existed in Hawaii. If anything the various Japanese organizations were more closely knit in Hawaii than on the mainland.

There is still another factor involved which has never been discussed in relation to the evacuation problem. The Japanese and the Japanese-Americans had a big economic stake in the security of the West Coast. Their holdings have been estimated as being in excess of $200 million. From a strictly economic point of view, what could they possibly hope to gain from a Japanese victory? Even the few deluded individuals who might have believed in the possibility of a Japanese victory must have realized, as did the Japanese war lords, that the most Japan could hope to achieve was a stalemate in the Pacific with Japan retaining a portion of its Far Eastern loot. How could even such a hypothetical victory improve the lot of the West Coast Japanese? Bad as their position was after the attack on Pearl Harbor, it would have become intolerable had Japan, let us say, achieved a stalemate in the Pacific. In such an eventuality, remote as it must have seemed, they could only have expected economic and physical annihilation on the West Coast. Most of the Issei had lived in this country from thirty to fifty years; they had, in a majority of cases, American-born children. Several thousand of these Nisei were serving in the United States Army on December 7, 1941. Assuming that there were strong currents of nationalism among some of the Issei leaders, it should not be forgotten that 72 percent of the Nisei have never been in Japan. The most powerful economic, family, and personal considerations dictated the necessity of continued allegiance to the United States.

ECONOMIC PRESSURES

While the position taken by the various groups before the Tolan Committee cannot be said to follow a clear line of economic interest, it is certainly true that special-interest groups were active in exerting pressure for mass evacuation. The shipper-grower interests in Washington were opposed to mass evacuation, while the Washington Commonwealth Federation, an ultraliberal group, favored it. But the California shipper-grower interests were definitely in favor of mass evacuation and for admittedly selfish reasons. Shortly after December 7, the Shipper-Grower Association of Salinas sent Mr. Austin E. Anson to Washington to lobby for mass evacuation. "We're charged with wanting to get rid of the Japs for selfish reasons," said Mr. Anson. "We might as well be honest. We do. It's a question of whether the white man lives on the Pacific Coast or the brown men. They came into this valley to work, and they stayed to take over."[29] Similarly, so-called "white interests" in the nursery and florist businesses were actively seeking mass evacuation as a means of eliminating unwanted competition.

To appreciate the position that these special-interest economic groups took, however, it is necessary to explain the situation as they saw it. By December 7, 1941, the Japanese had achieved a *tolerated* position in the industries in which they were concentrated, such as the produce industry, the floral industry, the nursery industry. They were tolerated because of an unofficial truce that had been declared: this far they might go, but no farther. But with prices rising after December 7, produce interests saw an opportunity to take over the Japanese holdings; for they foresaw that prices would continue to rise (particularly if the Japanese were ousted), thereby creating an opportunity for them to take over and operate successfully types of business which, in "normal" times or in a period of declining prices, they could not possibly hope to operate at a profit. They also realized that, once the Nisei came into possession and ownership of these businesses, they might expand out of the tolerated zone. For the Nisei were American citizens; they were exceptionally well educated; and they could not, therefore, be expected to stay within the confines into which their parents had been driven. To get all Japanese out of the state would eliminate, so they thought, this potential *future* competition.

These same special-interest groups have, moreover, continued to be most active in urging the permanent exclusion of the Japanese from the West Coast. High stakes are involved: the Japanese produce production in California had an estimated annual value of $35 million; their share of the florist business in Los Angeles alone was valued at around $4 million annually. In Washington, as I have indicated, the situation was somewhat different, because there the Japanese figured more prominently in the production of produce for interstate shipment, whereas in California they were largely confined to the production of fresh vegetables for the local markets. While there was this split in the ranks of the economic pressure groups—not all of whom favored mass evacuation—it is nevertheless incontestably true that certain groups stood to profit (momentarily at least) by the elimination of the Japanese; and that they played a very important behind-the-scenes role in securing mass evacuation.

THE EARTHQUAKE STRIKES

By the time the Tolan Committee arrived in California in February 1942, the social fault that I have mentioned had begun to jar the Japanese communities loose from their moorings. On July 26, 1941, the assets of Japanese nationals had been "frozen." The restrictions imposed on enemy aliens on December 7 and 8 had begun to hamper the Issei in their business activities, and a serious economic crisis had developed. The uncertainty of the situation had created a type of economic paralysis: business transactions were suspended, crops were not being planted, many activities were being held in *status quo*. Land-lords had begun to evict Japanese tenants; insurance policies were being canceled; social-security payments could not be released to Japanese na-tionals. Japanese firms were slowly losing patronage. No new employment fields were opening. The families of those individuals arrested on Presiden-tial warrants were in dire distress. Nisei were being discharged from their positions (they were summarily ousted from city, county, and state civil-service positions without hearings and with no charges being preferred against them). On January 17, 1942, it was reported that most of the Japa-nese firms in San Francisco would have "to close within a few months." This distress was apparent as early as August 1941; by January 1942 it had become acute.

The committee arrived in Los Angeles just in time to observe the disas-trous effects of the summary ouster of the Japanese fishing colony—five hundred families—from Terminal Island. On February 15, these families were told that they were expected to move within thirty days; later, they were given twenty-four hours in which to vacate. The utmost confusion prevailed as families sought to find places into which they might move and tried frantically to dispose of their effects. Most of these families were with-out resources. These two developments, the paralysis creeping over the Japanese communities and the ouster of families from spot strategic areas, merely indicated that an earthquake had struck along the fault.

There is one further aspect of the matter, however, that warrants con-sideration: between February 19 and March 27, 1942, the Japanese were at liberty to depart voluntarily from Military Area No. 1. The failure of vol-untary evacuation to effect the desired removal of all Japanese from the area was largely responsible for the subsequent orders for evacuation. Dur-ing the period mentioned, it is estimated that some 10,231 Japanese volun-tarily departed from Military Area No. 1, but, of this number, some 4,825 merely moved into Military Area No. 2. In some cases, this involved simply moving a few miles. It also had the effect of concentrating evacuees in cer-tain rural areas in central California where, by their presence, they aroused suspicion and tended to aggravate an already tense situation.

In the nature of things, voluntary evacuation could hardly have been suc-cessful, since few resident Japanese had friends or relatives in the Middle West or East, and they did not know where to go. Many of them lacked the neces-sary funds to finance a long-distance trip; and, besides, they were uncertain about the kind of reception they might meet. It was a question of fleeing from a known to an unknown evil. Of those who did voluntarily depart, some 5,396 went to areas outside both Military Areas Nos. 1 and 2, principally to Colorado and Utah. Of those who did move during the period of voluntary evacuation, it is estimated that 1,200 shortly returned to Military Area No. 1, thereby further complicating an already complicated situation.

In attempting to remove themselves beyond Military Areas Nos. 1 and 2, evacuees either had to cross through the intermountain states or to locate in this region. In February, Congressman Tolan had wired the governors of these (and other) states, inquiring about the possibilities of relocating the Japanese. With the exception of Governor Carr of Colorado (who was subsequently defeated in a political campaign), all replied unfavorably. Typical of the replies received was the comment of Governor Homer M. Adkins of Arkansas: "Our people are not familiar with the customs or peculiarities of the Japanese. We are always anxious to co-operate in any way we can, but our people, being more than 95 percent native born, are in no manner familiar with their customs and ways and have never had any of them within our borders, and I doubt the wisdom of placing any in Arkansas." I know of one family that had been located in New Mexico for almost thirty years prior to Pearl Harbor. Yet it is interesting to note that the pressures became so great in New Mexico (so many of whose soldiers were involved at Bataan) that this family voluntarily moved into a relocation center to secure protection. That this could happen in New Mexico is some indication of what might have happened in California if evacuation had not been ordered, once the flood of agitation had started.

Sentiment in these intermountain states not only was opposed to relocation, but was of such a character as to indicate the kind of reception that evacuees might face if they moved farther eastward. For example, Governor Payne Ratner of Kansas stated that "Japs are not wanted and not welcome in Kansas" and directed the state highway patrol to turn back any Japanese trying to enter the state.[30] One Japanese group consisting of seven adults and a baby was stopped at nearly every Colorado town in attempting to cross the state. On March 7, 1942, the press reported that Japanese attempting to cross through Arizona were stopped by state highway patrolmen. Similar incidents were reported throughout the area. Typical of the general reaction was the statement of the Nevada Bar Association: "We feel that if Japs are dangerous in Berkeley, California, they are likewise dangerous to the State of Nevada."

The *State-Tribune* of Wyoming stated in an editorial of March 8, 1942: "It is utterly unequitable and unfair to subject Wyoming to the bureaucratic dictum that it shall support and find employment for Japanese brought here from Pacific Coast defense zones." In its issues of March 2 and 9, 1942, the *Denver Post* carried similar editorial statements. The mere fact that the governors of these states had been queried on the possibility of relocation brought down upon them an avalanche of mail from irate constituents.

As they retreated eastward evacuees met with unpleasant incidents at many points and were constantly subjected to humiliating experiences. Signs posted in shops read: "This restaurant poisons both rats and Japs"; barbershops carried signs reading "Japs Shaved: Not Responsible for Accidents"; cards were placed in automobile windshields reading "Open Season for Japs"; stores, filling stations, restaurants, refused to serve evacuees.[31] The vigorous expression of such attitudes and the recurrence of such incidents clearly indicated, early in March 1942, that voluntary evacuation would not be successful. The same evidence indicated that evacuation would have to be federally supervised, that minimum measures of protection would have to be taken, and that further voluntary evacuation would have to be curtailed. As a consequence, the first "freezing" order was issued on March 27, 1942.[32]

"E DAY" ARRIVES

Just as the federal authorities were pushed into the program of evacuation, so they were compelled to improvise extraordinary devices and expedients to cope with the problem which they had inherited overnight. Not only were there no precedents to follow—no guideposts along the way—but the time element precluded the possibility of a studied consideration of various possibilities and alternatives. Having permitted themselves to be convinced that these people were a menace, it necessarily followed that prompt action was required. There is no evidence that the military had ever contemplated, in the event of war, such a measure; certainly they had no concealed Plan x to pull from their files. The whole program was evolved in response to external pressures and developments. It evolved dialectically: by internal and external compulsions.

It is important to remember, as Mr. Dillon Myer* has pointed out, that

---

* Dillon Myer was director of the National War Relocation Authority. In 1950 he was appointed commissioner of Indian Affairs.

"internment camps were never *intended* in relation to this program." All that was originally contemplated was an order excluding persons of Japanese descent from the area. When it became apparent that these persons were slow to move, that they needed assistance; and when it gradually dawned on the authorities that they did not even know where to move, then and only then were plans prepared which contemplated assistance, supervision, and control of the movement. Voluntary evacuation was then "frozen" and the Wartime Civil Control Administration was created as a branch of the Western Defense Command to supervise the removal of the evacuees. It was essentially WCCA's function to direct the removal—not the relocation—of these people. To this end it was deemed necessary to prevent further voluntary removals; to assemble all evacuees for removal; and to establish temporary reception or assembly centers.

Evacuation proceeded on a regular army timetable. Since removal was ordered on an area-by-area basis, as reception facilities were established, it did not occur simultaneously throughout the West Coast. Civil control stations were established in each area having a minimum of one thousand persons to be evacuated. Evacuees were registered at these stations and to these stations they reported on "E Day," the Army's designation of the date fixed for their removal. E Day will not soon be forgotten by the resident Japanese. The final decision in favor of total mass evacuation occurred only after weeks of uncertainty, debate, agitation, rumor, and conflicting reports. The decision itself came to most Japanese as almost as great a shock as Pearl Harbor. Until the very last moment there was always the hope of a respite or reprieve, or the possibility that some alternative plan might be adopted, or that only certain groups, such as the aliens, would be evacuated. To be forewarned of a disaster is not to be prepared for the disaster itself. As a group, the Japanese were stunned by the final decision; and to most of them it was a major disaster. It was as though they had been engulfed in a natural calamity, such as flood, or fire, or earthquake.

One Nisei underwent plastic surgery in an effort to have his features changed: "I was so ashamed," he said, "of my racial identity." Dreading to meet his Caucasian friends, Koji Kurokawa hid in the basement of his employer's home for twenty-three days. On a Fourth of July prior to evacuation, Hideo Murata, a veteran of the First World War, had been presented by the board of supervisors of Monterey County with a "Certificate of Honorary Citizenship" which read:

> Monterey County presents this testimony of heartfelt grati-
> tude, of honor and respect for your loyal and splendid ser-
> vice to the country in the Great World War. Our flag was
> assaulted, and you gallantly took up its defense.

When E Day was announced in Monterey County, Murata went to see his friend the sheriff and asked if it wasn't all a mistake, or perhaps just a practical joke. Finding that the order meant what it said, he went to a local hotel, paid for his room, and committed suicide. The sheriff found the certificate of honorary citizenship clutched in his hand. Not every Japanese, needless to say, felt this keenly about the matter. Most of them tried to accept the bitter intelligence itself in good spirit. Some volunteered to assist in the process; others attempted a show of high spirits about the entire procedure; all of them co-operated in the movement itself.

A curious aspect of E Day in California, as elsewhere on the West Coast, was the kindly complacence shown by the Caucasian residents of the area. While there had been weeks of agitation for the removal of the Japanese, this agitation had been conducted at a relatively high level. Uniformly the stress had been placed on considerations of national security, military necessity, and the well-being of these admirable people, the West Coast Japanese. The friendliest spirit prevailed in virtually every area. In more than one area this spirit verged on tenderness and remorse. Editorials appeared in which the evacuees were wished *bon voyage*; complimented on their excellent behavior; assured of a warm welcome upon their return; sentimental "sayonaras" echoed throughout the area. There were no harsh or strident or bitter denunciations. In areas which have since become hotbeds of anti-Japanese agitation, the departure of the Japanese was the occasion for the expression of heartfelt sentiments. There was virtually no realization, among the generality of citizens, that they were witnessing a unique departure from American tradition; for, those long proclamations ordering removal that appeared in the newspapers, were announced over the radio, and were tacked to telegraph poles and posted on bulletin boards referred to "all persons of Japanese ancestry." No exceptions were specified; no provision was made for cases involving mixed marriages; and one drop of Japanese blood brought a person within the category defined. Here a group was being singled out for discriminatory treatment *solely* upon the basis of race or ancestry. In Germany, as Dr. Morris Opler has pointed out, the Nazis merely pretended to discriminate against persons on the score of race or ancestry. They were well aware of the fact, as were the German people, that the Jews are not a race. But we premised the discrimination explicitly and solely upon the fact of race or ancestry; more particularly of "ancestry" since the Koreans and the Chinese belong to the same "race" as the Japanese. No phase of our tradition, particularly of our Western tradition, has been more firmly accepted than the proposition that a man is not responsible for his ancestors. Even to inquire about a person's ancestry, in the early days of the West, was to violate an unwritten prohibition firmly implanted in the mores of the people. The acquiescence of the Japanese in this singular procedure was wholly admirable; but the indifference to, the calm acceptance of the same procedure by their fellow citizens presents a somewhat different problem. It is, perhaps, only to be accounted for in terms of the fact that the Japanese, as such, had never been really accepted as a part of the community. Their removal was, therefore, accomplished with much the same smoothness that an easily detachable part is removed from a machine.

From the control stations, the evacuees were escorted to a series of hastily improvised assembly centers. In selecting sites for assembly centers, WCCA showed great ingenuity. Use was made of fairgrounds, parks, race tracks, and pavilions. In California, assembly centers were established at Marysville, Sacramento, Tanforan, Stockton, Merced, Turlock, Salinas, Fresno, Pinedale, Tulare, Santa Anita, Pomona, and Manzanar (the only assembly center that was constructed as a relocation project). In the Northwest, assembly centers were established in Portland and at Puyallup; and in Arizona at Cavecreek and Mayer Camp. On arriving at the assembly centers, the evacuees went through a process of induction (registration, baggage inspection, medical checkup) and were assigned to quarters. Before they really knew what had happened, they were inside the centers, the gates were locked, and the sentries had established their patrols.

In a period of 28 days, army engineers had constructed shelters in assembly centers for one hundred thousand people, and in a period of 137 days the same number of people had been moved into these centers. By June 8, 1942, the entire movement from points of residence in Military Area No. 1 to assembly centers had been effected; and shortly afterwards those remaining in Military Area No. 2 had likewise been removed. By that date, virtually every Japanese, citizen and alien alike, in the three West Coast states and portions of Arizona, was in an assembly center. The only exceptions were Japanese

EXODUS FROM THE WEST COAST ▍ 132

confined to institutions, such as hospitals, prisons, insane asylums, and or-
phanages. The rapidity and efficiency with which this movement was accomplished represents a major achievement for the Army. Colonel Karl
Bendetsen was well within the facts when he said that the entire movement had been effected "without mischance, with minimum hardship, and
almost without incident." All observers are in agreement on the proposition that the Army executed the assignment with tact, good judgment, and
remarkable efficiency. On June 8, 1942, the assembly-center population to-
taled 99,700 Japanese.

The efficiency of the Army, however, was matched by the excellent co-
operation of the evacuees. No incidents were reported in which the Japanese
failed to co-operate; on the contrary, all the evidence points to the fact that
they are justly entitled to a major share of the credit for the achievement
itself. It requires some measure of discipline, fortitude, and patience, on such
short notice, to close out businesses, to wind up affairs, to dispose of homes
and furnishings, to take care of the countless details which any move in-
volves, and to report, with a handful of possessions, on time for removal to
an unknown destination. Nor did the co-operation of the Japanese end with
their arrival in the centers. Many of these centers were not completed when
the evacuees began to arrive. The evacuees helped to build them; assisted in
making them livable; and quickly assumed major responsibilities in their
administration. The construction problem itself was of minor significance
when compared with the immediate problem of administration. Some of
these assembly centers were good-sized cities (there were eighteen thousand
evacuees in the Santa Anita center). The whole apparatus of municipal facilities—water system, sewer system, hospital, schools, police, post office, stores,
recreation, not to mention the detail of feeding eighteen thousand people
three times a day—had to be improvised overnight.

Faced with a problem of this magnitude, the administration would have
been completely paralyzed had it not been for the manner in which the evacuees co-operated in the entire undertaking. Imagine moving and relocating
one hundred thousand rank-and-file American citizens—of all classes, ages,
and occupations—under similar circumstances! It would have required several Army divisions to have accomplished such an assignment and these divisions would probably have had to cope with a new rebellion every fifteen
minutes. With no other group of similar size in our population could such a
feat have been possible. It is also important to remember that these people

were living under great emotional stress: they were fearful, bewildered, dis-
traught. The utmost confusion prevailed. While WCCA had attempted to
move entire families and entire communities intact to the same assembly
center, it was not possible to do so in all cases. Many of the evacuees were
completely alone among total strangers in the strangest world they had ever
known. The irritations and inconveniences, major and minor, were legion.
In Puyallup, there was one washroom for a hundred families; in Tanforan
and Santa Anita thousands of people were housed in stable stalls recently
occupied by horses; in Yakima, evacuees were "housed" in an abandoned
hop yard. The annoyances of the moment were dwarfed in significance by
mounting anxiety and by a growing concern about the future. It is against
this general background that the behavior and conduct of the Japanese must
be appraised. That they behaved as they did is a remarkable demonstration,
in itself, of their loyalty. Mr. Stimson has himself pointed out that "great
credit is due our Japanese population for the manner in which they responded
to and complied with the orders of exclusion."

ECONOMIC CONSEQUENCES

For a variety of reasons, it has been and will continue to be difficult to appraise the economic effect of the removal of the Japanese from the West
Coast. The rather boastful statements of California shipper-growers to the
effect that the removal of the Japanese occasioned no loss in farm production
are exceedingly misleading. The figures cited in substantiation of this and
similar statements usually have reference to total acreages and not to the
volume of production of a particular crop. They also relate to current abnormal price structures which have made possible a temporary shift in acreage
from Japanese-controlled to non-Japanese-controlled operations. Asked if the
Japanese were necessary factors in agricultural production in California, Mr.
Harold Ryan, Agricultural Commissioner of Los Angeles County, recently
testified: "Not unless we insist upon having cheap vegetables grown in great
quantities on small acreage of land." The qualifications noted in this statement are most significant. Later Mr. Ryan said that "it remains to be seen
whether the non-Japanese farmer can continue successfully in the growing
of miscellaneous vegetables on small acreages."

It can be definitely stated, however, that the removal of the Japanese has
had a most unfortunate effect on production insofar as consumers are concerned. In its annual report for 1942, the Federal-State Market News service

stated that Southern California consumers alone paid $10 million more for ten thousand truckloads less of perishable vegetables in 1942, by comparison with 1941.[33] Removal of the Japanese has created a chaotic situation in the wholesale produce markets in Los Angeles. Buyers complain that it is currently either "a feast or a famine"; tomatoes flood the market for a week and the next week cannot be obtained. The deterioration of quality is a self-evident fact to any Southern California consumer. In a report released on January 3, 1944, the State Director of Agriculture accused retailers of fresh fruits and vegetables in the state of charging prices ranging from "higher than necessary" to "wholly unwarranted and exorbitant." In some cases retailers, according to this report, have realized margins of from 50 to 450 percent above wholesale costs. Independent buyers of produce throughout the state complain that the removal of the Japanese has increased prices unnecessarily and has resulted in a definite consolidation of economic controls and a further extension in the direction of monopolistic price structures. It should be remembered that the removal of the Japanese occurred at a time when prices had begun to rise and when the population of the state was increasing in a most spectacular fashion.

That the Japanese sustained enormous economic losses as a result of evacuation cannot be denied. The whole evacuation program, as it developed, was so uncertain at the outset, and so summary in conclusion, that Japanese did not have time to dispose of their holdings. Their losses must be reckoned in the millions of dollars. Even after evacuation was a foregone conclusion, the federal government failed to set up any satisfactory system of property custodianship. The government agencies that were delegated responsibility in the matter in most cases either tried to evade this responsibility or joined in pressuring the Japanese to dispose of their holdings quickly and in a haphazard fashion. The grossest imposition was practiced upon the Japanese, ranging from petty chiseling to large-scale fraud.

Any number of suits are pending in the California courts today in which local interests are charged with the most serious fraud and, in some cases, with the most flagrant abuse of trust relationships. Considering that some of the individual Japanese holdings were quite large, it is possible to gain some idea of the amount of the stakes that are involved. Naturally the interests charged with fraud are among those most anxious to keep the Japanese from returning to the state. It is quite obvious that if a federal investigation is ever made of the manipulation that has already occurred, it will have the proportions of a national scandal.[34] In Santa Maria (in Santa Barbara County) local interests have been charged with bilking the Japanese out of holdings valued at $500,000.[35] In this instance, the Treasury Department was finally forced to intervene to protect the Japanese against a total dissipation of their holdings; but, as a result of extraordinary pressures brought to bear, the freezing order of the Treasury Department was subsequently lifted.

The creator of the fortune involved in this particular case, H. Y. Minami, Sr., came to California in 1905, to work for the Southern Pacific railroad as a day laborer. He laid the foundation for his considerable fortune by inducing the railroad to lease to him small acreages—then wholly unproductive—along its right-of-way. This is but one of many similar cases. It is out of such a murky background that much of the pressure for the permanent exclusion of the Japanese from the state stems at the present time. Gradually most of the Japanese holdings—urban and rural—are being liquidated. A recent report of their estimated holdings of $5 million in the city of Los Angeles indicates that virtually all of it will have been sold in another year. "It is expected that ultimately there won't be a parcel of Jap-owned real estate in Los Angeles."[36] It should also be remembered that those Japanese still remaining in relocation centers are being steadily pauperized. The small amounts that they earn are not sufficient to pay obligations of a fixed character, such as premiums on life insurance policies and other commitments. As a consequence, it is estimated that the residents of the two centers in Arizona alone are being pauperized at the rate of about $500,000 a year.

The removal of the Japanese has had other and, in some respects, rather amusing aspects. While the race purists of the state have been gloating over the removal of an "unassimilable" minority of around ninety thousand, the vacuum in the labor market occasioned by the removal of the Japanese is in part responsible for the current influx of Negroes from the Deep South. Approximately ninety thousand Japanese have been removed from the state and approximately one hundred and fifty thousand Negroes have been attracted into it. By and large, the Negroes have flooded into the Little Tokyo areas which were left vacant when the Japanese were removed. Little Tokyo in Los Angeles has recently been rechristened as Bronzeville. The influx of Negroes has created special problems of housing, education, and recreation and, at the same time, has contributed to the steadily mounting racial tensions.[37] As a matter of fact, the removal of the Japanese, coming as it did when defense production was increasing by leaps and bounds, artificially stimulated the already extended demand for manpower. What was accomplished, in terms of the war effort, by the removal of the Japanese was the elimination of a wholly theoretical hazard to the detriment of nearly every other aspect of the war....

ENDNOTES
1. See *Focus* for July 1938; *Friday,* May 9, 1941; *Life* for October 14, 1940—"Californians cast an anxious eye upon the Japanese-Americans in their midst" and *Click,* February 1941, "Japan Attacks the U.S. in 1941."
2. *Saturday Evening Post,* September 30, 1939.
3. *Preliminary Report,* Tolan Committee [House Select Committee Investigating National Defense Migration], March 19, 1942.
4. *Final Report: Japanese Evacuation from the West Coast,* Tolan Committee, 1943, p. 33.
5. See *Los Angeles Times,* January 7, 1944.
6. *PM,* July 9, 1943.
7. *Los Angeles Daily News,* June 14, 1939.
8. See *Sabotage!* by Sayers and Kahn, p. 193.
9. *Report,* p. 9.
10. *Pacific Citizen,* September, 1941; *Seattle Post-Intelligencer,* August 23, 1941; and series of articles in the *Los Angeles Daily News,* August 21, 22, and 23, 1941.
11. *Portland Oregonian,* for example, editorial of December 16, 1941.
12. *Survey,* January 1942.
13. *California Alumni Monthly,* April 1942.
14. *Assignment: U.S.A.,* 1943, p. 67.
15. *Sacramento Bee,* December 27, 1941.
16. *Los Angeles Times,* April 24, 1943.
17. *Report,* p. 9; italics mine.
18. See *Doho,* April 1940.
19. *Harper's,* October 1942.
20. *Report,* p. vii.
21. *Report,* p. 34.
22. Vol. 54, p. 9207. Italics mine.
23. See testimony of Mr. Paul Shoup, President of Los Angeles Merchants and Manufacturers Assn., before the Tolan Committee, p. 11866.
24. Tolan Committee hearings, p. 11015; italics mine.
25. See *Los Angeles: City of Dreams* by Harry Carr, 1935, pp. 329–330.
26. On the colony, generally, see "Friends of Spies on Terminal Island?" by Margaret Fowle Rogers, *International Baptist Magazine,* May 1941.
27. *Los Angeles Daily News,* August 21, 1941.
28. *Fact-Finding Committee Investigating Un-American Activities in California,* 1943, pp. 316–319.
29. *Saturday Evening Post,* May 9, 1942.
30. Reported in the *Las Vegas Daily Optic,* April 1, 1942.

31. See the *Christian Advocate,* October 15, 1942.

32. See also "The Problem People" by Jim Marshall, *Collier's,* August 15, 1942.

33. *Los Angeles Daily News,* February 17, 1943.

34. See, for example, the complaint in the matter of *Hiramatsu* vs. *L. R. Phillips* et al. [then] pending in the Superior Court of Santa Barbara County.

35. See *Santa Barbara News-Press,* October 27, 1943, p. A-2.

36. *Los Angeles Times,* December 5, 1943.

37. See the report of the San Francisco Grand Jury on conditions in its former Little Tokyo section as reported in the *San Francisco Examiner* of June 15, 18, and 19, 1943.

Storm Signals

1951

THE SEARCH FOR a new perspective on America's racial problem might well begin by a comparison of the race riots of World War I with those of World War II. Both wars had a revolutionary impact on the scheme of race relations, and the riots which occurred were the signal fires of social change. For, as Dr. Robert C. Weaver has pointed out, "A war is a social revolution....For society it means dislocation of temporary equilibriums incident to fundamental problems. In such a period, the basic, unsolved problems come to the fore and force our attention to them. We discover that many of the issues we had kept under cover can no longer be ignored."[1] We have somehow forgotten, in the shock and excitement of the race riots which came midway of the last war, that the riots of World War I were of much greater violence and destructiveness.

The first major riots of World War I occurred in East St. Louis, Illinois. The first of these riots, which started on May 28, 1917, lasted for two days and two nights, without an hour's cessation, and did not end until martial law was finally declared. The second riot, which began on July 1, was infinitely more violent. Witnesses, including a Congressman and an Army officer, told a Congressional committee of inquiry that over 500 Negroes were killed in this, the most savage of all American race riots. "Negroes were hunted through the streets like wild animals. A black skin became a death warrant."[2] The next major riot of World War I took place in Houston on August 16, 1917, when Negro troops at Camp Logan, enraged by reports of the mistreatment of Negro civilians, armed themselves and marched into the city. Thirteen people were killed, but, for a change, all but one were whites. In the savage reprisals which followed, 13 Negro soldiers were executed—presumably a life for a life—and 41 were given life imprisonment. Later in 1917, riots were reported at Chester, Pennsylvania, at Lexington, Kentucky, and at Waco, Texas.

In the year 1919, twenty-six race riots were reported in American communities, the first major riot occurring at Longview, Texas, on July 10, 1919, with 11 deaths being reported. Then, in rapid succession, came the race riot in Washington, D.C., of July 18, in which 7 persons were killed; the disastrous Chicago riot of July 27 to August 2, in which 38 persons were killed; the "sharecroppers' riot," which took place in Phillips County, Arkansas, on October 1, with 30 deaths (12 Negroes were later sentenced to death and 80 to long prison terms as punishment for the Negro participation in a riot in which no whites were arrested); and a final riot in Omaha, in which federal troops were used to restore order.[3] Although the statistics are incomplete, it is quite clear that the riots which occurred during and after World War I, and the great postwar upsurge of the Ku Klux Klan, were far more serious than the comparable disturbances which occurred during and after World War II.

World War II, however, had a much greater social, economic, and political impact on race relations than World War I. The Second World War, for example, completely upset the regional "balance" of the racial problem. Right off, approximately 110,000 Japanese-Americans were evacuated from the three West Coast states, creating a special shortage in an already tight wartime labor market and thereby stimulating a Negro migration from the states of Texas, Louisiana, and Oklahoma to the Pacific Coast. During the war it is estimated that 600,000 Negroes moved from rural to urban areas in the South, 300,000 Southern Negroes moved into the border and Northern states, 100,000 Negroes moved from the border states into other areas further north or west, and 250,000 Negroes moved to the West Coast. A large number of the Japanese-Americans have returned to the West Coast states, but few Negroes have returned to the South. In general this shifting of residence on the part of approximately 1.25 million Negroes, like the similar migration of nearly 1 million Negroes in the period from 1916 to 1929, has been a one-way movement with multiple consequences and interrelated effects.

During World War II, the West Coast suddenly became the nation's new racial frontier. As late as 1940, there was only one important Negro community in the eleven Western states—in Los Angeles. The other Negro communities were primarily small, isolated "Pullman car" colonies at the terminal points of the various transcontinental rail lines. Negroes constituted only 1½ percent of the total population of the three West Coast states in the pre-war period; but they made up 10 percent, or more, of the 2 million migrants who entered the region after 1940. Of ten major wartime production areas showing a 49 percent increase in the number of Negroes, five were located on the West Coast. Between 1940 and 1945, the Negro population in Los Angeles increased from 75,000 to 135,000 (it is much larger today); in San Francisco from 4,800 to 20,000; in Portland from 1,931 to 22,000; in Seattle from 3,789 to 16,000; in Vancouver (Washington) from 4 to 4,000; in Bremerton from 17 to 3,000. It should be noted, also, that Negroes have made a quicker and on the whole a far more satisfactory adjustment in the rapidly growing cities of the West Coast than in any area to which they have mi-grated. The West Coast migration has major historical significance, for it means that nowadays every major region of the nation for the first time has a significant Negro population; "the problem," in short, is now clearly na-tion-wide. Today Negroes outnumber all other racial minorities in the three West Coast states.[4]

It would take a volume to spell out the various social, economic, and political implications of these interregional shifts in the Negro population. Here I would merely point out, in passing, that the migration of Negroes to the West Coast has *reduced* the population of certain Southern states while, at the same time, it has *increased* the population of the three West Coast states. Not only does this mean more Negro voting strength in an area where Negroes can freely vote, but it also means greater representation in Con-gress, in the Electoral College, and in party conventions for areas outside the Deep South, and by the same token and to the same extent, a cut in the representation of the Bourbon Democrats.

The economic and industrial gains scored by Negroes in World War II completely dwarfed the comparable gains of World War I. The economic and industrial gains of World War II, moreover, were buttressed by impor-tant developments which had taken place during the period between the two wars, such as the birth of the CIO and the various New Deal health, housing, and education programs, including the effect of unionization and wage-and-hour legislation on wage-rate differentials. These supporting factors gave great meaning to the sudden and spectacular economic advances which racial mi-norities, and Negroes in particular, made in the period from 1940 to 1944. Over one million Negroes entered civilian employment during this period;

the number of Negroes employed at skilled jobs doubled, as did the number of single-skilled and semi-skilled workers; the number of Negro women employed as domestics was sharply curtailed; and, most important of all, thousands of Negroes began to enter industries and plants and occupations in which few Negroes had been previously employed. The number of Negro trade-union members was probably in excess of one million by the end of the war. "These changes in a period of four years," reports Dr. Robert C. Weaver, "represented more industrial and occupational diversification for Negroes than had occurred in the seventy-five preceding years."[5]

Although the employment and upgrading of Negro labor was impeded at first, it began to reach significant proportions by 1943 as witness the "hate strikes" in many industries in the spring of that year. As a matter of fact the race riots of midsummer 1943 are in part to be explained by the exceptionally rapid, and large-scale, industrial gains which Negroes were making. Every economic gain which Negroes scored during this period—every recognition which they achieved in the trade-union movement—automatically tended to augment their political power. The more political power Negroes acquired, the more jobs were opened to them, and as more and more Negroes moved into metropolitan industrial centers, in which industrial trade-unionism was a major social force, community attitudes toward the Negro began to change.

In World War I approximately 371,710 Negroes served in the armed forces (200,000 serving overseas); but in World War II, approximately 750,000 served in the Army (411,368 overseas), 100,000 in the Navy, 16,000 in the Marine Corps, and about 3,600 in the Coast Guard.[6] With the accompanying enhancement of political bargaining power and improvement in the quality of Negro leadership, it is not surprising that the fight for integration at all levels, in all branches of the services, including the auxiliary services, should have completely dwarfed the similar agitation of World War I in both volume and effectiveness.

On the eve of the Houston race riot of 1917, Senator James K. Vardaman of Mississippi had told his colleagues that "...one of the horrible problems which will grow out of this unfortunate war...is the training as a soldier which the Negro receives. Impress the Negro with the fact that he is defending the flag, inflate his untutored soul with military airs, teach him it is his duty to keep the emblem of the Nation flying triumphantly in the air—it is but a short step to the conclusion that his political rights must be respected....It was a mistake, against which I warned the administration when the President of the United States and the Congress called the Negroes of this country to arms."[7] The fears that Vardaman voiced in 1917 were echoed, of course, by Bilbo and Rankin in 1943.* At the same time, the logic of the situation, which had compelled the *New York World* to observe in the wake of the Washington riot of 1919 that "the Negro citizen is going to have his day in court; it ought not to be necessary for him to fight for it," compelled a similar admission, and from the same general sources, immediately following the race riots of midsummer 1943.

In World War II the general ideological ferment began to create a triple reaction: a great surge of hope and new aspiration among the racial minority groups; a somewhat similar reaching out for understanding and integration on the part of elements of the white majority; and a reflexive stiffening of resistance to change on the part of the traditionally most biased sections of the population. Each phase of this triple reaction affected every other: the more militantly Negroes pressed for their rights, the more active their white allies became, and the more defensive and "touchy" the Deep South became in its attitude. Conversely, each new affront to Negroes by the Bilbos and Rankins only spurred Negroes, and their allies, to greater efforts to win complete equality, not at some remote period, but here and now. American Negroes owe a great and most ironic debt to Bilbo and Rankin—gargoyles of Southern reaction inviting nationwide ridicule and scorn. At the same time, American Negroes began to find a new kind of ally quite unlike the philanthropists, the "gradualists," and the pussyfooting mediationists of the prewar period. For example, it would be impossible to exaggerate the importance of the role which Wendell Willkie played during the war years in forcing an honest approach to the problem of discrimination in American life.† The series of syndicated articles that he wrote in 1944 on the eve of the party conventions not only had great influence but represented the most statesmanlike approach to the problem of discrimination to be voiced by an American politician in our time. In large part, moreover, Willkie was a symbol of

---

* Congressman John Elliott Rankin and Senator Theodore Bilbo, Southern Democratic legislators known for racist, red-baiting, anti-labor, and anti-Semitic rhetoric.

† As the 1940 Republican presidential candidate, businessman and attorney Wendell Willkie received 45 percent of the popular vote but carried only ten states. After the United States entered World War II, he became Franklin D. Roosevelt's personal emissary abroad. His 1942 best-selling book, *One World,* was a plea for international cooperation, peace, and freedom.

the way in which a large element of the white majority was responding to the challenge of the times; he was driven to his conclusions by the pressure of events. "When we talk of freedom of opportunity for all nations," he said, "the mocking paradoxes in our own society become so clear that they can no longer be ignored....Our world is breaking to pieces. And with the break-up arises the opportunity to fashion a newer and a better life."[8]

ENDNOTES

1. "Racial Tensions in Chicago," by Robert C. Weaver, reprinted from *Social Service Year Book*, Chicago, 1943.

2. *Current Opinion*, vol. 63, pp. 75–77.

3. "Race Riots during and after the First World War," by Edgar A. Schuler, *The Negro History Bulletin*, April 1944; *The Negro in Chicago*, 1922; and "The Houston Race Riot, 1917," by Edgar A. Schuler, *Journal of Negro History*, July 1944.

4. *Common Ground*, Spring 1949; *Journal of Educational Sociology*, November 1945; series of articles by Horace R. Cayton, *Chicago Sun*, October 14, 15, 16, 1943; "The Negro in Portland," report of Portland City Club, July 20, 1945; "The Negro War Worker in San Francisco," May 1944.

5. *Negro Labor: A National Problem*, by Robert C. Weaver, 1946, p. 78.

6. *Leadership and the Negro Soldier*, Washington, D.C., 1944, p. 9.

7. *Congressional Record*, 55:6063.

8. *PM*, July 21, 1942.

3

THE ABUSE OF POWER

You can fool too many of the people too much of the time.

—James Thurber

Water! Water! Water!

1946

> Rain—the sweetest music to the California ear.
>
> —Theodore Van Dyke

SOUTHERN CALIFORNIANS are supposed to repeat the word "water" more often than Moslems say "Allah." Everyone knows, of course, that half of Los Angeles is wind, and the other half water. "God never intended Southern California to be anything but desert," a visitor once remarked. "Man has made it what it is." In a sense, the history of Southern California is the record of its eternal quest for water, and more water, and still more water. In the Los Angeles Basin of 1.4 million acres of habitable land (6 percent of the state's total) reside 45 percent of the inhabitants of California. But this same basin has only .06 percent of the natural stream flow of water in the state. Water is the life-blood of Southern California. Turn off the flow of water that now reaches the region from such remote sources as Owens Valley and the Colorado River, and the whole region would be bankrupt. The absence of local water resources is, indeed, the basic weakness of the region—its eternal problem.

It has always been difficult for visitors to Southern California, particularly since the turn of the century, to recognize the importance of water. Today the entire area from Santa Barbara to San Diego is an irrigated paradise. Water gurgles from irrigation pumps, water rushes along irrigation laterals and canals, and costly sprinkling systems spray a seemingly inexhaustible supply of water on elaborate lawns and gardens. Nowadays the land looks as though it had always been watered. But it is actually semi-arid. Not so long ago, it was a land of the *paisano*, or road-runner, the horned toad, the turkey buzzard; a land of dry brush and shabby-looking cactus. As late as 1870, a limited

147

number of windmills and surface wells barely sufficed to supply water for the livestock and the irrigated gardens of the ranches.

Throughout Southern California there is not a single river, as people ordinarily understand the term, not a single natural lake, not a single creek with a year-round flow of water. Disastrous droughts have, in years past, spread desolation and ruin in the region. Yet, in this paradoxical land, flood waters have probably caused more damage and loss of life than droughts. High mountain ranges wall the region off from the Central Valley and the desert. Dropping directly to sea-level plains, these towering mountains have always reminded me of the lines from a poem by Edmund Wilson:

> There where the waves are brought to heel,
> There where the Alps, no longer free,
> Come down like elephants to kneel
> Beside the glazed and azure sea.

Southern California is the land of the freak flood. In this semi-arid region, it can rain as nowhere else in America. In fact, it neither rains nor pours; the skies simply open up and dump oceans of water on the land. Pouring down the steep mountain ranges with the speed and fury of a mill race, rain waters convert the dry creek-beds or arroyos into raging infernos and then, on reaching the sandy soils of the plains, vanish as quickly as a mirage. While nearly all the rainfall occurs between November 1 and March 1 (it has seldom rained between May 1 and October 1), nevertheless, years of heavy rainfall have alternated with years of excessive drought. Thus, while there is a clearly defined rainy season, no one knows how much it will rain in any particular season, or just when the rains will come. To manage such a freakishly paradoxical environment has always required real insight into the basic character of the region, an insight difficult to cultivate in a land made up of newcomers and migrants.

IN SEARCH OF WATER

Originally, good-sized perennial streams flowed out onto the coastal plain. The first agricultural settlements and towns developed along the banks of these streams, in particular along the Los Angeles, San Gabriel, and Santa Ana Rivers. From an early date the waters from these streams were diverted for irrigation purposes. The first attempt to augment this supply of surface water took the form of drilling for artesian waters. In 1868 the first artesian well was bored near Compton, producing a seven-inch flow of water and demonstrating the existence of considerable underground sources in the Los Angeles Basin area. By 1910 approximately 1,596 artesian wells had been drilled. The entire coastal plain was at one time dotted with artesian wells that sprayed water into the air, for no pumping was then required. The first wells were drilled to a depth of from forty to no more than seventy feet, depending upon the location, but within two decades after 1868 the flow of artesian waters had begun to slacken. It then became necessary to drill new wells to a much greater depth, to conserve water by the use of cement pipes and other devices, and to apply electrically driven pumping systems.

By these and other methods, the use of underground waters was steadily increased. "One of the most noteworthy features during the past few years," wrote H. E. Brooks in 1904, "has been the utilization of an abundant subterranean water supply." Between 1899 and 1904, over 100,000 inches of water were developed from underground sources; between 1904 and 1907, 25,000 additional inches were added to the supply from the same source; and by 1910 still an additional 25,000 feet had been developed. At one time, California had 89.9 percent of all the farm acreage in America that is irrigated by artesian wells, and most of this acreage was located in the southern part of the state. From 140,000 acres thus irrigated in the South Coastal Basin in 1890, the number of acres increased to 342,400 by 1910. In 1905 Mendenhall estimated that two-thirds of the land under irrigation in Southern California tapped underground sources (by 1938 the figure had risen to 90 percent). Nowadays, however, it is the annual underground flow that is being tapped, not the accumulated artesian pools or reservoirs. In fact, the water plane has been lowered to such an extent, through excessive pumping, that but little remains of the original artesian areas. The artesian water supply was wasted, as a young spendthrift might dissipate a legacy, in a single generation.

Better utilization of water, more flexible legal arrangements for its proper management (such as mutual water companies and irrigation improvement districts), and the constant expansion of pumping systems served to keep the rural areas fairly well supplied with water from 1880 to 1910. The first real shortage was felt in the cities and towns. From the earliest date, Los Angeles had obtained its water supply from the Los Angeles River, the watershed of which embraces the entire San Fernando Valley. Water was diverted from the river by a system of *zanjas*, or open ditches, for irrigation and domestic consumption. Early residents of the city got their water either from the *zanjas* or from the water peddlers who roamed the town. The first attempt to conserve and to develop the available supply occurred in 1854, when the city appointed a *zanjero*, or water commissioner, to guard the *zanjas* and to keep them repaired. From its founding in 1781 until 1868, the city owned and operated its own water system. In the latter year, the city leased its water rights to the Los Angeles City Water Company, a private corporation, for a period of thirty years. Reacquiring control of the water system in 1899, the city has since operated its own municipal system.

During this hiatus from 1868 to 1899, I. N. Van Nuys and J. B. Lankershim, and others, had acquired vast holdings in the San Fernando Valley which were nearer to the sources of the Los Angeles River than was the City of Los Angeles. Relying upon the doctrine of riparian rights, these landowners asserted a prior claim on the waters of the Los Angeles River, both surface and underground, as owners of upstream lands along the river. The only thing that saved the city from this claim was the happy circumstance, which the city had been trying to forget for several decades, that it had been the one pueblo founded by the Spanish in Southern California. Under Mexican and Spanish law, pueblos were given a prior right to all waters within the watershed for domestic uses, and to supply manufacturing establishments and to irrigate lands within the pueblo limits. In a famous lawsuit between the City of Los Angeles and the land barons of San Fernando Valley, the Supreme Court ruled that Los Angeles had succeeded, by virtue of the Treaty of Guadalupe Hidalgo, to all the rights which it had enjoyed as a pueblo; therefore, its claim to the waters within the watershed was prior to that of all appropriators subsequent to 1781. In the same decision, it was also held that the city might put its water supply to uses not known under Mexican law, such as sewers, artificial lakes, and ornamental fountains. This decision saved the City of Los Angeles from disaster. Never did an American city owe more to the fortuitous circumstance of Spanish settlement.

Even with its watershed right firmly established, Los Angeles began to fear a future water famine. Although the city had enough water in 1900 for a population of 102,249, it began to be disturbed by the discrepancy between the available supply and the rate of population increase. In large part, however, this fear was artificially stimulated by a group of powerful "empire builders" of the period. In 1905 and later in 1910, a syndicate financed by Harry Chandler, General Harrison Gray Otis, Joseph F. Sartori (the banker), Henry

Huntington, E. H. Harriman, E. T. Earl, and M. H. Sherman acquired most of the former holdings of the Van Nuys and Lankershim families in the San Fernando Valley. In terms of what subsequently happened, it is important to note that M. H. Sherman, a member of this syndicate, was also a member of the city's water board. Eventually this group of men acquired control over 108,000 acres of land in the valley. Once in control of this vast acreage, they came to the water board of the City of Los Angeles with a typically grandiose proposal: that the city should build a 238-mile aqueduct to tap the waters of Owens Valley (located between the Sierra Nevada and the desert); and thereby hangs a tale.

THE OWENS VALLEY TRAGEDY

No one has ever seriously questioned the right of the City of Los Angeles to be concerned about its water supply, or, for that matter, to obtain water from Owens Valley.* The greatest good for the greatest number is, indeed, familiar American doctrine. But the Owens Valley project was conceived in iniquity. The citizens of Los Angeles knew nothing about the project at the time it was first proposed, for the members of the San Fernando Valley land syndicate controlled the press of the community. Even the City Council was kept completely in the dark. Worse than the conspiratorial silence, however, was the fact that the project was carried out by reprehensible tactics.

In 1903, J. B. Lippincott, Chief Engineer of the United States Reclamation Service in California, went to Owens Valley, ostensibly for the purpose of explaining to its hard-working pioneer settlers that the government was about to launch a vast reclamation project in the area. While purporting to work on this project, Lippincott acquired full information about water resources in the valley and even managed to induce many settlers to surrender priority claims on water. The following year, Fred Eaton, formerly Mayor of Los Angeles, appeared in Owens Valley. Representing himself as Lippincott's agent, he began to take options on lands riparian to Owens River. In possession of Lippincott's reports, he proceeded to checkerboard the area, that is,

---

* This is no longer true. One of the most visible effects of decades of diverting water from the Owens Valley is the dramatically lowered water level in Mono Lake. In 1983 the California Supreme Court ruled that the state has an obligation to protect places like Mono Lake "as far as feasible," even if it means reconsidering past water allocation decisions. A decade later, the State Water Resources Control Board put a stop to diverting water from Mono Lake until the water elevation reaches 6,392 feet. As of April 6, 2001, the water level was 6,383 feet. Plans are also under way to restore Owens Lake.

to take options on every other ranch on each side of the irrigation canals and along the Owens River. Once in possession of a sufficient number of options, he then exercised his right to buy the land. At the same time, Lippincott announced that the government had abandoned its "reclamation project," resigned from the service, and was promptly employed by the City of Los Angeles. The trap having been sprung, the *Los Angeles Times* broke a gentlemen's agreement with the other newspapers, and on July 29, 1905, plastered the news of the Owens Valley project on its front page. Traditionally opposed to all forms of public ownership, it is interesting to note that, in this instance, the *Times* worked hand in glove with the officials of the municipally owned water system of the City of Los Angeles.

Once the scheme was announced to the public—and for the first time to the City Council—the city agreed to float a bond issue of $25 million to build the Owens Valley aqueduct. In the ensuing campaign, only one newspaperman in Los Angeles had the courage and honesty to denounce the deceit which had been practiced on the residents both of Owens Valley and of Los Angeles. This lonely journalist, the late Samuel T. Clover, paid for his honesty by forfeiting control of his little weekly newspaper. In order to secure approval of the bond issue, the project sponsors resorted to strange and devious tactics. Thousands of inches of water were clandestinely dumped into the sewer system from reservoirs and storage dams, so as to create an artificial water famine. The water supply became so scarce that, on the eve of the election, an ordinance was passed forbidding people to spray their lawns and gardens. On September 7, 1905, the citizens of Los Angeles, by a heavy vote, approved the bond issue.

The sponsors of the Owens Valley project, however, were not interested in bringing water to the parched City of Los Angeles; they were concerned about 108,000 acres of previously unirrigated land in the San Fernando Valley which they had quietly bought up at prices of five, ten, and twenty dollars an acre. At the time the aqueduct was constructed, San Fernando Valley, as its historian Frank M. Keefer has pointed out, was "the logical and *only practical place* for the disposal of this *surplus* water" (italics mine). To the amazement of the residents of Los Angeles, who had just assumed a $25 million indebtedness, the aqueduct line was brought to the north end of San Fernando Valley, not into the City of Los Angeles, and there the terminal point still remains. With water available to irrigate the lands they had acquired in San Fernando Valley, the "men of vision" who had engineered this extraordinary deal proceeded to sell their holdings for $500 and $1,000 an acre, making an estimated profit of $100 million at the expense of the residents of Owens Valley and of Los Angeles. As late as 1930, eighty thousand acre-feet of Owens Valley water were still being used to irrigate San Fernando Valley farm lands, enough water to provide each and every one of the 1.3 million residents of Los Angeles with fifty gallons of water a day for one year. The facts concerning this amazing project have never been denied. The whole story is told with a wealth of detail in an excellent chapter in Morrow Mayo's book about Los Angeles,★ and is re-cited, in fictional form, in Mary Austin's novel *The Ford* (1917). As federal land agent in Owens Valley, Mrs. Austin's husband had intimate knowledge of this sordid scheme, which he tried by every means at his disposal to prevent. There is far more to the story than I have told here. For example, to keep homesteaders out of Owens Valley, Gifford Pinchot was prevailed upon in 1906 to declare most of the desert lands of Owens Valley a federal forest district! To facilitate the acquisition of a right of way for the aque-duct line, Congress was induced to pass special legislation upon assurances from the City of Los Angeles that the water would be used only for domes-tic purposes. When a provision to this effect was written into the bill, Sena-tor Frank Flint of Los Angeles asked President Theodore Roosevelt to have the section removed, since, as he said, some of the residents of Los Ange-les might want, occasionally, to water their gardens! At a later date, the City of Los Angeles proceeded to annex most of San Fernando Valley, thereby removing any question as to its right to use Owens Valley water for all purposes. What is of greater significance, however, is the fact that there existed, in Long Valley, a potential storage basin of sufficient capacity to have supplied the needs of both Los Angeles and Owens Valley. Not a single storage dam was built as part of the original aqueduct project; the waters of Owens Valley were simply funneled into the mouth of the aqueduct and piped to Los Angeles.

The acquisition of Owens Valley water by the City of Los Angeles ru-ined a prosperous farming community. Early in the spring of 1927, the rem-nants of the Owens Valley settlers published an advertisement in the Los Angeles newspapers under the heading: "We, the farming communities of Owens Valley, being about to die, salute you!" And die they did. Orchards

---

★ *Los Angeles,* by Morrow Mayo (A.A. Knopf, 1933)

withered, prosperous farms reverted to desert, and the blight of aridity reclaimed the valley. Failing to secure justice in their appeals to public opinion, to the legislature, and to the courts, the farmers of Owens Valley, in May 1924, blew up sections of the aqueduct, opened control gates, and for three years afterwards conducted a gallant fight against the City of Los Angeles. The sponsors of the Owens Valley project, however, knew how to cope with such stubbornness. The resistance in the valley had been financed by two pioneer bankers who, by manipulating their books in violation of the state banking act, were able to carry delinquent mortgages. Waiting until these leaders had become deeply involved, the powers-that-be then had them indicted and sentenced to San Quentin Prison. Having broken the resistance movement, the City of Los Angeles then proceeded, in 1931, to buy up most of the remaining lands in the valley. As late as 1945, the City of Los Angeles, and the *Los Angeles Times*, opposed state legislation designed to provide a small measure of belated justice to the ruined farmers of Owens Valley.

To this day, according to Mr. Mayo, "ninety percent of the people of Los Angeles have no idea of the colossal swindle which was put over on them, nor do they have the slightest inkling of what was done in Owens Valley." In fact, the conspiracy of silence still prevails. The highly important role played by the late Harry Chandler in the Owens Valley affair is never mentioned or discussed in Los Angeles. Morrow Mayo's book, which contained the first complete account of the rape of Owens Valley, was greeted by the almost audible silence of the Los Angeles press. Owens Valley remains one of those topics concerning which "the less said the better." One reason for the persistence of this attitude is that, although the Owens Valley project was conceived by a group of businessmen, it was actually executed by the municipally owned Department of Water and Power of the City of Los Angeles. Most of the reform leaders of Los Angeles, the men who had fought valiantly for public ownership, felt compelled to remain silent or actually to endorse the project. At various points in Los Angeles, one can today observe prominent statues, plaques, and memorials that have been erected in honor of the one-time *zanjero* of the Los Angeles water system, the engineer in charge of the Owens Valley project, William Mulholland. Just why the City of Los Angeles felt compelled to honor the engineer responsible for the Owens Valley fiasco, or even to mention Owens Valley, remains one of those curious examples of ambivalent civic ethics.

THE QUEST IS PURSUED

Because the Owens Valley project was unsound from an engineering stand-point, the City of Los Angeles got off to a bad start in its quest for water. The alternative project, namely the Long Valley reservoir, would have been a much sounder undertaking. Started in 1907, the Owens Valley project was not com-pleted until 1913. Two years later the city was again in search of water. This time its engineers went to the Mono Basin, even farther from Los Angeles than Owens Valley, and acquired an additional supply of 135 cubic feet per second. And, still later, the city sponsored the Boulder Dam Act, which was finally approved by Congress on December 21, 1928. Today water is brought by aqueduct from the Colorado River a distance of 242 miles to the Cajalco Reservoir near Riverside. To distribute Colorado River water, the Metropoli-tan Water District of Southern California was created in 1928, on the board of which thirteen Southern California cities are now represented. From the point of intake at Parker Dam to Los Angeles, the Colorado River aqueduct actually travels a distance of 392 miles. The inadequacy of the Owens River project is indicated not merely by the subsequent search of the City of Los Angeles for water, but by the fact that storage dams were not originally con-sidered in connection with the Owens Valley aqueduct. Even the matter of developing hydroelectric power came about, not as a basic aspect of the project, but as a more or less accidental by-product developed after the aque-duct was constructed.

Today the Metropolitan Water District has estimated the total water sup-plies, from all sources, for the 1.4 million acres in the South Coastal Basin (which includes all the arable lands from Santa Monica to Redlands, from the coast range to the sea) as follows:

Local water supply	0.5 in depth
Owens River and Mono Basin	0.2 in depth
Colorado River	0.7 in depth
Total future available supply	*1.4 in depth*

As Dr. Samuel B. Morris has pointed out, a supply of 1.4 feet in depth per acre of economically productive and usable lands is a gross figure with no allowances for losses in handling or distribution. As such it is "somewhat low for either irrigation or modest residential use" and is "quite insufficient for congested and industrial districts." It is, however, all the water that is in sight for the South Coastal Basin. When Colorado River water was finally obtained, the residents of Los Angeles were assured that the supply would be adequate at least until the year 1980. But this estimate did not take into consideration the fact that World War II was destined to convert Los Angeles into a great industrial center. As I write these lines, the *Los Angeles Times* carries a story under the caption: "Water Demands on Coast Zoom." The story quotes Colonel G. E. Arnold of the War Production Board to the effect that: "The curve of water consumption on the Coast went up sharply after Pearl Harbor and each seasonal peak has been higher than the last. This summer's peak has brought some communities near the danger point and a dry season would create some serious shortages." Obviously, the perennial problem of water has not been solved.

To a considerable extent, the problem of water in Southern California is a cultural problem. By this I mean that newcomers to the region, who have always made up a majority of the population, have never understood the crucial importance of water. Crossing the desert, they arrive in an irrigated paradise, in which almost anything can be grown with a quickness and abundance that cannot be equaled by any other region in America. There does not seem to be a water problem. Nor are they told that there is such a problem, for Southern California has always been extremely reluctant to discuss its basic weakness. As a consequence, there has been a truly amazing institutional lag in the culture of the region; that is, new institutional devices for coping with the eternal water problem have only been evolved years after the case for their establishment had been known to exist. It was years after California had been admitted to the union as a state before the courts and the legislature began to evolve a body of law to cope with water problems. It was not until 1887 that the legislature passed the Wright Act, which permitted communities to form, and to bond, irrigation districts—an act which has served as the basis for practically all similar legislation in the United States. It was not until 1911 that the Irrigation District Bond Commission Law was enacted; not until 1917 that the state began to supervise all dams built by irrigation districts; not until 1921 that the state passed the Water Storage District Act; and it was not until 1921 that the state appropriated $200,000 for a systematic inventory of its water resources.

Not only has the institutional lag been pronounced, but the culture of the region has only slowly and imperfectly been adapted to the physical factors of a semi-arid environment. The development of conservancy districts,

by which communities in Southern California pour surface water onto sandy
soils so that it may percolate to the underground storage basins, was a com-
paratively late innovation. Soil practices calculated to conserve water were
only evolved at a late date. A remarkable Southern Californian, William E.
Smythe, tried years ago to hammer home the point that a semi-arid environment necessarily requires a new orientation of an imported culture pattern.
His volume *The Conquest of Arid America,* first published in 1899, might well
be the bible of residents of Southern California. In particular, he insisted that
a semi-arid environment necessarily implied extensive collective action, a
subordination of private interests to the public welfare, and public ownership or control of water resources. He took a leading part in the formation of
the California Water and Forest Association around the turn of the century,
only to have the "private enterprise" advocates of the period completely sub-
vert the original purposes of the association. Some of his incidental papers,
such as the essay on "The Ethics of Irrigation," raise issues basic to the economy
of Western America. Like most prophets, however, Smythe was largely ignored.

That Southern California is an irrigated civilization largely accounts for
the breakdown between rural and urban distinctions. Irrigated settlements
naturally require a compact pattern of homes rather than scattered farm-
steads. The presence of running water, bathtubs, and electricity in the early
colony settlements is, in part, an aspect of irrigation development. "Rural"
life has never been precisely "rural" in Southern California. Irrigation requires
a heavy investment of capital and labor; it implies "co-operation of the many,"
through stable social organizations. It was this orientation that Smythe, with
his early background in the socialist movement and his training in the principles of Fourierism, sought to develop in his "little lander" projects, through
the irrigation congresses that he organized, and in his magazine, *The Irrigation Age.*

If ever a region had an important stake in co-operative organization, that
region is Southern California. Co-operative action is required to develop water
sources; to distribute, and to use, water efficiently; to introduce new tech-
nologies; to develop hydroelectric power. Nearly every major advance in the
region has been made possible not by greedy "men of vision"—the so-called
empire builders—but by the co-operative action of the people themselves,
through mutual water companies, irrigation and conservancy districts, co-
operative marketing agencies, and such instrumentalities as the Metropolitan Water District. Yet a general awareness of this fact does not exist.

FLOODS IN A DESERT

The general lack of cultural understanding in Southern California is strikingly shown in the neglect of forest resources, a matter intimately related to the ability of the region to husband its limited water supply. For the environment is dynamic as well as paradoxical and has always required careful management based upon accurate understanding. "No flood problems," writes Dr. Morris, "existed in primitive uninhabited California." Flood and forest problems arose in direct ratio to the increasing density of population. There is, for example, an almost perfect correlation between the number of forest fires and population increases. The damage caused by forest fires, particularly brush fires, in Southern California simply cannot be estimated. For many years, the brush fires have begun to burn each August and September. During these months, fires can usually be seen burning in a half-dozen areas of Los Angeles County. Following the first "Santa Ana" desert winds in May, similar fires frequently occur. For example, on May 17, 1945, the *Los Angeles Times* reported: "Firemen Kept Busy as Heat Again Hits 90." On this particular day, 388 grass fires were reported in the county. A glance at the scarred hillsides, in fact, is sufficient to indicate the damage caused by forest fires.

With so much of the sparse cover of the mountains having been removed by fires, it is not surprising to note a correlation between the increasing amounts spent on flood control and the number of forest fires. During the rainy season of late years, waters trumpet down the canyons and arroyos, causing extraordinary damage. In a five-day period in March 1938, eleven inches of rain fell, flooding thirty thousand square miles of land, taking a toll of 81 lives, and causing an estimated $83 million in property damage. Seeing no connection between forest fires and floods, the residents of the region perennially "solve" the problem by increasing the expenditures for flood control. Flood control has, in fact, become a major political setup in Los Angeles, the basis of which is to build more cement causeways so that surface waters may be carried to the ocean as swiftly as possible and with the minimum damage to extensive property holdings which have been built in areas that should have been zoned against occupancy. Through increasingly efficient flood control measures, Los Angeles has been wasting an ever-growing volume of surface waters.

In much the same manner, the flood hazard has been increased, in the past, by the construction of badly designed water storage dams at poorly selected sites. On March 12, 1928, the St. Francis Dam in the Santa Clara Valley, designed by William Mulholland and associates, fell apart, releasing a torrent of waters. In this particular disaster 1,240 homes were destroyed and 385 lives were lost. Most of the homes destroyed were occupied by Mexican citrus workers, and most of the lives lost were Mexican, for the Mexicans, of course, were permitted to live directly in the pathway of possible floods. Some time in advance of this disaster, the City of Los Angeles had knowledge of the weakness of the St. Francis Dam, yet nothing was done to relieve the mounting pressure of rain waters on the dam. For this folly, the city paid a heavy indemnity, but retained, and continued to honor, its chief engineer.

Although always in need of more and more water, Southern Californians hate moisture like cats and are probably the world's most incompetent rain-manipulators. Always praying for rain, they are invariably embarrassed and confused when Providence answers their petitions. A major rainstorm in Los Angeles has always spelt disaster for the community. When 4,761,548,800,000 pounds of rain fell from the skies in March 1938, one could read in the newspapers of perch being fished from downtown streets; of hail pellets the size of hen's eggs falling in the Arroyo Seco; of movie sets floating on Malibu Lake; of rowboats appearing in suburban areas; of marathon swimmers diving into the swirling waters of the proverbially "dry" Los Angeles River; of the "continuous cannonade of boulders, big as houses," rolling down from the mountains through the streets of Montrose. Cottages floated off their flimsy moorings; lots disappeared; alder and cottonwood trees bobbed in the streams; men in bathing suits rescued passengers from stalled automobiles; alligators washed out of the Lincoln Park Zoo splashed about in the streets, as elephants trumpeted, apes chattered, dogs went mad and jumped into the rivers, and birds bashed themselves to death against stone walls. The Hollywood Humane Society treated injured animals at the rate of thirty an hour, as hundreds of canaries, cats, goats, chickens, dogs, and even lions were rushed in for treatment. Overstuffed furniture, stoves, and tin cans bobbed along "fierce chocolate tributaries"; and airplanes flew south from San Francisco with relief supplies. Catching the excitement from afar, the *London Daily Mirror* reported that "people are frantically climbing the tops of trams and crowding into skyscrapers...the ultra-religious are campaigning among the refugees crowded by the hundreds in schools, crying to them, 'Repent! Repent! The Floods are a Judgment.'" A few days after the flood waters had begun to recede, the County Coroner sagely pronounced, after an open hearing, that the floods had been "an act of Providence and no one person can be held responsible." (Note: there is a vivid description of this particular flood in a novel by Rupert Hughes, *City of Angels,* published in 1941.) For weeks after The Great Flood of 1938, I watched the Los Angeles newspapers carefully to see if, by chance, one of the papers might possibly run an editorial on forest fires and forest resources. Needless to say, not a single editorial of this character appeared.

HATFIELD THE RAINMAKER

In a semi-arid land such as Southern California, it is not surprising that the first popular folk-hero should have been a rainmaker. Concerned by the delay of the rains, one reads that the residents of Santa Barbara in 1833 "besought the holy father of the Missions that the Virgin, Nuestra Señora del Rosario, might be carried in procession through the town whilst prayers and supplications should be offered for her intercession with the Almighty in behalf of their distress." If the rains did not appear on schedule, wrote an observer in 1887, "all classes of businessmen are at a white heat of anxiety." From the earliest date, the annals contain reference to "water magicians" and "precipitators" who used hazel wands and other devices. J. W. Potts—Prophet Potts as he was called—was a famous predictor and precipitator in early-day Los Angeles. The outstanding water magician of Southern California, however, was Charles Mallory Hatfield, "Hatfield the Rainmaker," who derived his ideas about "the science of pluviculture" from a treatise written by one Edward Powers in 1871. Such was the interest that this book aroused that, in 1891, Congress instructed General Robert Dyrenforth to make an official investigation of the subject and appropriated a sizable sum for the study.

Hatfield first began to experiment with rainmaking on his father's farm in San Diego around 1902. After making some sixteen experiments, he managed to produce, as he put it, "a slight precipitation." Always a modest man, Hatfield never contended that he could make rain. "The term is too broad," he objected. "I merely assist Nature. I only persuade the moisture to come down." As an experimenter, Hatfield was far in advance of the hazel-wand variety of rainmaker. When called into a drought-ridden area in Southern California, he would erect a few large "evaporating tanks" filled with "certain chemicals the character of which must necessarily remain secret." At the appropriate time, he would remove the lid from the tanks, thereby permitting the mysterious chemical fumes to mix with the air, "overturning the atmosphere" and precipitating rainfall. In the dry season, these Hatfield evaporators were once a familiar sight throughout Southern California.

Hatfield secured his first contract "to lend Nature just a little assistance" in Los Angeles in 1903. Setting up his evaporators, he produced an inch of rainfall in five days and was given twice his fee of $50 by a grateful and astonished landowner. Thereafter his rainmaking reputation quickly spread throughout the region and his services were in great demand. Over a period of years, he conducted five hundred rainmaking demonstrations in the region, for fees ranging from $50 to $10,000. For eight consecutive years, the farmers of the San Joaquin Valley contracted with Hatfield to "make rain"; and nearly every city government in Southern California, at one time or another, signed contracts with him "to precipitate moisture." He once signed a contract to fill the reservoir of the Lake Hemet Land and Water Company for a fee of $4,000. He was so successful, on this occasion, that he precipitated a downpour of eleven inches of rain, raising the water level of the dam by twenty-two feet. In Los Angeles, during the first four months of 1905, he produced eighteen inches of rainfall.

Hatfield's most fabulous exploit, however, occurred in 1916, when he signed a contract with the City of San Diego to fill its giant reservoir by a specified date. Large crowds gathered to watch Hatfield set up his evaporators and mix his mysterious chemicals. As the date for the expiration of his contract drew near, headlines in the local press counted off the days, and all of San Diego watched with bated breath to see if he would make good his agreement. With less than twenty-seven days left to run on the contract, the Great Rainmaker precipitated the mightiest downpour in the history of San Diego County. More than sixteen inches of rain fell in a two-day period. Not only did he fill the 18-million-gallon reservoir (it had never been more than one-third filled before), but a torrent of water rushed over the dam and caused great havoc in San Diego and environs. Railroad bridges were washed away, cities and towns were flooded, and attendance at the San Diego World's Fair fell to zero. "This was a phenomenon," said Hatfield, "that I was never able to repeat." The City of San Diego, indignant over the results of his experiment, refused to pay his fee. "We told you," the City Council said, "merely to fill the reservoir—not to flood the community."

In later years, the fame of Hatfield spread from Southern California throughout the world. He received fat contracts for rain-precipitation all the way from Texas to the Klondike, from Canada to Honduras. One of his last great feats was to produce forty inches of rainfall in three hours on the Mojave Desert near Randsburg. In fact, he was so successful that Southern California municipalities became fearful of his evaporators. The belief was widespread that Hatfield could not control his own magic. "I do not doubt," said Hatfield, "that my methods would have saved all the tremendous losses of the dust bowl, had they been called into play."

At the height of his fame, Hatfield was known throughout Southern California. The stories about him rival those told about Riley, and Paul Bunyan, and Pecos Bill. When I came to Southern California in 1922, municipalities were still signing contracts with him to make rain. As the newspapers counted off the number of days left to fulfill his contracts in screaming headlines, thousands of Southern Californians, scanning the skies, would speculate on whether "Hatfield was going to make it." The belief in his magic was well-nigh universal. In 1925, David Starr Jordan of Stanford University made an investigation of Hatfield's methods for *Science* magazine. According to Dr. Jordan, Hatfield was a close student of weather charts. His usual technique was to wait until the dry season was far advanced and the people were beginning to despair of rain. Then he would appear upon the scene, sometimes as late as mid-January, and obtain a contract to produce rain within, say, thirty or sixty days. And of course he never missed. But the cruel debunking by Dr. Jordan had no effect whatever upon the popular belief, particularly prevalent among newcomers, in Hatfield's magic. It was not until the City of Los Angeles finally secured Colorado River water that the Hatfield evaporators disappeared from the Southern California landscape. As nearly as I can determine, Hatfield secured no further contracts for rainmaking after the passage of the Boulder Dam Act in 1928.

Although Southern Californians do not understand the semi-arid environment in which they live, they are haunted by a vague and nameless fear of future disaster. Mary Austin was convinced that a stern God would someday visit just retribution upon the City of the Angels for the crime it had committed in Owens Valley. The belief in some awful fate that will someday engulf the region is widespread and persistent and has a history which cannot be chronicled here. "There is something disturbing about this corner of America," wrote J. B. Priestley, "a sinister suggestion of transience. There is a quality hostile to men in the very earth and air here. As if we were not meant to make our homes in this oddly enervating sunshine....California will be a silent desert again. It is all as impermanent and brittle as a reel of film."

It is the odd combination of almost perpetual sunshine with a lush, but not indigenous, vegetation that produces this impression of impermanence. Even newcomers are vaguely aware that the region is semi-arid, that the desert is near, and that all the throbbing, bustling life of Southern California is based on a single shaky premise, namely that the aqueduct life-lines will continue to bring an adequate supply of water to the region. The exotic has been superimposed on this semi-arid land; it is not native. "It ought to be exotic," a visitor once complained, "but somehow it really isn't exotic." The perpetual sunshine baffles, confuses, irritates, and eventually maddens the inhabitants. "This damnably monotonous sunlight," complained Denis Ireland. "Sometimes," observes a character in a novel by Carl Van Vechten, "I think I'll die if this sun don't stop shinin'. I wake up some mornings and I pull down the shades and turn on the electric lights to pretend it's rainin' outside." The hot-dry Santa Ana winds will not permit the residents to forget the nearness of the desert. "Shrieking and moaning," wrote George Randolph Chester in a novel published in 1924, "the wind swept in from the desert...it was one of those summer days rare to the Pacific Coast, but poignant, when through the yellow sunlight there sift vague phantom shapes of impalpable dust which bite the skin and smart the eyes, and are the prickling forerunners of a three-day withering heat from out the very heart of the vast shadeless inferno up yonder in the waste places...a day that lowers the vitality and depresses the spirits and sets the nerves on edge   No one knows what tremendous extent of folly and of tragedy may be chargeable to this same shrill, shrieking, moaning, sobbing wind from the deadly desert." Facing the ocean, Southern California is inclined to forget the desert, but the desert is always there, and it haunts the imagination of the region.

The Wheatland Riot

1939

THE ERRATIC AND VIOLENT DEVELOPMENT of agriculture in California has been paralleled by the sporadic turbulence which has characterized the history of farm labor in the state. The story of migratory labor is one of violence: harsh repression interrupted by occasional outbursts of indignation and protest. Nor is there much probability that the future will be one of peaceful adjustment to new social conditions; no one familiar with the dominant interests in California agriculture can have any illusions on this score. Violence, and more violence, is clearly indicated. It is indicated not only by the established patterns of industrialized agriculture, but, more explicitly, by the past record of violence in the industry. This record, it should be observed, stems from the early social behavior of the Californians. The history of the vigilance committees of 1850 and 1856 is well known and requires no repetition. While it is true that these early committees were organized to cope with crime, it is indisputable that they were largely representative of the "merchants and propertied" classes and that, at least in 1856, their activities were directed in part against organized labor. During the period when the vigilantes were in action, they completely usurped the functions of governmental officials, defied the Governor of the state, conducted their own trials, equipped and drilled an armed force, and operated in effect as an insurrectionary junta. The story of the vigilantes entered deeply into the consciousness of the merchants, businessmen, and industrialists of California. They never forgot the experience, and their successors have never hesitated to constitute themselves "vigilantes" whenever the occasion has demanded "action." In 1934 "vigilante committees" appeared in practically every city, town, and rural district in

California during the "red" hysteria of that year. The significance of this deeply rooted tradition of violence must constantly be kept in mind. Insurrection was once sanctioned—violence was once glorified in the historical annals of the state—these facts have been remembered. Hence present-day industrialists are quick to drape themselves in the cloak of the vigilante tradition. Mining camps throughout the West, in Montana, Idaho, and Nevada, quickly improvised vigilance committees, on the San Francisco pattern, when they were first faced with a strong labor movement. Vigilantism, as such, had its origin in California.

The eruptions of farm labor have been at infrequent intervals, and in every instance, they have been violently suppressed, each incident provoking a long chain of prosecutions in the courts. No tearful glorification of the occasional protests of farm labor, however, is to be found in the official histories. Whatever theoretical considerations may be entertained concerning the use of violence in labor disputes, it is evident that, from a historical point of view, migratory labor has made gains in California when it has been militant. It has been potentially militant for a great many years, but when strong protest movements have occurred, they have, in each instance, been directed by a clearly class-conscious leadership. One of the earliest instances of the stirring of deep-seated unrest in migratory labor was the Wheatland Riot, which occurred on the ranch of a large hop grower named Durst, near Wheatland, California, on August 3, 1913. Wheatland, clearly marked as one of the most significant episodes in the history of migratory labor in the West, also forms an important chapter in the social history of California. In the lurid illumination which the fires of the riot cast forth, the ugly facts about the condition of farm labor in California were, for the first time, thoroughly exposed. The riot and the subsequent trial attracted national attention (see *Harper's Weekly*, April 4, June 20, 1914; *The Outlook*, May 16, 1914; *Technical World*, August, 1914). It resulted in two important public documents bearing on the subject of farm labor (*Report on the Wheatland Riot*, issued June 1, 1914, and the section titled "The Seasonal Labor Problem in Agriculture," vol. v, *Reports of the United States Commission on Industrial Relations*), and one of the first serious studies of migratory labor (*The Casual Laborer*, by Carleton H. Parker, 1920).

The Wheatland affair marked the culmination of several years of agitational and organizational work on the part of the Industrial Workers of the World. To see the affair in proper perspective, therefore, it is necessary to indicate something of the background of these activities.

In the years between the Chicago convention at which the IWW was formed in 1905 and 1913, the wobblies had been active in the fields, along the highways, on the trains, and in the jungle camps, with their spectacular propaganda and vivid agitation. The roots of the IWW—if the organization may be said to have had any roots—were to be found among the migratory workers of the West. Not only were these workers unmercifully exploited—the conditions under which they worked making them highly susceptible to the inflammatory agitation of the wobblies—but they followed, in general, the routes pursued by the IWW organizers. Organizers, coming from the timber camps of the Northwest, drifted south into the agricultural fields. Always on the move, the wobblies, themselves essentially migratory, moved naturally into the currents of farm labor. Their organizational techniques— job action, organizing on the job, low dues or no dues at all—were well adapted to the circumstances under which farm labor was employed. They moved with the workers and organized them, so to speak, in transit.

During the years 1905 to 1913, the wobblies had demonstrated considerable strength in California. They had, for example, conducted two sensational "free-speech" fights: in San Diego and in Fresno. The fight in Fresno was of particular importance, as Fresno has long been the nerve center of agricultural labor in California, located as it is in the heart of the San Joaquin Valley. In Fresno the wobblies fought for the right to maintain a headquarters, to distribute literature, and to hold public meetings. For six months, through one fall and winter in 1910, they battled the Fresno authorities. As often as they were crushed, they launched new campaigns, finally succeeding in winning a kind of tolerance for their activities. The courage and tenacity of the wobblies in Fresno attracted the attention of many migratory workers and made a deep impression throughout the state.

The San Diego fight was, if anything, even more sensational. Beginning in January 1912, the San Diego authorities began to suppress wobbly meetings, the campaign culminating in a remarkable ordinance which outlawed free speech throughout the city (San Diego then had a population of about forty thousand). The wobblies promptly sent out word for a "concentration" on San Diego, the idea being to crowd the jails and to raise such a fracas that the city fathers would despair of making arrests. Newspapers, at the time, carried scare headlines about "thousands" of workers converging on San Diego; in fact, only about 150 wobblies were involved. To cope with the situation, the authorities sponsored a local vigilance committee which established camps and posted armed guards along the highways leading to San Diego (one of the first California "border patrols"), turning back all transients. In San Diego itself the vigilantes rounded up all persons even remotely suspected of being wobblies and marched them, one night, to Sorrento. There the wobblies were made to mount an improvised platform, kiss the American flag, and sing the national anthem, while hundreds of vigilantes stood about armed with revolvers, knives, clubs, blackjacks, and black snake whips. Then they were marched to San Onofre and driven into a cattle pen and systematically slugged and beaten. After a time, they were taken out of the pen and beaten with clubs and whips as, one at a time, they were made "to run the gantlet." One wobbly subsequently died in jail; scores received serious injuries. Not only was this performance sanctioned by the authorities, but the Merchants Association and the Chamber of Commerce passed resolutions praising the vigilantes. Speaking on behalf of San Diego, the *San Diego Tribune*, in its issue of March 4, 1912, spoke of the wobblies as follows: "Hanging is none too good for them and they would be much better dead; for they are absolutely useless in the human economy; they are the waste material of creation and should be drained off into the sewer of oblivion there to rot in cold obstruction like any other excrement." When one local editor protested, the vigilantes attempted to lynch him. The facts, as I have given them, merely summarize the findings of Mr. Harris Weinstock, who was appointed by Governor Hiram Johnson to investigate the incident.

After the San Diego free-speech fight, wobbly locals were established throughout California: in Fresno, Bakersfield, Los Angeles, San Diego, San Francisco, and Sacramento. From these locals, camp delegates were sent into the fields to organize workers "on the job." Many "job strikes" were called and, frequently, they were successful. Largely because of the sensational character of their propaganda and the militancy of their free-speech fights, the wobblies built up a reputation in California out of all relation to their actual numerical strength. The IWW had less than five thousand members in the state in 1913, and less than 8 percent of the migratory farm workers were members. Nevertheless, the wobblies were a great influence. Whenever "labor trouble" occurred in the fields or in the construction camps, it was usually discovered that a "camp delegate" had been on the ground. The songs of the IWW were frequently heard in the fields and in the jungle camps under the railroad bridges. To such an extent had this agitation permeated the mass of farm laborers that when the Wheatland incident occurred the IWW was able to assume complete leadership of the workers. Conditions similar to those which existed on the Durst ranch in 1913 had existed in California for twenty years or longer, but militant action awaited the arrival of the wobblies.

THE RIOT

Immediately prior to August 3, 1913, some 2,800 men, women, and children were camped on a low, unshaded hill near the Durst hop ranch at Wheatland. Of this number, approximately 1,500 were women and children. Over half the total number of workers in this miserable camp were aliens; at one of the subsequent mass meetings seven interpreters had to be used; and a field boss made note of twenty-seven nationalities represented in one working gang of 235 men on the ranch. Following the established practice of his fellow growers, Durst had advertised in newspapers throughout California and Nevada for workers. He had asked for 2,700 workers when, as he subsequently admitted, he could only supply employment for about 1,500. Within four days after his fanciful advertisements had appeared, this strange aggregation of workers had assembled. They came by every conceivable means of transportation; many of them had walked from nearby towns and cities. A great number had no blankets and slept on piles of straw thrown on tent floors. The tents, incidentally, were rented from Durst at seventy-five cents a week. Many slept in the fields. One group of 45 men, women, and children slept packed closely together on a single pile of straw. There were nine outdoor toilets for 2,800 people. The stench around the camp was nauseating, with children and women vomiting; dysentery was prevalent to an alarming degree. Between 200 and 300 children worked in the fields; and hundreds of children were seen around the camp "in an unspeakably filthy condition." The workers entered the fields at four o'clock in the morning, and by noon the heat was terrific, remaining, as it did, around 105 degrees. The water wells were "absolutely insufficient for the camp," with no means provided of bringing water to the fields. "Numerous instances of sickness and partial prostration among children from five to ten years of age were mentioned in the testimony." One reason for Durst's chariness about providing water was that his cousin, Jim Durst, had a lemonade concession, selling lemonade to the workers at a nickel a glass. There was no organization for sanitation, no garbage disposal. Local Wheatland stores were forbidden to send delivery wagons to the camp, so that the workers were forced to buy what supplies they could afford from a "concession" store on the ranch.

The commission of inquiry which investigated the incident found that Durst had intentionally advertised for more workers than he needed in order to force wages down, and that he purposely permitted the camp to remain in a filthy condition so that some of the workers would leave before the season was over, thereby forfeiting 10 percent of their wages, which he insisted on holding back. Carleton Parker stated that the amount paid per hundred pounds of hops picked fluctuated daily in relation to the number of workers on hand. Earnings varied between one dollar and seventy-eight cents a day. Over half the workers were destitute and were forced to cash their checks each night. Throughout the season, at least a thousand workers, unable to secure employment, remained idle in the camp.

The foregoing is a very meager and abbreviated statement of the conditions which were found to have existed at the camp, on and prior to August 3. Of the workers assembled, about a third came from California towns and cities; another third were "quasi-gypsies" from the Sierra foothills, with ramshackle wagons and carts; the remaining third were "hobos," or their "California exemplars, the fruit tramps," with many foreigners among this group, including Japanese, Hindus, and Puerto Ricans. Of this strange assortment, about a hundred men were IWW "card men," i.e. they had, at one time or another, carried a wobbly card. Some of the wobblies had organized a loosely formed local in the camp, in which some thirty workers had been enrolled. "It is a deeply suggestive fact," reads the official report, "that these thirty men, through their energy, technique, and skill in organization, unified and dominated an unhomogeneous mass of 2,800 unskilled laborers" within two days. It was subsequently estimated that about 400 workers of those assembled knew, in a rough way, something of the philosophy of the IWW, and could sing some of its songs. Of the hundred card men, some had been in the San Diego fight, some had been soap-boxers in Fresno. Among these men were Blackie Ford—an experienced IWW organizer—and Herman Suhr.

Resentment had been steadily mounting in the camp for several days prior to August 3. For the most part, the workers were indignant over living conditions; they were not primarily interested in wages. On August 3, the wobblies called a mass meeting, and Blackie Ford (he was unarmed) addressed the workers and, among other remarks, told them to "knock the blocks off the scissorbills."* He took a sick baby from its mother's arms and, holding it

* In IWW terminology, a worker who favored capitalism: a capitalist from the ears up and a worker from the ears down.

before the eyes of about two thousand workers, shouted: "It's for the kids we are doing this." The meeting had come to a close with the singing of "Mr. Block"—a wobbly song—when the Sheriff and his posse arrived with the District Attorney (who was, also, Durst's private attorney). The Sheriff and a few of his men started through the crowd to arrest Ford. One deputy, on the fringe of the crowd, fired a shot in the air "to sober the mob," and as he fired, the fighting started. The District Attorney, a deputy sheriff, and two workers, a Puerto Rican and an English boy, were killed, and many more persons were injured, in the riot which followed. The posse, apparently astonished at the resistance they had encountered, fled the scene. Shocked beyond measure by reports of the riot, the state was immediately up in arms. The Governor dispatched four companies of the National Guard to Wheatland. The guardsmen marched to the workers' camp, surrounded it, and assisted the local officers in arresting about a hundred workers. Most of the workers had left the camp the night of August 3, the "roads out of Wheatland being filled all that night with pickers leaving camp." The townspeople of Wheatland were so badly frightened by the incident that the National Guard remained on the scene for over a week.

Feeling that they had a revolutionary situation to cope with, the authorities were panic-stricken and promptly launched a campaign of wild and irresponsible persecution. The Burns Detective Agency was called in and a hundred or more of its operatives were deputized. There followed one of the most amazing reigns of terror that California has ever witnessed. Wobblies were arrested literally in every part of the state. No one was ever able to make an accurate estimate of the number of arrests; many cases were subsequently reported of men being arrested and held by local authorities incommunicado for seventy and eighty days. The total number of arrests ran well into the hundreds. Private detectives seized Suhr in Arizona (he was not even present when the riot occurred) and, without legal formalities, loaded him into a box car and brought him back to California. En route to Marysville, California, where the trial was held, Suhr was kept from consulting his attorney, being taken from hotel to hotel by night. Stool pigeons were placed with him to elicit confessions, and he was beaten on an average of once a night with rubber bludgeons. It was several weeks after his "arrest" before his attorneys could even discover his whereabouts. Many other defendants were arrested and hurried from county to county in order to elude defense attorneys who were scurrying about trying to find their clients. So terrible was the treatment of these prisoners that one committed suicide and another went insane. An operative of the Burns Agency was, in fact, later convicted in Contra Costa County for a violent assault upon one of the men who was arrested but never tried. Eight months after the Wheatland riot occurred, Ford and Suhr were convicted of murder and sentenced to life imprisonment, and this conviction was sustained on appeal (*People* v. *Ford*, 25 Cal. App. 388), the first California labor *cause célèbre*. During the trial sixty or more wobblies rented a house in Marysville, which they used as headquarters. Every day of the trial, they marched from this house to the courtroom. When Austin Lewis, the defense attorney, needed a witness, he merely scribbled the name and address of the witness on a card and handed it to one of these men. Sympathetic brakemen and conductors on the trains invariably honored the cards as passenger tickets and allowed wobblies to travel about the state hunting witnesses.

Wheatland was not a strike, but a spontaneous revolt. It stands out as one of the significant episodes in the long and turgid history of migratory labor in California. For the first time, the people of California were made to realize, even if vaguely, the plight of its thousands of migratory workers. It had been customary to assume the existence of these laborers, but never to recognize the fact of their existence. The deplorable conditions under which they lived and worked were also brought to light for the first time. Although the immediate public reaction was one of horror over the IWW menace, so-called, the incident made an impression. It created an opportunity for effective investigation by the Commission on Immigration and Housing in California, which, under the distinguished chairmanship of Simon J. Lubin, did much to improve living and housing conditions among migratory workers in the state. As the annual reports of this commission began to appear after 1914, the Californians were given some interesting facts about labor conditions in the state's most important industry. It was discovered, for example, that in 1914 there were about seventy-five thousand migratory farm laborers in the state; and that, when employed, these people worked on ranches "devoid of the accommodations given horses." Sample studies indicated that about a fourth of them were suffering from one type of sickness or another and that about an equal percentage were feebleminded.

KELLEY'S ARMY

Following the Wheatland affair, and during the winter of 1914, an incident occurred which, for the first time, threw considerable light on the question of what happened to seventy-five thousand migratory farm laborers during the winter months. The number of unemployed in San Francisco that winter was unusually large, and the city authorities soon discovered that "General Kelley," a gentleman of mysterious antecedents, had organized an army of the unemployed. About two thousand men had enrolled in the army and were living in abandoned warehouses and store buildings; quite a number were camped in tents in the Mission district. Kelley had his men organized into companies and squads and put them through regular military maneuvers. As the size of the army increased, Kelley became more outspoken in his demands upon the authorities for relief, or "charitable assistance," as it was then called. The officials and the business interests of the city soon became alarmed over the situation, and seizing upon Kelley's desire to stage a "march on the capitol," they escorted his army to the ferries and sent them across the bay to Oakland. The Mayor of Oakland, not at all delighted by this visitation of "rainsoaked, sick, and coughing" men, hurriedly arranged for their transportation to Sacramento. In Sacramento, they organized a "camp" and were preparing to march on the capitol building, fifteen hundred strong, when a rival "army" of eight hundred special deputy sheriffs arrived with pick handles and drove them across the river, burned their blankets and equipment, and mounted an armed guard along the bridge to keep them out. In the process of ousting the army, the deputies were none too gentle. E. Guy Talbott, a local clergyman, states that many of Kelley's men "were beaten into insensibility and the most atrocious and barbarous methods were used." Within three weeks the army, "rained on and starved out," melted away. For years afterwards, however, the story of Kelley's Army lingered in the social consciousness of the Californian as a grim portent of the days to come.

When the Industrial Relations Commission arrived in California in August 1914, they took testimony both on the Wheatland affair and on the strange rise and fall of General Kelley's army, and the connection between the two incidents was clearly indicated. "You can't analyze the Wheatland affair and the riot that took place," testified Carleton Parker, "or the problem of the unemployed in San Francisco last winter, without bringing into the analysis the seasonal character of employment in California." Testifying further, he said: "The fact that San Francisco is said to have in winter thirty-five to forty thousand men lying up until the earlier season when the first agricultural demand for labor occurs is explained by the fact that along in November and December, especially in November, agricultural work practically ceases. The state being fundamentally an agricultural state, the industrial life of the state not being of tremendous importance, and the fact that the state is geographically isolated means that we have to nurse our own casual labor class through the winter." Witness after witness testified as to the instability of employment, the lack of co-ordination, and the refusal of the agricultural interests of the state to assume any measure of responsibility for the situation which they had created. It is interesting to note that one witness did suggest that if the growers continued to shirk their responsibility, it might be well for the state to condemn some of their holdings and settle the unemployed on the land so that they could earn a living. At about the same time, San Diego, faced with a serious unemployment problem, took over four thousand acres of "waste" land and gave food and lodging to hundreds of unemployed, and paid them fifty cents a day while they worked in improving and cultivating the tract. The experiment was quite successful and was continued until 1916, when, the demand for labor increasing, it was abandoned. August Vollmer, describing the operation of the plan in the *Christian Science Monitor,* advocated its extension throughout the state and claimed that there were approximately eleven million acres of "waste" lands in the state that might be put to constructive social use in this manner.

The recognition of an acute social problem in migratory farm labor, a problem so serious as to shake the foundations of the state, which the Wheatland riot and the appearance of General Kelley's army had forced upon the people of California, was, unfortunately, destroyed by the world war. Both incidents passed into history. Even the beginning toward a solution of the problem, as indicated by the creation of the State Commission on Immigration and Housing, was soon nullified. Reactionary postwar administrations proceeded to undermine the work of the commission (Simon J. Lubin resigned in protest), and the blind chaos of former years once more prevailed.

The Pattern of Violence

1948

IN MARCH 1942, the Japanese were excluded from the West Coast and the remaining citizens found, rather to their surprise, that this drastic wartime measure had not solved all their social and economic problems as the more rampant West Coast newspapers had led them to believe. Problems which had existed before the Japanese exclusion still existed, intensified by the war activities which involved most of Southern California. In Los Angeles, where fantasy is a way of life, it was a foregone conclusion that Mexicans would be substituted as the major scapegoat group once the Japanese were removed. Thus within a few days after the last Japanese had left, the Los Angeles newspapers, led by the Hearst press, began to play up "Mexican" crime and "Mexican" juvenile delinquency, as though the Mexican element in crime and delinquency could be considered apart from the ordinary crime experienced by a large, congested metropolitan area in wartime.

A number of minor incidents in the spring of 1942 enabled the newspapers and the police to build up, within the short period of six months, sufficient anti-Mexican sentiment to prepare the community for a full-scale offensive against the Mexican minority. Once prepared, of course, this sentiment could be expected to assume violent expression with the first major incident. A young Mexican who had been arrested and sentenced to forty-five days in jail for having accosted a woman was, upon his release, taken before the Grand Jury and, if you please, reindicted for rape, on the same offense, and promptly sentenced to prison for twelve years! The case was quickly appealed and, of course, the conviction was reversed. A short time later, a group of Mexican men, celebrating a wedding, were arrested for playing a penny crap game, an offense usually ignored by the police as being inconsequential. But, in this instance, a "conspiracy" indictment was secured from the Grand Jury, thereby neatly converting a petty misdemeanor into a felony charge. On July 13, 1942, the press gave great prominence to a story involving a fight between two groups of Mexican boys, the Belvedere "gang" and the Palo Verde "gang." In all these preliminary "incidents," pointed mention was made of the "Mexican" character of the people involved. By these techniques, the groundwork was carefully prepared for the "big incident."

THE CASE OF SLEEPY LAGOON

On the afternoon of August 1, 1942, Henry Leyvas, a young Mexican-American, had taken his girl for a drive near a little pond in a gravel pit near what was called the Williams Ranch, on the east side of Los Angeles. In lieu of other recreational facilities, this abandoned gravel pit had long been used by Mexican youngsters in the neighborhood as a swimming pool. Early that evening, a Saturday night, Leyvas and his girl had been set upon by members of a rival "gang" and a fight had occurred. (Leyvas himself was a member of a group known as the 38th Street "gang.")

Later, the same evening, Leyvas returned to the gravel pit with members of his own gang, in several cars, to look for the troublemakers. Some of the members of this sortie knew that Leyvas intended "to get even," but others merely went along for the ride and a swim and a general good time. Finding the gravel pit deserted, they discovered that a party was in progress at a nearby house belonging to the Delgadillo family and decided "to crash the gate." Some fighting and scuffling occurred at the Delgadillo home and the invaders, after a time, left the scene of the party.

Early on the morning of August 2, the body of young José Diaz was picked up from a dirt road near the Delgadillo house and taken to the General Hospital, where Diaz died without ever regaining consciousness. The autopsy showed that he had met his death as the result of a fracture at the base of the skull. He had apparently been in a fight, for his hands and face were bruised but there were neither knife nor gun wounds on the body. The road where his body was found was well traveled and the autopsy showed that he was probably drunk at the time of his death. Diaz had left the Delgadillo home with two friends—presumably the last persons to have been with him prior to his death. *Never called as witnesses,* their version of what happened to Diaz is not known. The autopsy surgeon, it should be noted, testified that Diaz could have met his death by repeated hard falls on the rocky ground of the road and admitted that the injuries at the base of his skull were similar to those seen on the victims of automobile accidents. Such are the facts of the case.

With the prior background in mind, it is not surprising that the Los Angeles press welcomed the death of Diaz like manna from the skies. Around the essentially bare facts of the case, they promptly proceeded to weave an enormous web of melodramatic fancy. The old gravel pit was dubbed "The Sleepy Lagoon" by a bright young reporter, and the whole case was given an air of sordid mystery. Quick to cooperate, the police rounded up twenty-four youngsters, all alleged to be members of the 38th Street "gang," and charged them with the murder of Diaz. Two of them had the wit to demand separate trials, and the charges against them were later dropped. But to a fantastic orchestration of "crime" and "mystery" provided by the Los Angeles press, seventeen of the youngsters were convicted in what was, up to that time, the largest mass trial for murder ever held in the county.

In the process of "investigating" the case, the police severely beat up two of the boys. While testifying that he had been beaten by the police, one of the boys was shown a photograph by the prosecution. This photograph had been taken of him, purportedly, just prior to his entering the Grand Jury room and indicated that, at that time, he was unmarked and unbeaten. The boy then pulled from his pocket a photograph which had been taken by a newspaper photographer just as he was leaving the Grand Jury room. This untouched photograph showed him with severe bruises about the head and face. Anna Zacsek, attorney for Leyvas, testified that she had walked into a room at the police station where her client, handcuffed to a chair, was being beaten by the police, and that she found him barely conscious, smeared with his own blood. Held incommunicado while they were being "worked over" by the police, the defendants were then marched, en masse, to the Grand Jury, which proceeded to indict the lot of them for first-degree murder. When they appeared before the Grand Jury they were dirty, haggard, bruised—a thoroughly disreputable-appearing group of youngsters completely terrified by the treatment they had just received. Who were these "criminals"—these hardened "gangsters"?

Henry Leyvas, twenty, worked on his father's ranch. Chepe Ruiz, eighteen, a fine amateur athlete, wanted to play big-league baseball. In May 1942, his head had been cracked open by the butt of a policeman's gun when he had been arrested on "suspicion of robbery," although he was later found not guilty of the charge. In San Quentin Prison, where he and the others were sent after their conviction in the Sleepy Lagoon case, Ruiz won the admiration of the warden, the prison staff, and the inmates when he continued on in a boxing match after several of his ribs had been broken. Robert Telles, eighteen, was working in a defense plant at the time of his arrest. Like many Mexican youngsters on the east side, he had remarkable skill as a caricaturist and amused his co-defendants during the trial by drawing caricatures of the judge, the jury, and the prosecutor. Manuel Reyes, seventeen, had joined the Navy in July 1942 and was awaiting induction when arrested. Angel Padilla, one of the defendants most severely beaten by the police, was a furniture-worker. Henry Ynostrosa, eighteen, was married and the father of a one-year-old girl. He had supported his mother and two sisters since he was fifteen. Manuel Delgado, nineteen, also a woodworker, was married and the father of two children, one born on the day he entered San Quentin Prison. Gus Zamora, twenty-one, was also a furniture-worker. Victor Rodman Thompson, twenty-one, was an Anglo youngster who, by long association with the Mexican boys in his neighborhood, had become completely Mexicanized. Jack Melendez, twenty-one, had been sworn into the Navy before he was arrested. When a dishonorable discharge came through after his conviction, he said it was "like kicking a guy when he's down." John Matuz, twenty, had worked in Alaska with the U.S. Engineers.

These, then, were the "criminals," the "baby gangsters," the "murderers" who provided Los Angeles with a Roman holiday of sensationalism, crime-mongering, and Mexican-baiting. From the very outset, a "gang" was on trial. For years, Mexicans had been pushed around by the Los Angeles police and given a very rough time in the courts, but the Sleepy Lagoon prosecution capped the climax. It took place before a biased and prejudiced judge (found to be such by an appellate court); it was conducted by a prosecutor who pointed to the clothes and the style of haircut of the defendants as evidence of guilt; and was staged in an atmosphere of intense community-wide prejudice which had been whipped up and artfully sustained by the entire press of Los Angeles.

From the beginning the proceedings savored more of a ceremonial lynching than a trial in a court of justice. The defendants were not allowed to sit with their counsel—there were seven defense attorneys—and were only permitted to communicate with them during recesses and after adjournment.

For the first weeks of the trial, the defendants were not permitted to get haircuts, and packages of clean clothes were intercepted by the jailer on orders of the prosecutor. As a consequence of this prejudicial order, the defendants came trooping into the courtroom every day looking like so many unkempt vagabonds. Following a trial that lasted several months and filled six thousand pages of transcript, they were convicted on January 13, 1943: nine were convicted of second-degree murder plus two counts of assault and were sentenced to San Quentin Prison; others were convicted of lesser offenses; and five were convicted of assault and sentenced to the county jail.

Following the conviction, the Sleepy Lagoon Defense Committee was formed and raised a large fund to provide new counsel and to appeal the case. I served as chairman of this committee, and Harry Braverman, a member of the Grand Jury who had tried to stop the indictment, served as its treasurer. On October 4, 1944, the District Court of Appeals, in a unanimous decision, reversed the conviction of all the defendants, and the case was later dismissed "for lack of evidence." In its decision, the court sustained all but two of the contentions which our defense committee had raised, castigated the trial judge for his conduct of the trial, and scored the methods by which the prosecution had secured a conviction. On October 24, when the charges were finally dismissed after the defendants had served nearly two years in San Quentin Prison (we had been unable to provide bonds during the appeal), hundreds of Mexicans crowded the corridors of the Hall of Justice to greet the boys. "Hysterical screams and shrieks," reported the *Los Angeles Times*, "laughter and cries of jubilation welled from the crowd. The atmosphere was electric with excitement as the liberated men were besieged by well-wishers who enthusiastically pumped their hands and slapped their backs. Tears flowed unashamedly." For the first time in the history of Los Angeles, Mexicans had won an organized victory in the courts, and, on this day, bailiffs and deputy sheriffs and court attachés were looking rather embarrassed in the presence of Mexicans.

The work of the Sleepy Lagoon Defense Committee received nationwide attention and was hailed as an important contribution to the war effort by ex-President Cárdenas of Mexico and by the Mexican consul-general. In Mexico City, the magazine *Hoy* devoted a three-page spread in its issue of September 30, 1944, to the work of the defense committee. During the time the committee was in existence, we received hundreds of letters from GIs, from posts in Guam, New Guinea, Hawaii, the Fiji Islands, the Aleutians; in fact, from all over the world. Soldiers with names like Livenson, Hart, Shanahan, Hecht, Chavez, Scott, Bristol, Cavouti, and Burnham enclosed dimes, quarters, and dollars for the work of the committee. Marine Corps Captain M. A. Cavouti wrote us from New Guinea: "This war is being fought for the maintenance and broadening of our democratic beliefs and I am heartily in accord with any effort to apply these principles by assisting in obtaining a review of this case. Please accept my modest contribution." From Hawaii, Corporal Samuel J. Foreman, a Negro, wrote: "I saw in the *Pittsburgh Courier* that you were leading the fight for victims of aggression. We members of the colored race are sympathetic to your worthwhile and moral fight to free these Mexican boys." Dozens of letters came from Mexican-Americans in the service.

Everyone liked what we had done, except, of course, the dominant cliques in Los Angeles. Since the initial suggestion for the formation of the committee had come from LaRue McCormick, a member of the Communist Party, we were systematically red-baited. The press accused us of "inciting racial prejudice," scoffed at the charge of bias during the trial, and lauded the trial judge and the prosecutor. Even the unanimous decision of the District Court of Appeals sustaining the charges we had made failed to bring so much as a mumbled retraction of the accusations that had been made against the boys or so much as a grudging acknowledgment that we had been right.

While the case was pending on appeal, several members of the committee, including myself, were subpoenaed by the Committee on Un-American Activities in California, headed by Senator Jack Tenney, and grilled at great length. Naturally these various grillings were reported in the press in a manner calculated to make it most difficult for us to raise money for the appeal. The Assistant District Attorney who conducted the prosecution threatened the First Unitarian Church of Los Angeles with the removal of its tax-exempt status if it permitted the committee to hold a meeting on its premises. In fact, permission to hold the meeting was, at the last minute, revoked by the church in response to this pressure. That I had expressed opposition to segregation and had testified that I was opposed on principle to miscegenation statutes was actually cited by the Tenney Committee on page 232 of its report as *proof* (!) of Communistic inclinations!

As a postscript to this section, I should add that not long after his release from prison Henry Leyvas was convicted of a criminal offense after receiving a fair trial. So far as Leyvas was concerned, he had been con-victed of being a Mexican long years ago and the damage was done. Need-less to say, his general morale and attitude were not improved by his experiences in the Sleepy Lagoon case.

CAPTAIN AYRES: ANTHROPOLOGIST

To appreciate the social significance of the Sleepy Lagoon case, it is neces-sary to have a picture of the concurrent events. The anti-Mexican press cam-paign which had been whipped up through the spring and early summer of 1942 finally brought recognition, from the officials, of the existence of an "awful" situation in reference to "Mexican juvenile delinquency." A special committee of the Grand Jury, shortly after the death of José Diaz, was ap-pointed to investigate "the problem." It was before this committee, within two weeks after the arrest of the defendants in the Sleepy Lagoon case, that Captain E. Duran Ayres, chief of the *Foreign* Relations Bureau" of the Los Angeles Sheriff's office, presented a report presumably prepared under the instructions of his superiors.

"Mexicans as a whole, in this county," reads the report, "are restricted in the main only to certain kinds of labor, and that being the lowest paid. It must be admitted that they are discriminated against and have been hereto-fore practically barred from learning trades....This has been very much in evi-dence in our defense plants, in spite of President Roosevelt's instructions to the contrary....Discrimination and segregation, as evidenced by public signs and rules, such as appear in certain restaurants, public swimming plunges, public parks, theaters, and even in schools, cause resentment among the Mexican people....There are certain parks in this state in which a Mexican may not appear, or else only on a certain day of the week. There are certain plunges where they are not allowed to swim, or else only on one day of the week, and it is made evident by signs reading to that effect, for instance, 'Tues-days reserved for Negroes and Mexicans.' ...Certain theaters in certain towns either do not allow Mexicans to enter, or else segregate them in a certain section. Some restaurants absolutely refuse to serve them a meal and so state by public signs....All this applies to both the foreign and American-born Mexicans."

So far, in the report, Captain Ayres was simply drawing a true picture of conditions in Los Angeles County. But, since his real purpose was "to ex-plain" the causes of Mexican juvenile delinquency, he soon began to draw some extraordinary conclusions. "The Caucasian," he went on to report, "especially the Anglo-Saxon, when engaged in fighting, particularly among youths, resort to fisticuffs and may at times kick each other, which is considered unsportive: but this Mexican element considers all that to be a sign of weakness, and all he knows and feels is a desire to use a knife or some lethal weapon. In other words, his desire is to kill, or at least let blood. That is why it is difficult for the Anglo-Saxon to understand the psychology of the Indian or even the Latin, and it is just as difficult for the Indian or the Latin to understand the psychology of the Anglo-Saxon or those from northern Europe. When there is added to *this inborn characteristic* that has come down through the ages the use of liquor, then we certainly have crimes of violence." (Emphasis added.)

This passage should, perhaps, be compared with similar conclusions drawn by another amateur anthropologist. "Race," wrote Adolf Hitler, "does not lie in the language but exclusively in the blood. A man may change his language without any trouble but...his inner nature is not changed." The close agreement between these two experts was shown after the publication of the Ayres Report, when Radio Berlin, Radio Tokyo, and Radio Madrid quoted passages from the report to show that Americans actually shared the same doctrines as those advocated by Hitler. The Los Angeles Sheriff, who had previously made much fuss over his "Latin blood" and his "early California background," was sufficiently embarrassed by these broadcasts to suggest to a reporter from the *New York Daily News* that the Japanese, upon being evacuated, had incited the Mexican population of Los Angeles to violence. Thus the Sheriff, who had always identified himself with the Mexican population on Cinco de Mayo and the Sixteenth of September, inferentially charged that the Mexicans, his own people, had become agents of the Japanese government!

In considering the subsequent pattern of events, it is important to remember that the Ayres Report had been formally presented to the Grand Jury by the Sheriff and had presumably represented the official views, candidly expressed, of law enforcement officers in Los Angeles. Thus the chief law enforcement agency in the county had given voice to the view that the Mexican minority possessed an inborn tendency to criminal behavior and to crimes of violence. Being primarily men of action, the law enforcement officials proceeded to act in accordance with this belief. Essentially, therefore, there is nothing incredible about their subsequent behavior and conduct.

PLOTTING A RIOT

If one spreads out the span of one's right hand and puts the palm down on the center of a map of Los Angeles County with the thumb pointing north, at the tip of each finger will be found a community where the population is predominantly Mexican. In each of these neighborhoods, moreover, a majority of the juveniles living in the area will be found to be first-generation Mexican-Americans, sons and daughters of the Mexican immigrants who came to Southern California during the 1920s.

Now, if one believes that Mexicans have an inherent desire to commit crimes of violence, the logical first step in a crime prevention program is to arrest all the people living in these areas. Unfortunately for the practice of this cozy little theory, there are well over a hundred thousand people living in these areas who are of Mexican descent. The maximum capacity of the Los Angeles jails being somewhat under this figure, it therefore becomes necessary to proceed on a more selective basis. If one group of Mexicans, say, the young people, could be selected for token treatment, and if sufficient arrests could be made from this group, perhaps this would serve as an example to all Mexicans to restrain their inborn criminal desires....

If this sounds a bit fantastic, consider the following letter which Captain Joseph Reed sent to his superior on August 12, 1942:

> C. B. Horrall,
> Chief of Police.
> Sir:
> The Los Angeles Police Department in conjunction with the Sheriff, California Highway Patrol, the Monterey, Montebello, and Alhambra Police Departments, conducted a drive on Mexican gangs throughout Los Angeles County on the nights of August 10th and 11th. All persons suspected of gang activities were stopped. Approximately 600 persons were brought in. There were approximately 175 arrested for having knives, guns, chains, dirks, daggers, or *any other implement that might have been used in assault cases*....(Emphasis added)
> Present plans call for drastic action....
>
> Respectfully,
> JOSEPH F. REED
> Administrative Assistant

On the nights in question, August 10 and 11, 1942, the police selected the neighborhoods which lay at our fingertips on the maps and then blockaded the main streets running through these neighborhoods. All cars containing Mexican occupants entering or leaving the neighborhoods were stopped. The occupants were then ordered to the sidewalks, where they were searched. With the occupants removed, other officers searched the cars for weapons or other illicit goods.

On the face of it, the great raid was successful, for six hundred people were arrested. The charges? Suspicion of assault, suspicion of robbery, suspicion of auto thefts, suspicion of this, suspicion of that. Of the 600 taken into custody, about 175 were held on various charges, principally for the possession of "knives, guns, chains, dirks, daggers, or any other implement that might have been used in assault cases." This is a broad statement, indeed, but it is thoroughly in keeping with the rest of this deadly serious farce. For these "other" implements consisted, of course, of hammers, tire irons, jack handles, wrenches, and other tools found in the cars. In fact, the arrests seem to have been predicated on the assumption that all law-abiding citizens belong to one or another of the various automobile clubs and, therefore, do not need to carry their own tools and accessories.

As for those arrested, taking the names in order we have, among those first listed, Tovar, Marquez, Perez, Villegas, Tovar, Querrero, Holguín, Rochas, Aguilera, Ornelas, Atilano, Estrella, Saldana, and so on. Every name on the long list was obviously either Mexican or Spanish and therefore, according to the Ayres Report, the name of a potential criminal. The whole procedure, in fact, was entirely logical and consistent once the assumptions in the report were taken as true.

Harry Braverman, a member of the Grand Jury who had opposed returning the indictment in the Sleepy Lagoon case, was greatly disturbed by these mass dragnet raids and by the manner in which the Grand Jury was being used as a sounding board to air the curious views of Captain Ayres. Accordingly, he arranged for an open Grand Jury hearing on October 8, 1942, at which some of the damage caused by the Ayres Report might, if possible, be corrected. At this hearing, Dr. Harry Hoijer of the University of California; Guy T. Nunn of the War Manpower Commission (who later wrote, on his return from a German prison camp, a fine novel about Mexican-Americans called *White Shadows*); Manuel Aguilar of the Mexican consulate; Oscar R. Fuss of the CIO; Walter H. Laves of the Office of the

Coordinator of Inter-American Affairs; and myself all endeavored to create in the minds of the Grand Jurors at least a doubt that everything that Captain Ayres had said was true. To appreciate the incomparable irony of this situation, suffice it to say that here we were having to defend "the biological character" of the Mexican people months after Mexico had declared war on Germany, Italy, and Japan on May 22, 1942; after the first shipment of fifteen hundred Mexican workers—the vanguard of an army of one hundred thousand workers that Mexico sent to this country during the war—had arrived in California on September 29, 1942; and after Henry Wallace, then Vice-President of the United States, had declared to a great Sixteenth of September celebration in Los Angeles that "California has become a fusion ground for the two cultures of the Americas...."

On the occasion of this hearing, representatives of the Coordinator of Inter-American Affairs made the rounds of the newspapers, calling attention to the serious harm being done the war effort and the Good Neighbor Policy by the newspaper campaign against resident Mexicans. In the interest of winning the war, these officials had suggested, there might well be some abatement in this campaign: we were fighting the Germans and the Japanese, not the Mexicans. With stated reluctance, and obvious misgivings, the newspapers promised to behave, and from October to December 1942, the great hue and cry either disappeared from the press or was conducted *sotto voce*. That the campaign had seriously interfered with the war effort, there can be no doubt. When the Sleepy Lagoon defendants were convicted, for example, the Axis radio beamed the following message, in Spanish, to the people of Latin America:

> In Los Angeles, California, the so-called City of the Angels, twelve Mexican boys were found guilty today of a single murder and five others were convicted of assault growing out of the same case. The 360,000 Mexicans of Los Angeles are reported up in arms over this Yankee persecution. The concentration camps of Los Angeles are said to be overflowing with members of this persecuted minority. This is justice for you, as practiced by the "Good Neighbor," Uncle Sam, a justice that demands seventeen victims for one crime. (Axis broadcast, January 13, 1943).

The representatives of the Coordinator's Office urged the newspapers in particular to cease featuring the word "Mexican" in stories of crime. The press agreed, but true to form quickly devised a still better technique for baiting Mexicans. "Zoot-suit" and *"pachuco"* began to appear in the newspapers with such regularity that, within a few months, they had completely replaced the word "Mexican." Any doubts the public may have harbored concerning the meaning and application of these terms were removed after January 13, 1943, for they were consistently applied, and only applied, to Mexicans. Every Mexican youngster arrested, no matter how trivial the offense and regardless of his ultimate guilt or innocence, was photographed with some such caption as "Pachuco gangster" or "Zoot-suit hoodlum." At the Grand Jury hearing on October 8, 1942, some of us had warned the community that, if this press campaign continued, it would ultimately lead to mass violence. But these warnings were ignored. After the jury had returned its verdict in the Sleepy Lagoon case and Mr. Rockefeller's emissaries had left Los Angeles, the campaign, once again, began to be stepped up.

On the eve of the zoot-suit riots in Los Angeles, therefore, the following elements were involved: first, the much-publicized "gangs," composed of youths of Mexican descent, rarely over eighteen years of age; second, the police, overwhelmingly non-Mexican in descent, acting in reliance on the theories of Captain Ayres; third, the newspapers, caught in a dull period when there was only a major war going on, hell-bent to find a local scapegoat, "an internal enemy," on which the accumulated frustrations of a population in wartime could be vented; fourth, the people of Los Angeles, Mexican and non-Mexican, largely unaware that they were sponsoring, by their credulity and indifference, a private war; and, fifth, the men of the armed services stationed in or about the city, strangers to Los Angeles, bored, getting the attitudes of the city from its flamboyant press. They entered the plot, however, only at the climax. Knowing already of the attitude of the police and of the press, let's examine the Mexican "gang."

THE ORIGIN OF *PACHUQUISMO*

In Los Angeles, in 1942, if a boy wished to become known as a "gangster" he had a choice of two methods. The first, and by far the more difficult, was to commit a crime and be convicted. The second method was easier, although it was largely restricted to a particular group. If you were born of Mexican parents financially unable to move out of certain specific slum areas, you could be a gangster from birth without having to go to all the trouble of committing a crime. For Los Angeles had revised the old saying that "boys will be boys" to read "boys, if Mexican, will be gangsters." The only reservation to be noted, of course, consists in the definition of a "gang."

Adolescent boys in the United States are among the most gregarious groups in our society. American boys traditionally "hang out with the gang." Their association is based, of course, on common interests. The boys in the "gang" may go to the same school, live in the same neighborhood, or have the same hobbies. There is, however, a difference in the degree to which the members of various "gangs" feel a sense of solidarity. A boy who belongs to a club for those who make model airplanes may have little loyalty toward the club. It serves a particular interest, and beyond this interest he must have other associations. But a "gang" of Mexican boys in Los Angeles is held together by a set of associations so strong that they outweigh, or often outweigh, such influences as the home, the school, and the church.

The various teen-age clubs in the better parts of Los Angeles often get together and spend an evening dancing in Hollywood. But the respectable places of entertainment will often refuse to admit Mexicans. The boys and girls who belong to the "Y" often make up theater parties. But the "best" theaters in Los Angeles have been known to refuse admission to Mexicans. Many youngsters like to go roller-skating or ice-skating; but the skating rink is likely to have a sign reading "Wednesdays reserved for Negroes and Mexicans." Wherever the Mexicans go, outside their own districts, there are signs, prohibitions, taboos, restrictions. Learning of this "iron curtain" is part of the education of every Mexican-American boy in Los Angeles. Naturally it hits them hardest at the time when they are trying to cope with the already tremendous problems of normal adolescence. The first chapters are learned almost on the day they enter school, and as time passes and the world enlarges, they learn other chapters in this bitter and peremptory lesson.

Most of the boys are born and grow up in neighborhoods which are almost entirely Mexican in composition, and so it is not until they reach school age that they become aware of the social status of Mexicans. Prior to entering school, they are aware, to a limited extent, of differences in background. They know that there are other groups who speak English and that they will someday have to learn it, too. But it is at school that they first learn the differences in social rank and discover that they are at the bottom of the scale. Teachers in the "Mexican" schools are often unhappy about their personal situation. They would much rather be teaching in the sacrosanct halls of some Beverly Hills or Hollywood school. Assignment to a school in a Mexican district is commonly regarded, in Los Angeles, as the equivalent of exile. Plagued by teachers who present "personality problems," school administrators have been known to "solve" the problem by assigning the teacher to "Siberia." Neither in personnel nor equipment are these schools what they should be, although a definite attempt to improve them is now under way.

Discovering that his status approximates the second-rate school has the effect of instilling in the Mexican boy a resentment directed against the school, and all it stands for. At the same time, it robs him of a desire to turn back to his home. For the home which he knew prior to entering school no longer exists. All of the attitudes he has learned at school now poison his attitude toward the home. Turning away from home and school, the Mexican boy has only one place where he can find security and status. This is the gang made up of boys exactly like himself, who live in the same neighborhood, and who are going through precisely the same distressing process at precisely the same time.

Such is the origin of the juvenile gangs about which the police and the press of Los Angeles were so frenetically concerned. Gangs of this character are familiar phenomena in any large city. In Los Angeles, twenty years ago, similar gangs were made up of the sons of Russian Molokan immigrants. They have existed in Los Angeles since the city really began to grow, around 1900, and they will continue to exist as long as society creates them. Thus "the genesis of *pachuquismo*," as Dr. George Sanchez has pointed out, "is an open book to those who care to look into the situations facing Spanish-speaking people" in the Southwest. In fact, they were pointed out over a decade ago in an article which Dr. Sanchez wrote for the *Journal of Applied Psychology*.[1]

The *pachuco* gang differs from some other city gangs only in the degree to which it constitutes a more tightly knit group. There is more to the *pachuco* gang than just having a good time together. The *pachucos* suffer discrimination together and nothing makes for cohesiveness more effectively than a commonly shared hostility. Knowing that both as individuals and as a group they are not welcome in many parts of the city, they create their own world and try to make it as self-sufficient as possible.

While the fancier "palladiums" have been known to refuse them, even when they have had the price of admission, there are other dance halls, not nearly so fancy, that make a business of catering to their needs. It should be

noted, however, that Mexican boys have never willingly accepted these inferior accommodations and the inferior status they connote. Before they have
visited the "joints" on Skid Row, they have first tried to pass through the
palatial foyers on Sunset Boulevard. When they finally give up, they have few
illusions left about their native land.

It should also be remembered that *pachuquismo* followed a decade of
important social change for Mexicans in Los Angeles. During the depression
years, thousands of Mexicans had been repatriated, and those remaining
began to adjust to a new mode of existence. The residence of those who had
been migratory workers tended to become stabilized, for residence was a
condition to obtaining relief. Thousands of Mexicans were replaced, during
these same years, by so-called Okies and Arkies in the migratory labor movement. A greater stability of residence implied more regular schooling, better
opportunities to explore the intricacies of urban life, and, above all, it created
a situation in which the Mexican communities began to impinge on the larger
Anglo-American community.

During the depression years, one could watch the gradual encroachment of Mexicans upon downtown Los Angeles. Stores and shops catering
to Mexican trade crossed First Street, moving out from the old Plaza district, and gradually infiltrated as far south as Third or Fourth Streets. The
motion picture theaters in this neighborhood, by far the oldest in the city,
began to "go Mexican," as did the ten-cent stores, the shops, and the small
retail stores. Nowadays the old Mason Opera House, in this district, has
become a Mexican theater. Being strangers to an urban environment, the
first generation had tended to respect the boundaries of the Mexican communities. But the second generation was lured far beyond these boundaries into the downtown shopping districts, to the beaches, and above all,
to the "glamour" of Hollywood. It was this generation of Mexicans, the
pachuco generation, that first came to the general notice and attention of
the Anglo-American population.

Thus, concurrently with the growth of the gangs, there developed a new
stereotype of the Mexican as the *"pachuco* gangster," the "zoot-suiter. " Many
theories have been advanced and reams of paper wasted in an attempt to
define the origin of the word *"pachuco."* Some say that the expression originally came from Mexico and denoted resemblance to the gaily costumed
people living in a town of this name; others have said that it was first applied
to border bandits in the vicinity of El Paso. Regardless of the origin of the

word, the *pachuco* stereotype was born in Los Angeles. It was essentially an easy task to fix this stereotype on Mexican youngsters. Their skin was dark enough to set them apart from the average *Angeleno*. Basically bilingual, they spoke both Spanish and English with an accent that could be mimicked by either or both groups. Also, there was an age-old heritage of ill-will to be exploited and a social atmosphere in which Mexicans, as Mexicans, had long been stereotyped. The *pachuco* also had a uniform—the zoot-suit—which served to make him conspicuous.

Mexican-American boys never use the term "zoot-suit," preferring the word "drapes" in speaking of their clothes. "Drapes" began to appear in the late thirties and early forties. In general appearance, "drapes" resemble the zoot-suits worn by Negro youngsters in Harlem, although the initiated point out differences in detail and design. The costume is certainly one of the most functional ever designed. It is worn by boys who engage in a specific type of activity, namely, a style of dancing which means disaster to the average suit. The trouser cuffs are tight around the ankles in order not to catch on the heels of the boy's quickly moving feet; the shoulders of the coat are wide, giving plenty of room for strenuous arm movements; and the shoes are heavy, serving to anchor the boy to the dance floor as he spins his partner around. There is nothing esoteric about these "sharp" sartorial get-ups in underprivileged groups, quite apart from their functional aspect. They are often used as a badge of defiance by the rejected against the outside world and, at the same time, as a symbol of belonging to the inner group. It is at once a sign of rebellion and a mark of belonging. It carries prestige.[2]

For the boys, peg-topped pants with pleats, high waists up under the armpits, the long, loose-backed coat, thick-soled bluchers, and the duck-tailed haircut; for the girls, black huaraches, short black skirt, long black stockings, sweater, and high pompadour. Many of the boys saved their money for months to buy one of these get-ups. The length of the coat and the width of the shoulders became as much a mark of prestige as the merit badges of the Boy Scout. But, it should be noted that the zoot-suit was not universal among Mexican boys. Some never adopted it, while others never adopted it completely. There were all varieties of acceptance. The newspapers, of course, promptly seized upon the zoot-suit as "a badge of crime." But as one zoot-suited boy said to me, with infallible logic, "If I were a gangster, would I wear a zoot-suit so that everyone would know I was a gangster? No, I'd maybe dress like a priest or like everyone else; but no zoot-suit."

With the backdrops all in place, the curtain now rolls up on an interesting tableau in Our City the Queen of the Angels, which was founded in the year 1781 by Mexican *pobladores* under the direction of Spanish officers who wore costumes far more outlandish than those worn by the most flamboyant *pachucos*.

ENDNOTES

1. See comments by Dr. George Sanchez, *Common Ground,* Autumn 1943, pp. 13–20.
2. See comments by Albert Deutsch, *PM,* June 14, 1943; *Racial Digest,* July 1943, pp. 3–7; *New York Times,* June 11, 1943.

Blood on the Pavements

1948

ON THURSDAY EVENING, June 3, 1943, the Alpine Club—made up of youngsters of Mexican descent—held a meeting in a police substation in Los Angeles. Usually these meetings were held in a nearby public school, but since the school was closed, the boys had accepted the invitation of a police captain to meet in the substation. The principal business of the meeting, conducted in the presence of the police captain, consisted in a discussion of how gang-strife could best be avoided in the neighborhood. After the meeting had adjourned, the boys were taken in squad cars to the street corner nearest the neighborhood in which most of them lived. The squad cars were scarcely out of sight when the boys were assaulted, not by a rival "gang" or "club," but by hoodlum elements in the neighborhood. Of one thing the boys were sure: their assailants were not of Mexican descent.

Earlier the same evening a group of eleven sailors, on leave from their station in Los Angeles, were walking along the 1700 block on North Main Street, in the center of one of the city's worst slum areas. The surrounding neighborhood is predominantly Mexican. On one side of the street the dirty brick front of a large brewery hides from view a collection of ramshackle Mexican homes. The other side of the street consists of a series of small bars, boarded-up store fronts, and small shops. The area is well off the beaten paths and few servicemen found their way this far north on Main Street. As they were walking along the street, so they later stated, the sailors were set upon by a gang of Mexican boys. One of the sailors was badly hurt; the others suffered minor cuts and bruises. According to their story, the sailors were outnumbered about three to one.

When the attack was reported to the nearest substation, the police adopted a curious attitude. Instead of attempting to find and arrest the assailants, fourteen policemen remained at the station after their regular duty was over for the night. Then, under the command of a detective lieutenant, the "Vengeance Squad," as they called themselves, set out "to clean up" the gang that had attacked the sailors. But—miracle of miracles!—when they arrived at the scene of the attack they could find no one to arrest—not a single Mexican—on their favorite charge of "suspicion of assault." In itself, this curious inability to find anyone to arrest—so strikingly at variance with what usually happened on raids of this sort—raises an inference that a larger strategy was involved. For the raid accomplished nothing except to get the names of the raiding officers in the newspapers and to whip up the anger of the community against the Mexican population, which may, perhaps, have been the reason for the raid....

Thus began the so-called "Zoot-Suit Race Riots," which were to last, in one form or another, for a week in Los Angeles.

THE TAXICAB BRIGADE

Taking the police raid as an official cue—a signal for action—about two hundred sailors decided to take the law into their own hands on the following night. Coming down into the center of Los Angeles from the Naval Armory in Chavez Ravine (near the "Chinatown" area), they hired a fleet of twenty taxicabs. Once assembled, the "task force" proceeded to cruise straight through the center of town en route to the east side of Los Angeles, where the bulk of the Mexicans reside. Soon the sailors in the lead car sighted a Mexican boy in a zoot-suit walking along the street. The "task force" immediately stopped, and in a few moments the boy was lying on the pavement, badly beaten and bleeding. The sailors then piled back into the cabs and the caravan resumed its way until the next zoot-suiter was sighted, whereupon the same procedure was repeated. In these attacks, of course, the odds were pretty uneven: two hundred sailors to one Mexican boy. Four times this same treatment was meted out and four "gangsters"—two seventeen-year-old youngsters, one nineteen, and one twenty-three—were left lying on the pavements for the ambulances to pick up.

It is indeed curious that in a city like Los Angeles, which boasts that it has more police cars equipped with two-way radio than any other city in the world (Los Angeles Times, September 2, 1947), the police were apparently unable to intercept a caravan of twenty taxicabs loaded with two hundred uniformed, yelling, bawdy sailors as it cruised through the downtown and east-side sections of the city. At one point the police did happen to cross the trail of the caravan, and the officers were apparently somewhat embarrassed over the meeting; for only nine of the sailors were taken into custody and the rest were permitted to continue on their merry way. No charges, however, were ever preferred against the nine.

Their evening's entertainment over, the sailors returned to the foot of Chavez Ravine. There they were met by the police and the Shore Patrol. The Shore Patrol took seventeen of the sailors into custody and sent the rest up to the ravine to the Naval Armory. The petty officer who had led the expedition, and who was not among those arrested, gave the police a frank statement of things to come. "We're out to do what the police have failed to do," he said; "we're going to clean up this situation….Tonight (by then it was the morning of June 5) the sailors may have the marines along." [1]

The next day the Los Angeles press pushed the war news from the front page, as it proceeded to play up the pavement war in Los Angeles in screaming headlines. "Wild Night in L.A.—Sailor Zooter Clash" was the headline in the *Daily News*. "Sailor Task Force Hits L.A. Zooters," bellowed the *Herald-Express*. A suburban newspaper gleefully reported that "zoot-suited roughnecks fled to cover before a task force of twenty taxicabs." None of these stories, however, reported the slightest resistance, up to this point, on the part of the Mexicans.

True to their promise, the sailors were joined that night, June 5, by scores of soldiers and marines. Squads of servicemen, arms linked, paraded through downtown Los Angeles four abreast, stopping anyone wearing zoot-suits and ordering these individuals to put away their "drapes" by the following night or suffer the consequences. Aside from a few half-hearted admonitions, the police made no effort whatever to interfere with these heralds of disorder. However, twenty-seven Mexican boys, gathered on a street corner, were arrested and jailed that evening. While these boys were being booked "on suspicion" of various offenses, a mob of several hundred servicemen roamed the downtown section of a great city, threatening members of the Mexican minority without hindrance or interference from the police, the Shore Patrol, or the Military Police.

On this same evening, a squad of sailors invaded a bar on the east side and carefully examined the clothes of the patrons. Two zoot-suit customers drinking beer at a table were peremptorily ordered to remove their clothes. One of them was beaten and his clothes were torn from his back when he refused to comply with the order. The other—they were both Mexicans—doffed his "drapes," which were promptly ripped to shreds. Similar occurrences in several parts of the city that evening were sufficiently alarming to have warranted some precautionary measures or to have justified an "out-of-bounds" order. All that the police officials did, however, was to call up some additional reserves and announce that any Mexicans involved in the rioting would be promptly arrested. That there had been no counterattacks by the Mexicans up to this point apparently did not enter into the police officers' appraisal of the situation. One thing must be said for the Los Angeles police: it is above all consistent. When it is wrong, it is consistently wrong; when it makes a mistake, it will be repeated.

By the night of June 6 the police had worked out a simple formula for action. Knowing that wherever the sailors went there would be trouble, the police simply followed the sailors at a conveniently spaced interval. Six carloads of sailors cruised down Brooklyn Avenue that evening. At Ramona Boulevard, they stopped and beat up eight teenage Mexicans. Failing to find any Mexican zoot-suiters in a bar on Indiana Street, they were so annoyed that they proceeded to wreck the establishment. In due course, the police made a leisurely appearance at the scene of the wreckage but could find no one to arrest. Carefully following the sailors, the police arrested eleven boys who had been beaten up on Carmelita Street; six more victims were arrested a few blocks further on, seven at Ford Boulevard, six at Gifford Street—and so on, straight through the Mexican east-side settlements. Behind them came the police, stopping at the same street corners to "mop up" by arresting the injured victims of the mob. By morning, some forty-four Mexican boys, all severely beaten, were under arrest.

OPERATION "DIXIE"

The stage was now set for the really serious rioting of June 7 and 8. Having featured the preliminary rioting as an offensive launched by sailors, soldiers, and marines, the press now whipped public opinion into a frenzy by dire warnings that Mexican zoot-suiters planned mass retaliations. To insure a riot, the precise street corners were named at which retaliatory action was expected, and the time of the anticipated action was carefully specified. In effect these stories announced a riot and invited public participation. "Zooters Planning to Attack More Servicemen," headlined the *Daily News*; "Would jab broken bottlenecks in the faces of their victims....Beating sailors' brains out with hammers also on the program." Concerned for the safety of the Army, the Navy, and the Marine Corps, the *Herald-Express* warned that "Zooters…would mass five hundred strong."

By way of explaining the action of the police throughout the subsequent rioting, it should be pointed out that, in June 1943, the police were on a bad spot. A man by the name of Beebe, arrested on a drunk charge, had been kicked to death in the Central Jail by police officers. Through the excellent work of an alert police commissioner, the case had finally been broken, and at the time of the riots, a police officer by the name of Compton Dixon was on trial in the courts. While charges of police brutality had been bandied about for years, this was the first time that a seemingly airtight case had been prepared. Shortly after the riots, a Hollywood police captain told a motion- picture director that the police had touched off the riots "in order to give Dixie [Dixon] a break." By staging a fake demonstration of the alleged necessity for harsh police methods, it was hoped that the jury would acquit Dixon. As a matter of fact, the jury did disagree, and on July 2, 1943, the charges against Dixon were dismissed.

On Monday evening, June seventh, thousands of *Angelenos*, in response to twelve hours' advance notice in the press, turned out for a mass lynching. Marching through the streets of downtown Los Angeles, a mob of several thousand soldiers, sailors, and civilians proceeded to beat up every zoot-suiter they could find. Pushing its way into the important motion-picture theaters, the mob ordered the management to turn on the house lights and then ranged up and down the aisles dragging Mexicans out of their seats. Streetcars were halted while Mexicans, and some Filipinos and Negroes, were jerked out of their seats, pushed into the streets, and beaten with sadistic frenzy. If the victims wore zoot-suits, they were stripped of their clothing and left naked or half-naked on the streets, bleeding and bruised. Proceeding down Main Street from First to Twelfth, the mob stopped on the edge of the Negro district. Learning that the Negroes planned a warm reception for them, the mobsters turned back and marched through the Mexican east side, spreading panic and terror.

Here is one of numerous eye-witness accounts written by Al Waxman, editor of *The Eastside Journal*:

> At Twelfth and Central I came upon a scene that will long live in my memory. Police were swinging clubs and servicemen were fighting with civilians. Wholesale arrests were being made by the officers.

Four boys came out of a pool hall. They were wearing the zoot-suits that have become the symbol of a fighting flag. Police ordered them into arrest cars. One refused. He asked: "Why am I being arrested?" The police officer answered with three swift blows of the night-stick across the boy's head and he went down. As he sprawled, he was kicked in the face. Police had difficulty loading his body into the vehicle because he was one-legged and wore a wooden limb. Maybe the officer didn't know he was attacking a cripple.

At the next corner a Mexican mother cried out, "Don't take my boy, he did nothing. He's only fifteen years old. Don't take him." She was struck across the jaw with a night-stick and almost dropped the two-and-a-half-year-old baby that was clinging in her arms....

Rushing back to the east side to make sure that things were quiet here, I came upon a band of servicemen making a systematic tour of East First Street. They had just come out of a cocktail bar where four men were nursing bruises. Three autos loaded with Los Angeles policemen were on the scene, but the soldiers were not molested. Farther down the street the men stopped a streetcar, forcing the motorman to open the door, and proceeded to inspect the clothing of the male passengers. "We're looking for zoot-suits to burn," they shouted. Again the police did not interfere....Half a block away...I pleaded with the men of the local police substation to put a stop to these activities. "It is a matter for the Military Police," they said.

Throughout the night the Mexican communities were in the wildest possible turmoil. Scores of Mexican mothers were trying to locate their youngsters, and several hundred Mexicans milled around each of the police substations and the Central Jail, trying to get word of missing members of their families. Boys came into the police stations saying: "Charge me with vagrancy or anything, but don't send me out there!" pointing to the streets where other boys, as young as twelve and thirteen years of age, were being beaten and stripped of their clothes. From affidavits which I helped prepare at the time, I should say that not more than half of the victims were actually wearing zoot-suits. A Negro defense worker, wearing a defense-plant identification badge on his workclothes, was taken from a streetcar and one of his eyes was gouged out with a knife. Huge half-page photographs showing Mexican boys stripped of their clothes, cowering on the pavements, often bleeding profusely, surrounded by jeering mobs of men and women, appeared in all the Los Angeles newspapers. As Al Waxman most truthfully reported, blood had been "spilled on the streets of the city. "

At midnight on June 7, the military authorities decided that the local police were completely unable or unwilling to handle the situation, despite the fact that a thousand reserve officers had been called up. The entire downtown area of Los Angeles was then declared "out of bounds" for military personnel. This order immediately slowed down the pace of the rioting. The moment the Military Police and Shore Patrol went into action, the rioting quieted down. On June 8 the city officials brought their heads up out of the sand, took a look around, and began issuing statements. The District Attorney, Fred N. Howser, announced that the "situation is getting entirely out of hand," while Mayor Fletcher Bowron thought that "sooner or later it will blow over." The Chief of Police, taking a count of the Mexicans in jail, cheerfully proclaimed that "the situation has now cleared up." All agreed, however, that it was quite "a situation."

Unfortunately "the situation" had not cleared up; nor did it blow over. It began to spread to the suburbs, where the rioting continued for two more days. When it finally stopped, the *Eagle Rock Advertiser* mournfully editorialized: "It is too bad the servicemen were called off before they were able to complete the job....Most of the citizens of the city have been delighted with what has been going on." County Supervisor Roger Jessup told the newsmen: "All that is needed to end lawlessness is more of the same action as is being exercised by the servicemen," while the District Attorney of Ventura, an outlying county, jumped on the bandwagon with a statement to the effect that "zoot-suits are an open indication of subversive character." This was also the opinion of the Los Angeles City Council, which adopted a resolution making the wearing of zoot-suits a misdemeanor! On June 11, hundreds of handbills were distributed to students and posted on bulletin boards in a high school attended by many Negroes and Mexicans which read: "Big Sale. Second-Hand Zoot Suits. Slightly Damaged. Apply at Nearest U.S. Naval Station. While they last we have your size."

Egging on the mob to attack Mexicans in the most indiscriminate manner, the press developed a fine technique in reporting the riots. "44 Zooters Jailed in Attacks on Sailors" was the chief headline in the *Daily News* of June 7; "Zoot Suit Chiefs Girding for War on Navy" was the headline in the same paper on the following day. The moralistic tone of this reporting is illustrated by a smug headline in the *Los Angeles Times* of June 7: "Zoot-Suiters Learn Lesson in Fight with Servicemen." The riots, according to the same paper, were having "a cleansing effect." An editorial in the *Herald-Express* said that the riots "promise to rid the community of...those zoot-suited miscreants," while Mr. Manchester Boddy, in a signed editorial in the *Daily News* of June 9, excitedly announced that "the time for temporizing is past....The time has come to serve notice that the City of Los Angeles will no longer be terror-ized by a relatively small handful of morons parading as zoot-suit hoodlums. To delay action *now* means to court disaster later on." As though there had been any "temporizing," in this sense, for the prior two years!

But once the Navy had declared the downtown section of Los Angeles "out of bounds," once the Mexican Ambassador in Washington had addressed a formal inquiry to Secretary of State Hull, and once official Washington began to advise the local minions of the press of the utterly disastrous inter-national effects of the riots—in short, when the local press realized the con-sequences of its own lawless action, a great thunderous cry for "unity" and "peace" and "order" went forth. One after the other, the editors began to disclaim all responsibility for the riots which, two days before, had been hailed for their "salutary" and "cleansing" effect.

Thus on June 11 the *Los Angeles Times,* in a pious mood, wrote:

> At the outset, zoot-suiters were limited to no specific race; they were Anglo-Saxon, Latin, and Negro. The fact that later on their numbers seemed to be predominantly Latin was in itself no indictment of that race at all. No responsible per-son at any time condemned Latin-Americans as such.

Feeling a twinge of conscience, Mr. Boddy wrote that "only a ridiculously small percentage of the local Mexican population is involved in the so-called gang demonstrations. Every true Californian has an affection for his fellow citizens of Mexican ancestry that is as deep-rooted as the Mexican culture that influences our way of living, our architecture, our music, our language, and even our food." This belated discovery of the Spanish-Mexican cultural heritage of California was, needless to say, rather ironic in view of the fact that the ink was not yet dry on Mr. Boddy's earlier editorial in which he had castigated the Mexican minority as "morons." To appreciate the ironic aspects of "the situation," the same newspapers that had been baiting Mexicans for nearly two years now began to extol them.[2]

As might have been expected, this post-mortem mood of penitence and contrition survived just long enough for some of the international repercussions of the riots to quiet down. Within a year, the press and the police were back in the same old groove. On July 16, 1944, the *Los Angeles Times* gave front-page prominence to a curious story under the heading: "Youthful Gang Secrets Exposed." Indicating no source, identifying no spokesman, the story went on to say that "authorities of the Superior Court" had unearthed a dreadful "situation" among juvenile delinquents. Juveniles were using narcotics, marijuana, and smoking "reefers." Compelled to accept drug addiction, "unwilling neophytes" were dragooned into committing robberies and other crimes. Young girls were tattooed with various "secret cabalistic symbols" of gang membership. The high pompadours affected by the *cholitas*, it was said, were used to conceal knives and other "weapons." Two theories were advanced in the story by way of "explaining" the existence of these dangerous gangs: first, that "subversive groups" in Los Angeles had organized them; and second, that "the gangs are the result of mollycoddling of racial groups." In view of the record, one is moved to inquire, what mollycoddling? By the police? By the juvenile authorities? By the courts? Backing up the news story, an editorial appeared in the *Times* on July 18 entitled: "It's Not a Nice Job But It Has To Be Done." Lashing out at "any maudlin and misguided sympathy for the 'poor juveniles,'" the editorial went on to say that "stern punishment is what is needed; stern and sure punishment. The police and the Sheriff's men *should be given every encouragement* to go after these young gangsters" (emphasis mine).

Coincident with the appearance of the foregoing news story and editorial, the Juvenile Court of Los Angeles entered a most remarkable order in its minutes on July 31, 1944. The order outlined a plan by which Mexican wards of the Juvenile Court over sixteen years of age might be turned over to the Atchison, Topeka, and Santa Fe Railroad for a type of contract employment. A form of contract, between the parents of the youngsters and the railroad, was attached to the order. The contract provided that the ward was to work "as a track laborer" at 58½¢ per hour; that $1.03 per day was to be deducted for board, $2.50 per month for dues in a hospital association, and 10¢ a day for laundry. It was also provided that one-half of the pay was to be turned over to the probation officers, to be held in trust for the ward. That this order was specifically aimed at *Mexican* juveniles is clearly shown by the circumstance that the court, prior to approving the arrangement, had first secured its approval by a committee of "representative" leaders of the Mexican-American community.

THE STRANGE CASE OF THE SILK PANTIES

All of this, one will say—the Sleepy Lagoon case, the riots, etc.—belongs to the past. But does it? On the morning of July 21, 1946, a thirteen-year-old Mexican boy, Eugene Chavez Montenegro, Jr., was shot and killed by a deputy sheriff in Montebello Park on the east side of Los Angeles. The deputy sheriff later testified that he had been called to the area by reports of a prowler. On arriving at the scene, he had stationed himself near a window of the house in question and had played his flashlight on the window. A little later, he testified, "a man" lifted the screen on the window, crawled out, and ran past him. When the "man" failed to halt on order, he had shot him in the back. At the coroner's inquest, the same deputy also testified that he had seen another officer remove a pair of "silk panties" from the dead boy's pocket, and that the boy was armed with "a Boy Scout's knife."

While incidents of this kind have been common occurrences in Los Angeles for twenty years, in this case the officers had shot the wrong boy. For it turned out that young Montenegro was an honor student at St. Alphonsus parochial school; that his parents were a highly respectable middle-class couple; and that the neighbors, Anglo-Americans as well as Mexicans, all testified that the boy had an excellent reputation. Accepting the officers' version of the facts, it was still difficult to explain why they had made no effort to halt the boy, who was five feet, three inches tall, when he ran directly past them within arms' reach. Before the hearings were over, the "silk panties" story was exposed as a complete fake. Despite a gallant fight waged by Mr. and Mrs. Montenegro to vindicate the reputation of their son, nothing came of the investigation. "Raging Mother Attacks Deputy Who Slew Son" was the *Daily News* headline on the story of the investigation.

On January 23, 1947, the Attorney General of California ordered the removal of two police officers for the brutal beating of four Mexican nationals who, with eight hundred of their countrymen, had been brought to Oxnard to harvest the crops....On March 30, 1946, a private detective killed Tiofilo Pelagio, a Mexican national, in a café argument. On the same day affidavits were presented to the authorities that confessions from four Mexican boys, all minors, had been obtained by force and violence. Esther Armenta, sixteen years of age, complained to her mother that she was being mistreated by Anglo-American classmates in a Los Angeles junior high school. "They would spit on her," said Mrs. Catalina Armenta, the mother, "and call her a 'dirty Mex.' Esther would come home in tears and beg me to get her transferred." A few weeks later the girl was in juvenile court, charged with the use of "bad language." She was then sent to the Ventura School for Girls, a so-called correctional institution. When Mrs. Armenta finally got permission to visit her daughter, in the presence of a matron, the girl had "black and blue marks on her arm" and complained that she had been whipped by one of the matrons. On April 10, 1946, Mrs. Michael Gonzales complained to the Federation of Spanish-American Voters that her daughter had been placed in the Ventura School without her knowledge or consent, and that when she had protested this action she had been threatened with deportation by an official of the juvenile court. On the basis of a stack of affidavits, the San Fernando Valley Council on Race Relations charged on May 16, 1947, that the police had broken into Mexican homes without search warrants; that they had beaten, threatened, and intimidated Mexican juveniles; and that they were in the habit of making "wholesale roundups and arrests of Mexican-American boys without previous inquiry as to the arrested boys' connection—if any— with the crime in question." In 1946 a prominent official of the Los Angeles schools told me that she had been horrified to discover that, in the Belvedere district, Mexican-American girls, stripped of their clothing, were forced to parade back and forth in the presence of other girls in the gym as a disciplinary measure. (For a detailed account of still another "incident," see *Justice for Salcido* by Guy Endore, published by the Civil Rights Congress of Los Angeles, July 1948.)

THE POLITICS OF PREJUDICE

I reported the zoot-suit riots in Los Angeles for *PM* and *The New Republic* and had a hand in some of the hectic events of that memorable week. Following the June 7 rioting, I chaired a meeting of a hundred or more citizens at which an emergency committee was formed to bring about, if possible, a return to sanity in Los Angeles. That same evening we communicated with Attorney General Robert W. Kenny in San Francisco by telephone and urged him to induce Governor Earl Warren to appoint an official committee of inquiry. The next day the Governor appointed a committee of five, which included four names from a panel which I had submitted. The fifth member was the Governor's own selection: Mr. Leo Carrillo. Mr. Carrillo, like the Sheriff of Los Angeles, is a descendant of "an early California family." The committee immediately assembled in Los Angeles, where Mr. Kenny presented to them a proposed report, with findings and recommendations, which I had prepared at his request. With some modifications, this report was adopted by the committee and submitted to the Governor. Out of the work of our emergency committee there finally emerged, after a year of negotiation, the present-day Council of Civic Unity.

Praising the report of the Governor's committee—which I had prepared—the *Los Angeles Times* devoted several harsh editorials to certain "reckless" individuals, myself included, who had suggested that "racial prejudice" might have had something to do with the riots! "When trouble arose," said the *Times* in an editorial of June 15, 1943, "through the depredations of the young gangs attired in zoot-suits, it was their weird dress and not their race which resulted in difficulties. That is a simple truth which no amount of propaganda will change." In the same editorial, the charges of unfairness which I had raised in connection with the Sleepy Lagoon case were branded as "distortions," "wild charges," and "inflammatory accusations" (charges later confirmed in minute detail by the District Court of Appeals).

When Mrs. Eleanor Roosevelt innocently remarked in her column that the zoot-suit riots were "in the nature of race riots," she was severely taken to task by the *Times* in an editorial of June 18 under the caption: "Mrs. Roosevelt Blindly Stirs Race Discord." Even the president of the Los Angeles Chamber of Commerce felt compelled to reply to Mrs. Roosevelt. "These so-called 'zoot-suit' riots," he said, "have never been and are not now in the nature of race riots....At no time has the issue of race entered into consideration....Instead of discriminating against Mexicans, California has always treated them with the utmost consideration."[3]

The zoot-suit riots in Los Angeles were the spark that touched off a chain-reaction of riots across the country in midsummer 1943. Similar "zoot-suit" disturbances were reported in San Diego on June 9; in Philadelphia on June 10;

in Chicago on June 15; and in Evansville, Indiana, on June 27. Between June 16 and August 1, large-scale race riots occurred in Beaumont, Texas, in Detroit, and in Harlem. The Detroit riots of June 20 to 21 were the most disastrous riots in a quarter of a century. The swift, crazy violence of the Harlem riot resulted, in a few hours' time, in property damage totaling nearly a million dollars. The rapid succession of these violent and destructive riots seriously interfered with the war effort and had the most adverse international repercussions. The spark that ignited these explosions occurred in *El Pueblo de Nuestra Señora La Reina de Los Angeles de Porciúncula*, founded by Felipe de Neve in 1781, settled by Mexican *pobladores*.

None of these disturbances had more serious international consequences than the zoot-suit riots. On April 20, 1943, President Roosevelt had held his historic meeting with President Camacho on the soil of Mexico. At the time the riots occurred, Mexico was our ally in the war against Germany, Italy, and Japan. Large-scale shipments of Mexican nationals had just begun to arrive in the United States to relieve the critical manpower shortage. "Our two countries," President Roosevelt had said, "owe their independence to the fact that your ancestors and mine held the same truths to be worth fighting for and dying for. Hidalgo and Juárez were men of the same stamp as Washington and Jefferson." President Camacho, replying to this toast, had said that "the negative memories" of the past were forgotten in the accord of today. And then in the largest city in the old Spanish borderland had come this explosion of hatred and prejudice against Spanish-speaking people.

In response to a request from the Mexican Ambassador, Secretary of State Hull had asked Mayor Fletcher Bowron for an official explanation. With a perfectly straight face, the Mayor replied that the riots were devoid of any element of prejudice against persons of Mexican descent! The same edition of the newspapers that carried this statement also carried another statement by the Mayor under a headline which read: "Mayor Pledges 2-Fisted Action, No Wrist Slap"—a reference to police action contemplated against the Mexican minority. On June 9 Mr. Churchill Murray, local representative of the Coordinator of Inter-American Affairs, wired Mr. Rockefeller that the riots were "non-racial." "The frequency of Mexican names among the victims," he said, "was without actual significance." If all this were true, asked Dan G. Acosta in a letter to the Los Angeles press, "Why are we consistently called hoodlums? Why is mob action encouraged by the newspapers? Why did the city police stand around saying very nonchalantly that they could not intervene and even hurrahed the soldiers for their 'brave' action? Not until these questions are answered will the Mexican population feel at ease."

What the riots did, of course, was to expose the rotten foundations upon which the City of Los Angeles had built a papier-mâché façade of "Inter-American Good Will" made up of fine-sounding Cinco de Mayo proclamations. During the riots, the press, the police, the officialdom, and the dominant control groups of Los Angeles were caught with the bombs of prejudice in their hands. One year before the riots occurred, they had been warned of the danger of an explosion. The riots were not an unexpected rupture in Anglo-Hispano relations but the logical end-product of a hundred years of neglect and discrimination.

The riots left a residue of resentment and hatred in the minds and hearts of thousands of young Mexican-Americans in Los Angeles. During the rioting, one Los Angeles newspaper had published a story to the effect that the *cholitas* and *pachucas* were merely cheap prostitutes, infected with venereal disease and addicted to the use of marijuana. Eighteen Mexican-American girls promptly replied in a letter which the metropolitan press refused to publish: "The girls in this meeting room consist of young girls who graduated from high school as honor students, of girls who are now working in defense plants because we want to help win the war, and of girls who have brothers, cousins, relatives, and sweethearts in all branches of the American armed forces. We have not been able to have our side of the story told." The letter, with a picture of the girls, was published in Al Waxman's *Eastside Journal* on June 16, 1943. Still another group of Mexican-American girls—real *pachucas* these—bitterly protested the story in another letter which the metropolitan press did not publish. These girls insisted that they should be examined, as a group, by an officially appointed board of physicians so that they could prove that they were virgins. Long after the riots, I have seen Mexican-American boys pull creased and wrinkled newspaper clippings from their wallets and exhibit the slanderous story with the greatest indignation. Four years have now passed since the riots, but the blood has not yet been washed from the pavements of Los Angeles.

ENDNOTES

1. *Los Angeles Herald-Express,* June 5, 1943.
2. "Imported Mexican Workers Save Millions in Citrus Crops," reads a headline, *Los Angeles Times,* June 30, 1943.
3. *Los Angeles Times,* June 18, 1943.

4

THE PRACTICE OF POLITICS

VOTE, n. The instrument and symbol of a freeman's power to make a fool of himself and a wreck of his country.

—Ambrose Bierce, *The Devil's Dictionary*

Strange Doings in California

February 1945

POLITICALLY, California is one of the liveliest states in the union—a state in which "anything can happen"; it has been the scene of some fantastic political shenanigans during the past fifteen years. Even seasoned political observers, however, were stunned by Governor [Earl] Warren's message to the legislature on January 8. Boldly seizing the initiative, the Governor has proposed a liberal, if by no means comprehensive, social program. Among its items are a compulsory health-insurance bill, large plans for preventive medical care, the establishment of a school of industrial relations at the University of California, the creation of a commission of inquiry into race relations, and a liberalization of unemployment-insurance legislation, including—miracle of miracles!—an extension of unemployment-insurance benefits to agricultural workers. Since as late as 1942 persons who advocated the inclusion of agricultural workers in the unemployment-insurance program were automatically denounced as "Communists," a practice in which the Governor actively participated. It is small wonder that his message has been referred to as a "bombshell" that "rocked the legislature." Coupled with the Governor's sudden, and total, reversal of attitude on the Japanese evacuee question,* his message is important political news, and has been so interpreted in the West. To appreciate its effect one should realize that it came as a distinct surprise to most factions, including apparently his own stand-pat Republican backers, and is markedly at variance with his 1943 program and, indeed, with his entire political record to date.

---

* In 1942, Earl Warren, then Attorney General of California, had played a major role in the World War II internment and incarceration of over 120,000 Japanese Americans, most of them U.S. citizens.

Unquestionably the decisive factor in this sudden reversal was the November 1944 election. There can be no doubt of the current liberal trend in California politics—the people gave President Roosevelt a plurality of 500,000—and Governor Warren apparently read the meaning of the election correctly. Prior to November he had given no hint of the kind of program he intended to sponsor, but between the election and January 8 he seems to have determined to make a bold bid for liberal support. His program shows evidence of hasty improvisation; the compulsory health-insurance legislation, for example, has not yet been drafted. It also indicates that the Governor, an ambitious man, is playing for national stakes. His message was quickly interpreted on the West Coast as a bid for re-election in 1946 as the necessary pre-condition to capturing the Republican nomination for the Presidency in 1948.

Governor Warren's current appearance as a liberal represents, under the circumstances, the minimum change consistent with political survival. For the Governor is in an exceptional predicament. He was elected in 1942 as a Republican running on a "non-partisan" platform. The "non-partisan" character of the campaign was stressed for the reason that a sizable majority of the registered voters of California were then, and still are, members of the Democratic Party. He was elected, in fact, by a defection of Democratic votes. He is in the position, therefore, of being a Governor who represents a minority party, despite the fact that the Republicans control both houses of the legislature. To maintain this precarious position, it is necessary for him to hold the Old Guard Republican support, which has always been his, and at the same time to snare a good many Democratic votes. Agility is the prime requisite of a politician occupying such a position.

His January 8 message knocked the Democrats off balance, but that is not in itself a major accomplishment. For the Democratic Party in California represents to an extravagant degree the incongruous elements that make up the party nationally. In California the Democrats are not so much a political party as a loose federation of disparate groups. The party leadership in the legislature is divided, inept, and furtively reactionary. Its initial response to the Governor's message was characteristic—bitter complaints that he had "stolen" the Democrats' program. When the Democratic leaders had recovered from the shock, they proceeded to do precisely what the Governor wanted them to do: they announced that henceforth they would be the "economy bloc" in the legislature.

But if the Democrats were shocked, "all has not been peaches and cream on the Republican side of the legislature," to quote Chester G. Hanson, veteran political correspondent for the *Los Angeles Times*. From the bewildered manner in which the Republicans behaved, it is apparent that they had no more warning of the new dispensation than their Democratic colleagues. It is extremely doubtful, in fact, whether even the Old Guard within the Republican Party received advance information; there is no evidence that they were consulted. The prevailing tone in the Republican press has been one of mild consternation mingled with cautionary admonitions. The *Los Angeles Times,* in commenting on the compulsory health-insurance program, declared there was much to be said on the matter "pro and con," pointed to "a wide diversity of opinion," and suggested "further study" of the proposal with postponement of actual consideration until after the war. If Governor Warren is on a hot spot, the Old Guard also occupies a rather embarrassing position. For Warren is their candidate—hand-picked, carefully trained, skillfully promoted. At this late hour there is no other candidate to whom they could turn if they should feel compelled to dump him. If they cannot support his program in its entirety, and they have given no indication that they intend to do so, still they can hardly afford to oppose it openly....*

---

* Earl Warren was re-elected in the 1946 election against Democratic candidate Robert Walker Kenny.

The Education of Evans Carlson

December 1945

ON SEPTEMBER 28, 1945, California newspapers carried an inconspicuous paragraph announcing that the Point Loma Democratic Club of San Diego had gone on record as urging Colonel Evans Fordyce Carlson, of Carlson's Raiders fame,* "to make himself available for the position of United States Senator from California in 1946." Other Democratic clubs in San Diego promptly echoed the resolution. While Colonel Carlson has not agreed to run, he has expressed "a very real sense of obligation to work in the postwar years for the full realization of the objectives for which we fought the recent global war," and he has said that he expects to be released from active service as soon as his present hospitalization at the San Diego Naval Hospital is completed. This has proved sufficient encouragement for the San Diego Democrats, and a Carlson-for-Senator movement is now under way in California.

The "talk about Carlson" in California politics has an interesting genesis. On his release from the Marine Corps, Michael Blankfort, the Hollywood screenwriter and novelist—at present engaged on a biography of Colonel Carlson—wrote several letters to Robert Walker Kenny, Attorney General of California, calling attention to the great political possibilities of Carlson. Though accustomed to discount such suggestions, Kenny met Blankfort at the California Club in Los Angeles and was apparently convinced without too great difficulty that Carlson was "a great guy." By midnight they were both on the telephone rousing Hollywood liberals from

---

* Marine battalion renowned for guerrilla-like tactics in the Pacific during World War II.

their sleep to announce the new political discovery. Since then the "talk about Carlson" has been persistent and increasingly enthusiastic. Recently I drove down to Escondido to spend a Sunday with Colonel Carlson, with the intention of finding out, if possible, how a professional soldier had managed to acquire a democratic social, economic, and political philosophy.

A NEW KIND OF DEMOCRAT

Colonel Carlson is not the easiest person in the world to interview. Since he is still in the service, he cannot take part in political activity, and he scrupulously respects this restriction. But he is quite willing, painfully modest man that he is, to talk about his experience with people in China and Nicaragua. Ironically, the education of Evans Carlson in democracy has taken place outside the United States. I am convinced that this education has been unusually thorough and that his unique experience has revealed to him a basic weakness in our conception of democracy. Should he run for the Senate, as I believe he will, he will represent a new kind of democrat in American politics. To understand his point of view, it is necessary to know something about his career—about his education in realism.

Although Colonel Carlson was born in Vermont, a distinct handicap in California politics, he has his roots deep in California. His father was "the first white child born in Alpine County, California"—Native Sons and Daughters please note—and was christened Thomas Alpine Carlson. Still living, the father is a retired minister of the Congregational faith. That Colonel Carlson is the son of a minister provides, I believe, the first clue to an understanding of the man. Point Loma Democrats have stressed his "moral integrity" and his "ethical qualifications for public leadership," and these are the qualities one first notices in him. One gathers, however, that Colonel Carlson at an early age became dissatisfied with some of the answers given by his father to his questions about matters of faith, for at sixteen he ran away from home and enlisted in the Army.

He served as a private with a field-artillery unit in the Philippines and Hawaii from 1912 to 1915. When his period of enlistment was up, he was advised to apply for a commission, but was rejected when, for the first time, he revealed his true age. After working for a year or so as an engineer with the Highway Commission in Riverside, California, he reentered the Army in 1916 for service on the Mexican border. Commissioned a second lieutenant in 1917, he was later promoted to first lieutenant and then to captain, served in France with the Eighty-seventh Division, and for a time was Assistant Adjutant General of the Third Army (the army of occupation). In 1919 he resigned his commission and got a job in California. A few years later he entered the Marine Corps, becoming a captain in 1935. It was in the Marine Corps that his real education began.

SHANGHAI AND NICARAGUA

Attached to the staff of Major (now General) Vandergrift, Carlson accompanied the Third Battalion, Fourth Marines, to Shanghai in 1927, and served as regimental intelligence officer there until 1929. As an intelligence officer, he believed that it was incumbent upon him to know something about China—its people, its customs, its politics, and its culture. This first assignment in China was therefore really a freshman course in Far Eastern affairs.

In 1930 Carlson applied for service with the Guardia Nacional in Nicaragua, giving as his reason a desire to work with native peoples. His experience in Nicaragua supplied the second chapter of his socio-economic education. Among his assignments was a term as chief of police of a Nicaraguan town. Since the agreement under which the Marines were in Nicaragua stipulated that the courts were not under our control, the judges reflected the prevailing anti-Yankee sentiment of the people and Carlson found it extremely difficult to secure convictions. Realizing that the courts would not cooperate, he decided to take the problem of law enforcement directly to the people. First of all he sought to win their confidence by demonstrating that the rich and well-born were not immune from arrest—something of a novelty in Nicaraguan life. He also set about establishing direct, personal contact with the people, and to this end proceeded to teach himself the language.

"YOU CAN TRUST THE PEOPLE"

Before his term of office was over, he was functioning as chief dispenser of justice and personal adviser to the people. It was in Nicaragua that he first got a pervading sense of confidence in the people and in the workings of the democratic process; he learned, he says, that "you can trust 'the people.'" When he left Nicaragua, he was awarded the Medal of Merit by the President for his relief work after the earthquake of March 31, 1931, and the Medal of Distinction as a token of the esteem in which he was held by the people. Listening to him recount his experiences with all sorts and conditions of people in Nicaragua, one realizes that for him Nicaragua was a fine training school in the techniques of democratic leadership.

Returning to China in 1933, Carlson resumed his post as intelligence officer at Shanghai. During his previous assignment in China (1927 to 1929), he had closely studied the Kuomintang government then being established in Nanking. Now he requested a transfer to Peking so that he might have a better opportunity to study the Chinese language and the cultural and historical background of the Chinese people. From 1933 to 1935 he served as adjutant of the guard at the Peking legation. One might assume that such an experience would tend to make a man an authoritarian, but for Carlson, who carried a well-worn edition of Emerson's "Essays" on all his travels, these were particularly fruitful years.

When he first went to Peking, the marines spent most of their leisure hours carousing and pushing Chinese "coolies" off the street. Carlson thought it would be a good idea to cultivate their interest in China and thereby improve their morals. With the assistance of his old friend, Edgar Snow, he organized a forum program for the marines which soon became a popular adult-education center. He even induced the men to learn a little Chinese. Once the marines were assigned the task of digging a deep excavation for an installation. Knowing that the site had archaeological interest, Carlson got the men interested in what they might discover. As the excavation proceeded, they found and carefully preserved numerous coins, artifacts, ceramics fragments, and the like. All these items were laid aside, catalogued by experts in the presence of the men, and later shown as a special Marine Corps exhibit. For Carlson, these years in Peking were a kind of post-graduate course in Chinese history and culture. Among his personal acquisitions was an expert knowledge of Chinese ceramics.

Back in America in 1935, Carlson served as aide-de-camp to General Charles H. Lyman at Quantico and got permission to attend night classes at George Washington University in international law and politics, with special emphasis on the Far East. As part of his studies he wrote a thesis on Japanese expansion which concluded with a prediction that in the near future Japan would attack the United States. In November of 1935 Carlson became commander of the Marine detachment assigned to guard President Roosevelt at Warm Springs. It was there that he got to know the President as a friend. Although it is not generally known, Carlson served the President as a special intelligence officer on Far Eastern affairs when he returned to China in 1937, reporting directly to the White House.

THE LESSON OF YENAN

During this third assignment in China, Carlson was an observer with the Chinese armies at the battles of Nanking and Hankow. On his own initiative he covered more than twenty-five hundred miles with the Chinese Communist forces behind the Japanese lines in North China and Mongolia, the first foreign military observer to study the tactics and training methods of these famous guerrilla fighters. His experience was graphically described in his book *Twin Stars of China*, published by Dodd, Mead in 1940. Of particular interest are his accounts of his interviews with such leaders as Chu Teh, Mao Tse-tung, and Chou En-lai. From his experience in North China, superimposed on his Nicaraguan experience, Carlson got the ideas about democratic indoctrination and training that he put to such effective use in his Marine Raider battalion.

Carlson resigned from the service in 1938 to join the American Committee for Non-Participation in Japanese Aggression—the Stimson committee—which was trying to mobilize American opinion to demand an embargo on the shipment of scrap iron and war materials to Japan. In a speech before the Foreign Policy Association in Boston on March 2, 1940, he warned against "a surprise attack from the air," which he characterized as "more imminent than a surprise attack through any other medium," urged an ethical indoctrination of our military personnel, and called for a foreign policy "designed to convince other nations of our desire to meet them on terms of equality, which will assure them of our integrity, of our sense of justice, and of our good-will toward all nations."

In July 1940, he returned to China to make a four-thousand-mile tour of the Chinese industrial cooperatives with Rewi Alley. He interviewed Chiang Kai-shek at Chungking and continued to report directly to President Roosevelt on Chinese affairs. Early in 1941 he hastened back to America convinced that Japan intended to strike soon for Singapore. Commissioned a major in the Marine Corps in April 1941, he later organized the famous Second Marine Raider Battalion of gung-ho fame. He landed with the Second Marine Division at Tarawa, accompanied the assault units in the Marshall Islands operations, and took part in the battle for Saipan, where he was wounded. He has received about all the decorations the services have to offer—the Navy Cross (three times), the Legion of Merit, two Purple Hearts, and three Presidential Unit Citations, for Guadalcanal, Tarawa, and Saipan.

UNIQUE QUALIFICATIONS FOR SENATOR

It is apparent that Colonel Carlson would bring to the United States Senate some unique qualifications—an expert knowledge of Far Eastern and Central American affairs and of the people of those areas, an expert knowledge of our military establishment together with some ideas about the necessity for democratizing the services, a realistic knowledge of the kind of world we live in, a profound faith in democracy, and great skill, based on wide experience, in the techniques of democratic leadership. After Hiram Johnson, James Phelan, and Samuel Shortridge, who did so much to undermine American prestige in Asia, California might well take pride in a Senator who actually understood the peoples of the Far East. (A Senator who speaks both Chinese and Spanish would be, I take it, a rather exceptional figure on the hill.)

In the course of our conversation, Colonel Carlson said that the American people must renounce the "success myth," with its emphasis on individual achievement, and acquire something that they now seem to lack, namely, a sense of identification with the democratic process. By this he means not merely the formal identification expressed by going to the polls at stated intervals to cast a ballot, but a living, creative, participating identification with democratic processes in personal and family relationships and social conduct. He constantly emphasizes the necessity for self-discipline in a democracy, the kind of self-discipline that he found in the Eighth Route Army. Essentially, his concept of democracy is that of John Collier—"democracy livingly, immanently experienced." Both men apparently acquired this concept of democracy from their experience with non-industrial, or rather pre-industrial, peoples; Collier from his life among American Indians, Carlson in Nicaragua and China. It is a concept of democracy that industrialism has damagingly corroded in the Western democracies and that only the vigorous self-discipline advocated by Colonel Carlson seems able to restore.

Recently I asked Staff Sergeant Willard D. Darling for his impressions of the Colonel. In reply he wrote: "I find that words are of no use to me. When the Colonel is mentioned you don't think, you feel things inside of you that you were not aware of, that become a part of your life while you are with him. There was never a man who left his outfit who did not grit his teeth to keep the tears back, and some couldn't. He is the kind of man you would go to hell for should he tell you to, and never ask the reason why." A man who can inspire this feeling in those he commands has demonstrated his capacity for democratic leadership.

Colonel Carlson frequently quotes these words from a speech which President Roosevelt was prevented by death from delivering: "Today we are faced with the preeminent fact that if civilization is to survive, we must cultivate the science of human relationships—the ability of all peoples, of all kinds, to live together and work together in the same world, at peace." Our problem, in other words, is to create a real democracy based upon individual self-discipline and cooperative effort.*

---

* Evans Carlson ran in the 1946 Senatorial election until a heart attack forced him out of the campaign. He died in 1947 at the age of 51.

Mr. Tenney's Horrible Awakening

July 1949

THOUGH STATE LEGISLATURES are showing increasing interest in "un-American" activities, the oldest of the "little Dies committees,"* the Tenney committee in California, has recently suffered a stunning defeat. An account of its rise and decline provides an interesting case history of the politics of red-baiting.

The California legislature first became interested in "subversive" activities during the administration of Governor Culbert L. Olson. In 1940 an Assembly committee, with Sam Yorty as chairman and Jack B. Tenney as its most active member, was appointed to inquire into the extent of Communist influence in the state relief program. Although the committee failed to make a case, it did succeed in its primary purpose of pinning a red label on the Olson administration. The following year a joint fact-finding committee on un-American activities was created, and Tenney, composer of "Mexicali Rose" and once charged with actual membership in the Communist Party by two witnesses testifying before the Dies committee, was made its chairman.

In the eight years of its existence the Tenney committee has received appropriations of $153,000 from the state Senate, but few if any legislative enactments have been chalked up to its credit. Other states now considering the appointment of similar committees might well ponder the following appraisal of the work of the Tenney committee by the *Los Angeles Daily News*

---

* The Dies committee was the Special House Committee to Investigate Un-American Activities and Propaganda in the United States, 1938–1944, chaired by Martin Dies, an extremely conservative Democrat from Texas. It was the forerunner of the well-known House Un-American Activities Committee.

(June 13, 1949): "We believe that our Un-American Activities Committee, as directed by its chairman, Senator Jack B. Tenney, not only has failed to serve the purpose for which it was intended but has been used more effectively than any other governmental institution in the state of California to aid, assist, and develop communism in this state."

How did the committee happen to stray so far from its stated purposes and objectives? The answer is to be found in what might be called the law of diminishing returns as applied to red-baiting in American politics. Professional politicians should familiarize themselves with the workings of this interesting principle.

"Un-American" committees must constantly broaden the scope of their inquiries, just as placer miners are forced farther and farther into the marginal sands as the rich diggings are exhausted. Once such a committee has examined the obvious witnesses and worked over the most fertile fields of inquiry, it is driven to summon witnesses who are progressively less vulnerable to attack; as the most likely issues are explored and abandoned, increasingly fanciful issues must be tackled. And the wider the dragnet thrown out, the more numerous the opposition becomes. For example, as long as Communist leaders are under investigation, the opposition will generally be limited to Communists, but if the committee goes farther afield, it will have to subpoena witnesses of considerable standing in the community. Once witnesses of this kind are brought before the inquisition, two concurrent developments are usually noted: the opposition is strengthened, and the position of the committee is undermined, for it begins to look ridiculous even in the eyes of the less progressive elements of the community.

One would think that those who direct inquisitorial agencies would be on their guard against this danger, but the opposition usually assumes real substance before the inquisitors realize that they are less popular than they had imagined. Emboldened by their initial successes, they become drunk with power and develop a remarkable blindness to changes in public opinion. It happens also that the chairman begins to take "menace" seriously, and once this happens he forfeits any competence he may have possessed. Thus Senator Tenney, who started out as a cynical turncoat liberal, reached such a pitch of self-indoctrination that he made maudlin speeches warning his colleagues that "the eyes of Cardinal Mindszenty are upon you."* If a chairman

* József Mindszenty (1892–1975), a passionate opponent of Communism, had been arrested by the Hungarian government in 1948 for treason and illegal monetary transactions and sentenced to life imprisonment.

succumbs to his own demagoguery, he becomes obtuse and unmanageable. By a curious irony, the more "sincere" he becomes, the less useful he is to those who sponsored his show in the first place. If he persists in his "sincerity," he will ultimately be repudiated by the very elements that selected him for the role of inquisitor. The failure to realize this basic fact of political life proved the undoing of Senator Tenney.

When the California legislature convened in January 1949, the Tenney committee faced the necessity of sounding the usual alarms in order that it might secure a new appropriation. But the committee had already filed four reports, running into many millions of words, and it found it difficult to invest a new one with the right sense of "urgency" and "menace." A fresh sensation had to be manufactured for the legislators, and an unjaded scribe, someone who also could inject real fervor into his work, was needed. For this assignment Senator Tenney selected one Ed Gibbons, at a salary of $200* a week. Once amanuensis to Willie Bioff, the racketeer, Gibbons had become a member of the anti-subversive public-relations firm of Jacoby and Gibbons, publishers of a smear sheet called *Alert*. While working on the report, Gibbons published in the May 2 issue of *Alert* an article in which he charged that a long list of prominent Democrats were "fellow-travelers, dupes, or dopes." The Gibbons list included Mrs. Edward H. Heller, Democratic national committeewoman from California; Oliver Carter, state chairman of the Democratic Party; State Senators George Miller and Gerald J. O'Gara; Mrs. Helen Gahagan Douglas; Edmund Brown, District Attorney of San Francisco; Colonel James Roosevelt; and others of similar standing. The smearing of these individuals, of course, provided the new sensation, but the sensation quickly backfired. Senators O'Gara and Miller demanded an investigation of the employment of Gibbons, and protests against the Tenney committee began to pour into Sacramento.

Apparently annoyed by this resistance, Senator Tenney proceeded to oppose the nomination of Daniel G. Marshall and W. J. Bassett to the Social Welfare Board on the ground that their "philosophies" were repugnant to him. Mr. Marshall is a prominent Los Angeles attorney who is extremely well thought of in Catholic circles; and W. J. Bassett is the conservative secretary of the Los Angeles Central Labor Council (AF of L). In opposing these

---

* Adjusted for inflation, about $1400 a week in 2001.

appointments, Tenney also attacked the Citizens' Committee for Old Age Pensions out of pique because the oldsters had refused to support him for Mayor of Los Angeles (he had run a poor fifth in this race). Obviously Tenney had become "punchy"; in one brash outburst he had antagonized the Catholic Church, the American Federation of Labor, and the best-organized section of the pension movement.

Just at this time, however, the industrious Gibbons pen had completed the writing of the Fifth Report of the committee. Released on June 8, the document created an immediate furor. To their horror, Tenney's sponsors discovered that he had divided the newspapers of the state into two categories—those that looked with favor on the Tenney committee and those that did not. Among the latter were listed the *San Francisco Chronicle,* the *San Francisco News,* and the *Los Angeles Daily News.* The *Chronicle* promptly replied with an editorial attacking the "razzle-dazzle, headline-grabbing, witch-hunting techniques" of the committee.

Then, just to insure the effectiveness of the coalition that was forming against him, Senator Tenney went on to introduce thirteen "anti-subversive" bills, two of which would have required test oaths from lawyers and teachers, and to release a long list of persons said to be within "Stalin's orbit." On this list was the name of Judge Isaac Pacht, president of the Los Angeles Jewish Community Council. The council promptly passed a resolution castigating Tenney for his "vicious, unjust, and completely untrue" charge. By these moves Tenney had succeeded in antagonizing the two best-organized professional groups in the state and the Jewish community of Los Angeles. The introduction of his ambitiously conceived "thought control" program greatly alarmed his backers and manipulators. As one of these behind-the-scenes individuals complained: "We hired someone to tell us of the presence of our enemy, to keep our house in order, and he has mistook [sic] his mission." The lobbyists were immediately alarmed, fearing that Tenneyism might become a major, and unmanageable, issue in 1950.

Almost before Tenney realized what had happened, a group of legislators, acting on the orders of the lobbyists, decided that the time had come "to blow the whistle" on the Tenney committee. In the last days of the session Assemblyman Sam Yorty, who had once initiated Tenney in the rites of red-baiting, moved that the remaining undefeated Tenney bills be tabled, and the motion was carried by a vote of fifty-five to sixteen. While he was still groggy from this blow, Tenney discovered that the Rules Committee had decided to remove him as chairman of the Un-American Activities Committee. Tenney was a victim of the illusion that political power is inherent in red-baiting, *per se,* rather than in the forces that find it convenient to use red-baiting for their particular purposes. A power in the state one day, Tenney woke up the next morning to find that he was "out." In his humiliation there is a lesson for all politicians who fail to see that certain political forces encourage red-baiting for purposes not necessarily connected with belief in "the red menace." If a red-baiter gets in their way, he will promptly discover who runs the show.

California is now, somewhat ahead of the nation, entering upon the new phase of "controlled" red-baiting. The more extreme forms of it have been repudiated, not because they are ugly or unfair, but because the powers that be have discovered that red-baiting caters to a constantly shrinking political market; each succeeding dividend is lower than the one which preceded it. Tenney was thrown overboard to appease public opinion, and now a new set of rules has been adopted to prevent the cruder indignities of such committees and salvage red-baiting as a technique. The new rules provide (1) that witnesses shall have the right to submit statements; (2) that individuals whose names are brought into the record may file a statement concerning such testimony or appear before the committee and testify in their own behalf; 3) that such individuals also have the right to secure the appearance of the witnesses whose testimony adversely affected them and to cross-examine these witnesses within reasonable limits, either personally or by counsel; and (4) that no reports are to be issued until approved by a majority of the committee. Whether these rules and the elimination of the odious Tenney will have the effect of rehabilitating red-baiting remains to be seen. In the meantime, Jack B. Tenney is probably pondering an editorial entitled "Will He Be Missed?" which appeared in the *Fresno Bee,* a newspaper that Tenney had fondly included in the "loyal" category. "Building mountains out of mole-hills," to quote from this editorial, "is another thing which has served to detract from the value of its work [the Tenney committee's]. It has shouted wolf so often and so long when no wolves could be seen that people have lost confidence in its warning cries."

Bungling in California

November 1950

FROM FIRST TO LAST the California political campaign has been a monumental irrelevance. No significant issues have been raised. Though a record vote will probably be cast, few elections in this state have aroused less rank-and-file enthusiasm.

The Democratic ticket is weak where it should be strong, in the center of the line, where the nominee for Governor stands. Edmund "Pat" Brown, District Attorney of San Francisco, is a strong candidate for the attorney-generalship and should win. Mrs. Helen Gahagan Douglas is a strong candidate for the senatorship, has conducted a first-rate campaign, and under more favorable circumstances would surely defeat Representative Richard Nixon. But she has been confronted, since the primary, with an extremely difficult situation.

The trouble is that James Roosevelt's campaign against Governor Warren has come apart at the seams. Warren's total vote in the primary was almost seven hundred thousand greater than Roosevelt's. In addition, Warren, with an eye on the Presidency, has been "pouring it on," in the hope of rolling up a huge vote in November. With his usual skill—here is one politician who never campaigns too soon—the Governor has planned a smashing finale. His opponent's campaign has been as oddly incompetent as the Governor's has been well planned and cleverly conducted. Nearly everything Roosevelt has done or said has somehow confirmed the public's initial impression that he was a lightweight in the ring with a heavyweight champion. His blows have been tossed about in a frivolous and opportunistic fashion. Not once has he managed to break down Warren's guard and land a real punch.

No one seems to know just who is responsible for the Roosevelt campaign—it is apparently the handiwork of Russell Birdwell, a Hollywood public-relations counselor. Bringing Mrs. Eleanor Roosevelt to California merely emphasized the candidate's ineffectiveness. The spectacle of Mother rushing out West to defend Son against the Big Boy was by local standards a bit ludicrous. Herbert L. Phillips, political editor of the McClatchy newspapers, summed up a week's activities quite accurately in these words: "Roosevelt's record for the week: Running attack—slowed up noticeably by rugged Warren line; kicking—frequent but inaccurate; fumbles recovered—none; passes attempted—eight; passes incomplete—eight; total ground gained from political scrimmages—not enough to net him even a single first down."

Concerned about the all-important Senatorial campaign, the [Truman] Administration has sent a parade of important speakers to California, including Maurice Tobin, Vice-President Barkley, and Attorney General McGrath, with Oscar Chapman, Charles Brannan, W. Averell Harriman, and Representative Wright Patman en route. All of them so far have been cautious if not downright cagey about supporting Roosevelt. "I'm not in California to attack the Republicans," said Vice-President Barkley. "I have great respect for the Governor of this state. I am not attacking Governor Warren." It is doubtful whether this oblique strategy has helped Mrs. Douglas, for it has confirmed the weakness of the center. Had she been able to induce Harold Ickes to visit California and devote his splendid powers of denunciation to a subject worthy of them—namely, the brazen demagoguery of Richard Nixon—the effect would have been greater than that produced by this parade of big names.* Ickes, I understand, has not wanted to come to California because he is not enthusiastic about James Roosevelt.

Despite Mrs. Douglas's fine efforts to conduct an intelligent campaign, the issue which has shaped up as the decisive one in the Senatorial struggle is: Do California voters approve of the voting record of Vito Marcantonio?†

---

* Harold Ickes, appointed Secretary of the Interior by Franklin D. Roosevelt, was one of the most progressive thinkers of the Roosevelt administration. This may be a reference to a scathing indictment of Harry Truman's architectural taste that Ickes published after Truman proposed to make alterations to the White House.

† Vito Marcantonio was a left-wing representative from New York. Douglas and Marcantonio had both opposed the creation of the House Un-American Activities Committee, but most of the 354 votes they held in common were on nonsubstantive issues, such as declaring October National Poultry Month or what time to convene on the following day. This tactic of Nixon's led to the epithet "Tricky Dick."

To outsiders this question may seem unrelated to California politics, but it is the only one Nixon has raised. His every speech and statement have pounded home the argument that Mrs. Douglas has lined up on the same side as Marcantonio more often than has Nixon. His own voting record is a distinct liability in a basically liberal state; on most issues Congressman Nixon has been several paces to the right of Senator Knowland. Mrs. Douglas has tried to combat this trickery by a consistently sensible and dignified rebuttal but has not yet managed to launch the counter-attack which might break the hypnotic rhythm of the Nixon theme song: "Helen Douglas is a red."

A dapper little man with an astonishing capacity for petty malice, Nixon might best be described as a distinctly third-rate Tom Dewey.* In this campaign he enjoys the support of virtually every newspaper in the state, including the *San Francisco News*—which was a bit of a surprise....

Some weeks ago the *Daily News* finally came out for Mrs. Douglas, but in a curiously left-handed way. It sagely told its readers that it did not consider Richard Nixon a fascist and that it was by no means thoroughly convinced that Mrs. Douglas was a Communist. On the basis of this remarkable statement, its readers were at liberty to infer that they could, if they wished, vote for Mrs. Douglas with reasonable assurance that she would not commit treason....

Governor Warren seems certain to be reelected by a handsome margin; the odds are five to one in his favor. The Nixon-Douglas fight will be close, but Mrs. Douglas should win. Brown, too, will probably be successful.†...

---

* Thomas Dewey (1902–1971) began his career as a prosecuting attorney. Popular for his successful racket-busting efforts, he was elected Governor of New York for three terms (1943–1955). He was the Republican presidential nominee in 1944 and 1948 but lost in both elections.

† Brown and Warren were elected, and Helen Gahagan Douglas lost to Richard M. Nixon. This was Earl Warren's third term as Governor. When he was appointed to the U.S. Supreme Court by President Eisenhower in 1953, Lieutenant Governor Goodwin Knight succeeded him.

The Old Fresno Magic

February 1954

THE CITY OF FRESNO, almost equidistant from San Francisco and Los Angeles, has been the birthplace of the only successful popular political movements that present-day Californians have ever known. It was the home of Chester Rowell, leader of the Hiram Johnson Progressives in 1910, the central meeting ground of the Upton Sinclair Epics in 1934, and the launching place of the CFPU (California Federation for Political Unity), which carried Culbert L. Olson into the Governor's chair in 1938. Since then California has not been nourished by popular movements arising in Fresno—or anywhere else.

When the California Democratic Council was scheduled to meet in Fresno on February 6, it was assumed that, as usual, the James Roosevelt forces would dominate the meeting. Three days before it met, Mr. Roosevelt's untimely flair for epistolary reminiscence landed him on the nation's front pages.* He did not attend the Fresno meeting and ultimately withdrew his candidacy for Congress.

The result was that the amateurs promptly took over the Fresno meeting and did such a good job that California now has its first chance in sixteen years to elect a Democratic Governor. In the nominations they carried every office except that of the candidate to oppose United States Senator Thomas Kuchel, appointed by Warren to fill the Nixon vacancy.† This nomination was given to Representative Sam Yorty, Los Angeles Democrat, who in 1939 was chairman

---

* James Roosevelt (oldest son of Franklin D. Roosevelt) had signed a letter in 1945 admitting to infidelities with a number of women. Newspaper coverage of its contents when his wife sued for a legal separation led him to withdraw from the election.
† The vacancy occurred when Nixon was elected Vice-President, serving for two terms under Eisenhower.

of the state legislature's "little Dies committee." But the only reason that Yorty won was that the amateurs did not have any candidate against him.

The "amateurs" are the thousands of new people who have come into the Democratic Party in California during and since the Stevenson campaign.* There were hundreds of brand-new faces at Fresno, new voters who had just come of age or only recently come to California.

Richard Graves, who was the choice for Governor, is the best-informed man on government in the state and will make a great campaign against reactionary Governor Knight. Having spent twenty years as executive secretary of the League of California Cities, a mutual-aid organization of which every one of California's hundreds of small incorporated cities is a member, he can appeal to a nucleus of supporters in all the fifty-eight counties. A lot of the Warren Republicans are also going to vote for Graves.

The hero of the convention was State Senator George Miller, Jr. He is the first Democratic leader in years who has not been trying to lead the people in his own direction. He was not a candidate for anything himself, but he was the man who induced Graves to make the race.

The choice of Edward Roybal, Los Angeles City Councilman, for Lieutenant Governor was a stroke of genius. It will bring to a focus the drive to obtain participation for Mexican voters, a long-dormant political force.

The distinctive thing about the 1954 election, in addition to the absence of Warren's smooth-running leadership of the GOP, will be the fact that the state will have held the first primaries under the new rules. In November 1952, the voters adopted a modified anti-cross-filing proposal which will require Republican cross-filers in the Democratic primary to carry the word "Republican" after their names. The old masquerade has thus been outlawed, and not many people who take the trouble to vote in the June 8 primary are going to vote for candidates of the opposite party. As a result, there will be run-offs in November for nearly all the contested offices. This will serve to bring out a much larger Democratic vote in an off-year gubernatorial election.

The California Democratic Party is ready to sail again with a new progressive crew. Most of the old patronage-hunting and pseudo-liberal barnacles dropped off in the fresh waters of Fresno. The old Fresno magic of unity may be at work once again.

---

* Adlai Stevenson, known for wit, intelligence, and supporting liberal causes, lost two presidential elections to Eisenhower. He was reluctant to run in the second (1956), but a "Draft Stevenson" movement gained him the nomination and generated massive grass-roots support.

The Kennedys Take Over

July 1960

SENATOR JOHN F. KENNEDY, his family, his friends, and his superb organization have scored a resounding triumph here in Los Angeles, where despite the smog, you can still see Catalina Island on a clear day. The Senator is an excellent campaigner, his attractive family constitute a distinct political asset, and his organization is a thing to marvel at. But while the Kennedys have scored a personal family triumph, they have also filled an enormous leadership vacuum in the Democratic Party. The house was not vacant, but it was not defended; and the Kennedys, all of them, led by Jack and brother Bobby, simply moved in and took over. How they were able to take over so easily is the story of this odd convention.

Start with the amazing fact that the Kennedys met with only a kind of token opposition. Nowadays, primaries are important less for the delegates that the winners acquire than for the publicity they get. Senator Kennedy used the primaries, with the active help of the press, to score a personal publicity triumph. In the primaries he was opposed only by Senator [Hubert] Humphrey (the skirmish with Senator [Wayne] Morse hardly counted). Senator Humphrey, for all his virtues, had obvious political weaknesses as a candidate for the Presidency, one of which was that he could not muster his potential support, a large part of which remained loyal to Adlai Stevenson. Senators [Lyndon] Johnson and [Stuart] Symington stayed out of the primaries. The Kennedys filled the vacuum, and that was that. Late in the game, when the opposition realized what was happening, it refrained from organizing a "stop Kennedy" movement not out of chivalry, but because it knew that any such movement would be said to rest solely on Senator

Kennedy's religion, which the Senator had converted into a formidable defense weapon.

Another factor was Governor Brown's inept political fan dance in California. The concept of a favorite-son delegation in California made sense. It was a means of creating unity within a divided delegation and, at the same time, of protecting the California Congressional delegation, which, with a session coming up soon and many key state measures at stake, did not want to oppose [vice-presidential candidate Lyndon] Johnson overtly. For a time, Brown took himself seriously as a candidate for either the Presidency or Vice-Presidency. He gave interviews, on the hour, to every itinerant journalist who showed up in Sacramento. What he said was confusing; he wavered from day to day. Then he conducted personal polls which he ignored when they revealed remarkable strength for Stevenson. At zero hour, he attempted to come out for Kennedy personally without releasing the delegation—thus infuriating that part of the Congressional delegation not pledged to Kennedy. And it forced a delegation split which fragmented the state's potential influence in the convention. Add the fact that he removed Paul Ziffren as national committeeman for what seemed to be a most inconsistent reason—i.e., that Ziffren had urged Kennedy to enter the California primary. The end result was that California's strategic strength was never brought into play effectively. Solidly pledged to Brown, California alone could have stopped the Kennedy *putsch*. But here, too, the Kennedys are entitled to credit; it is hard to escape the conclusion that Brown had a working agreement with Senator Kennedy from the outset. Kennedy knew he could not win the entire California delegation, so he settled for Brown's support; and the *quid pro quo* was his agreement to stay out of the California primary. Many reports circulate about a meeting between Brown and Joe Kennedy at Lake Tahoe at which the protocol was negotiated....

The odd thing about the Kennedy drive was that it was based on only two "popular" elements: Catholic support, particularly among the politically influential Irish-Americans, and younger elements, including older persons who think we need "young" leadership. Many young people do respond to Kennedy; but at Los Angeles, the young were for Stevenson. One of the most interesting aspects of this odd convention was the excitement which the pro-Stevenson youngsters engendered and reflected. And they were wonderfully attractive: exuberant, eager, undiscouraged, confident (not of winning, just confident generally), articulate, full of bounce, world-minded....The pro-Stevenson youth were "pre-mature," which is what makes them outsiders; they are the "students" of whom Kenneth Rexroth wrote in the July 2 issue of *The Nation,* the vanguard of the new political forces of the 1960s. The Kennedy "young men" are young junior executives; they feel they have it made. They may be young in years and energy, but they are not young ideologically.

So the paradox of this convention has been that a young man without an impressive political record, without a program, without broad rank-and-file support, backed by not a single interest group with the possible exception of labor, not merely won the nomination of a great party without substantial opposition, but took possession of it, lock, stock, and barrel....

Has Success Spoiled Dick Nixon?

June 1962

CALIFORNIA, booming and bouncing as never before, goes to the polls on June 5 in the first round of an election of extraordinary local and national interest. In terms of issues, it would be rated dull: there really are none. But the stakes are high: the short-term future of the Republican Party in California—and, it well may be, its long-term future nationally. As one state leader told the *Wall Street Journal* recently, California may well be "the crucible for the future of the Republican Party." As an added feature, another chapter—it may well be the last—is being written in the soap-opera political career of Richard M. Nixon. What California can make, California can unmake—and often does. Nixon's career began here—it could only have happened in California—and it may well end here.

Nixon's decision to run for Governor was a desperate gamble. If he is defeated in November, he is through. True, he may retain an influence, even a major one, in the Republican Party; but as a Presidential contender he will have had it. No one knows this better than Nixon. When he finally announced on September 27, after a long period of uncertainty, the decision was probably dictated as much by pressures and circumstances over which he had no control as by his own cool judgment. The time had come, his financial backers said, for the pay-off; in all the years since his first story-book election to Congress he had needed them; now they needed him. The party organization was a shambles. Governor Brown had defeated former Senator Knowland by more than a million votes in 1958. A leadership vacuum existed. Someone had to fill it. Nixon was the strongest candidate the party could field in California. Eight new seats in Congress were up for grabs, and a strong man at the head of the ticket might help the party to capture some of them. Even so, Nixon might not have decided to make the gamble had it not been that the odds seemed to be shifting in his favor; last June he held a sixteen-point margin over Governor Brown in the polls. The party was in bad shape—this he knew—but he had carried the state in 1960; and no one could have realized, last fall, the depth and bitterness of the intra-party tensions which his candidacy has brought to light.

Nixon's troubles began with the spectacular upsurge of the Radical Right in California. As might be expected, his handling of the issue has been highly opportunistic. At the outset, he publicly congratulated the *Los Angeles Times* for a series of articles "exposing" the John Birch Society.* But a long silence then ensued; he was not quite sure which way to jump. Subordinates, attending Robert Welch's first big meeting in Los Angeles, reported to Nixon that the audience was made up of types that normally make good Republican precinct workers. In the meantime, Governor Brown and Attorney General Stanley Mosk had smartly seized the initiative and made Birchism an issue by their blistering attacks on the society.

It was not until the first Field Report (a local polling service) had demonstrated that the support of the Birchites was a real liability that Nixon decided to hazard still another gamble. When the twelve hundred delegates to the California Republican Assembly (CRA) gathered in Berkeley in March, Nixon startled a group of his backers at a closed-door luncheon by reading a resolution—it had not previously been discussed—which he insisted that they should present to the convention. In effect it read the Birchites out of the party. The luncheon over, he then departed in haste for Southern California, leaving his supporters to face the music. In a secret ballot battle that tied up the convention longer than any resolution fight in the thirty-year history of the assembly, a modified version of the resolution was finally forced through after extremely bitter debate. As adopted, the resolution condemned Robert Welch and urged all members of the CRA to get out of the Birch Society; as originally drafted, the resolution had ordered the Birchites out of the party. Senator Thomas Kuchel, up for re-election this year, supported the Nixon resolution and was booed; when Nixon's name was mentioned, there was hissing and booing. Nevertheless, the convention endorsed Nixon for Governor by a

---

* In 1958, candy manufacturer Robert Welch formed the ultraconservative John Birch Society to combat "the infiltration of Communism into American life." The organization was named for a missionary / intelligence officer killed by Communists in China.

vote of 276 to 176 (for Joe Shell); in committee, the vote had stood at 34 to 25. The same convention endorsed Senator Kuchel by a vote of 220 to 112 for Howard Jarvis, and 107 for Loyd Wright (beloved by the ultras).

It is generally agreed that Nixon paid a heavy price for the Birch Society resolution. It brought into the open, and intensified, the seething undercurrent of bitterness and tension that had been building up in the Republican Party for a long time. The way in which the matter was handled antagonized many moderates and conservatives who felt that Nixon had tossed them a hot potato and then walked out. The young moderates muttered "hierarchy" and "dictation," while an ultra shouted: "All Communists will now vote for the resolution." A member of the resolutions committee, Howard Koester, an aeronautical engineer and an admitted member of the Birch Society (it is interesting to note that many lower-echelon Birchites are connected in one way or another with defense industries), resigned from the CRA and stalked out of the meeting. Nixon's endorsement for the governorship, while a victory, was, as Carl Greenberg reported in the *Los Angeles Times*, "hardly an overwhelming landslide for a former Vice-President of the United States pitted against a lowly Assemblyman."

On the face of it, Nixon's final stand on the Birch Society might seem to do him credit; for once he appeared to have taken the high road of principle. But the appearance is illusory. The November ballot in California may contain a severely repressive, anti-communist initiative measure known as the Francis Amendment. Governor Brown has denounced it as patently unconstitutional, and Nixon has questioned its wisdom, but for different reasons. What Nixon is up to is clear enough; in fact, he has been at some pains to make it clear. He wants to make a major campaign issue out of "fighting communism," at which he modestly assures all and sundry that he "rates better than passing grades"; at the same time, he wants to appear to be quite "responsible" about the issue. Seen in this perspective, the anti-Birchite resolution was simply a tactic designed to set the stage for the grand post-primary crusade against communism. So, too, is Nixon's opposition to the Francis Amendment.

In the meantime, Nixon has coasted along in the primary campaign, shaking hands, probing for issues, trying to avoid embarrassing commitments. He is not repeating the mistake he made in 1960 of "peaking" his campaign too soon. On strictly state issues, Governor Brown has the advantage; he has made a good record and Nixon knows it. So to avoid talking about critical state issues, on which he could not hope to match Brown's liberalism without alienating conservative Republican votes, Nixon proposes instead to "fight communism," which is how he got started in politics in the first place. Somehow—by some black magic—he must capture 90 percent of the Republican vote and about 20 percent of the Democratic vote in order to win in November. His tactics are tailored to this necessity.…

In a bitter fight, Nixon lost control of the Young Republicans in Los Angeles (where he has also lost control of the county Central Committee); and he came within a few ballots of losing control of the Young Republicans state-wide. Robert Gaston, son-in-law of Charles S. Jones of Richfield Oil and president of the Young Republicans of Los Angeles, who today calls himself a "Goldwater-Tower-Rousselot" Republican, was a Nixon precinct worker in 1960. The April convention of the California Young Republican College Federation (four thousand members) at the Statler-Hilton ended in a brawl; police had to be called in to quell Shell partisans who contended that the credentials committee had been stacked with Nixonites. These Young Republicans are important; they make good precinct workers. Many of them are in Shell's camp.

Aside from the Young Republicans, a party official told the *Wall Street Journal* that the most common GOP precinct worker is the middle-aged Los Angeles widow, fairly well off, with loads of time, who tends to be very, very conservative. Many of these good ladies are aligned with the Shell-Goldwater faction. In fact, about the only elements in the GOP who are enthusiastically for Nixon other than his top backers are the Class of '47, who "went up the ladder with Dick." In a crude effort to cover up this dearth of "activists," Nixon's managers are flooding newspapers with press releases announcing the appointment of Mrs. X as "coffee-hours chairman," Mrs. Y as chairman of "campaign costume jewelry," Miss Y as chairman of "Nixonettes costuming," etc.; but no one is fooled.

Oddly enough, upper-income Republicans of the kind that you see in the Pacific Union Club in San Francisco or meet in San Marino make a point of expressing their hostility to Nixon. One of Nixon's key advisers—a real "pro" in California politics—told me that "top management" locally and nationally was critical of both Nixon and Kuchel to a remarkable degree. I spoke with some of those elements and was surprised at the extent to which they seem out of touch with political realities; they appear to have no realization of what a Republican nominee must do to win in California. Like dinosaurs, they suffer from an over-specialization of function. A former longtime top

GOP manager in California told me, wearily, sadly, that these big wheels, even the self-made ones, have a habit of ignoring "the human heart"....

Success must have spoiled Dick Nixon. He should have known that, despite his prestige, he was the person least likely to unify the Republican Party in California. Actually, his candidacy has intensified all of the tensions that have been building up in the party for the last decade. Today, unlike the past, the "soreheads," the malcontents, the ultras, the noise-makers, are in the GOP....

Up from Sunset Boulevard in Beverly Hills is the new luxury subdivision of Trousdale Estates, founded by Paul Trousdale and reverently regarded by most Southern Californians as a kind of hillside Versailles. Here, late the other night, the latest and most celebrated of all the "celebrity homes" in the tract was pointed out to me: the new mansion of Dick and Pat Nixon, their two daughters, and faithful Checkers. It has seven baths, three fireplaces, and a 900-square-foot, S-shaped swimming pool.

The question is not what did it cost, but what did Nixon pay for it? Trousdale says that the lot was sold to Nixon for $35,000, but would now sell for $50,000. "We built him a home on contract for $100,000 and he added $25,000 in extras and $25,000 in landscaping. He paid us around $125,000." Maybe. But estimates suggest that the mansion as it stands—lot, landscaping and furnishings included—represents an investment of around $300,000. That it was sold as a "celebrity deal" is conceded, but it is not known what Nixon's price was—in concessions, shaded prices, and the rest. Currently Nixon is trying to make an issue of the fact that the Teamsters Union is backing Governor Brown; but Teamster pension funds, to a total of more than $6 million, assisted in financing the Trousdale Estates.

It is to this curiously mixed-up social scene, in which Teamsters finance lush subdivisions and home construction provides the new gravy train, that Dick Nixon has returned after his fast ride to fame and fortune in American politics. Characteristically, he sees nothing improper in permitting Trousdale to exploit the "celebrity aura" that attaches to those who have occupied the office of Vice-President. As in 1952, the faceless, amoral Nixon is still on the make, still "fighting communism," still full of tricks, haunted as always by the lack of self-knowledge, of identity, that makes everything he says sound empty of meaning and turns everything he touches into putty. But from way up there, high in the upper reaches of Trousdale Estates, the lights sparkle clear and bright for Dick and Pat; win or lose, they have it made—at last. Every night, for a full week, they can bathe in a different bathroom.

The Politics of Personality

October 1962

THE MOST EXPENSIVE—and the noisiest—campaign in California's political history is drawing to a close without having aroused voters to the fever pitch. It would seem to be a rule of modern TV politics that the more expensive a campaign is, the less rank-and-file interest and participation it is likely to arouse. With three-hour (Nixon) and ninety-minute (Brown) telethons, the exhausted viewer-voter apparently feels that there is very little need for him to "talk it up" in neighborhood, shop, or office. Then, too, there are really no issues in the California campaign; or, to state it another way, the only issue is Richard M. Nixon. Also, big-league baseball—the exciting play-off between two California teams and the protracted World Series—has diverted attention....

Tactically, Nixon has not been effective. He has nothing to offer in the way of a rival program (some of his suggestions have been extremely silly), and his "slashing attacks" on the Brown administration have not slashed very deeply.

The plain fact is that Brown has been a good Governor—better by most accounts than Governor Knight and with more legislative accomplishments in one term than Earl Warren managed to chalk up in three. Brown is a real expert on California issues, Nixon a novice.

In large part because he is the kind of man he is, the Governor has enjoyed a much better press than Democratic nominees usually enjoy in California. He will run very well in the northern part of the state, while Nixon will have a slight edge in Southern California, particularly in San Diego County. But even in Southern California, the big blocs are pro-Brown: labor, the minorities (Negroes, Mexican-Americans, Jews), and the senior

243

citizens. Factors which might elect Nixon are: the volatile new voters, some last-minute "emotionalism" tagged to headlines (a blow-up in Cuba or something of the sort), and possible apathy—for, as noted, there is less interest in the campaign than the noise heard at a distance would indicate.

The biggest "sleeper" factor is the well-timed, last-minute visit of President Kennedy, which could add enough momentum to the campaign to elect the entire slate of Democratic nominees for state offices and Richards as well…

Predictably, a last-minute red-baiting gimmick has been injected into the campaign. One cannot prove that the Chotiner-Nixon team authored it, but it is certainly out of their familiar bag of tricks.* The first manifestation was the appearance, in suspiciously large numbers, of a booklet entitled "California: Dynasty of Communism," by Karl Prussion, who has appeared at some of the "anti-communist" schools. More recently, a rather mysterious organization calling itself the "Committee for the Preservation of the Democratic Party in California" has been raising funds to send out mailings to registered Democrats. The propaganda is all geared to the suggestion that the California Democratic Clubs (CDC), with a membership of sixty thousand, are about to take over the Democratic Party in the state. The smear is aimed at the CDC on the ostensible ground that the organization has refused to erect a specific bar against "reds"—meaning those accused of being reds. Reports indicate that as many as a million copies of this poisoned dart will be aimed at registered Democrats between now and November 6…

---

* Los Angeles lawyer Murray Chotiner, as the first of the professional political consultants as we know them today, imparted his mastery of merchandising and public relations techniques to the campaigns and crises of Richard Nixon's career.

Mr. Nixon and the Press

November 1962

IN HIS DRAMATIC TIRADE against the press, Richard M. Nixon demonstrated a degree of inconsistency and ingratitude that can fairly be characterized as shocking.* The press, he snarled, has always kicked him around. It has been unfair to him. Even the *Los Angeles Times,* which has supported him in all his campaigns—in season and out, through thick and thin—was not excepted, and drew a searing rebuke. Yet if ever a politician had occasion to be grateful to the press, if ever there was a politician whose entire public career has been fostered and furthered by the press, however unwittingly—that man is Richard M. Nixon. An unknown young man in Congress, he was catapulted into national limelight by the well-known incapacity of the press to resist the news bait of "charges" and "denunciations." Now, with a truly amazing lack of perception, Nixon complains that "since the Alger Hiss case," the press has been his enemy.† This particular snarl suggests the ancient tag line "man bites dog." For it was the manner in which the American press made a sensation of the Alger Hiss case that launched Nixon's national political career. Even earlier, it was the built-in disposition of the press to handle "charges" in a manner that keeps the calumniated forever in pursuit of the calumniator that resulted in his triumphs over Jerry Voorhis and Helen

---

* The tirade referred to is the famous post-election speech in which Nixon, eight years before he was elected President, told the press, "You won't have Nixon to kick around anymore."

† It was at Congressional hearings investigating accusations that high-level State Department employee Alger Hiss was a spy for the U.S.S.R. that Nixon, then a Congressman from California, first gained national coverage in the news media.

Gahagan Douglas. Individual reporters and columnists have no doubt disliked Nixon, but publishers, by and large, have always been in his camp; in his latest and final campaign, the press, with rare exceptions, was on his side.

But to underscore the lack of insight demonstrated in the extraordinary flare-up at the Beverly Hilton, the former Vice-President—for years a heartbeat from the Presidency—said: "Thank God for radio and television." But it was television that, in a famous Presidential campaign debate, revealed to the American people more sharply than the press had ever succeeded in doing, and in a matter of minutes, the real Nixon: not the black-jowled villain of the Herblock cartoons, or the haloed hero of the far Right, but an empty, faceless, insecure, weak, almost abject opportunist striving mightily, with no sense of values and a most uncertain sense of self-identity, to claw his way to the top by fair means or foul. In brief, Mr. Nixon is an American tragedy in the classic pattern, but it took television to reveal the truth.

And in Nixon's final seventeen-minute press conference it was television, not the press, that managed to catch once again the true character of the man. His words seem lifeless on the printed page, but the image on the television screen conveyed the unmistakable lineaments of the man's true character. To this day he does not understand, he will never understand, that it was the circumstance that Governor Brown's "image" happened to be the man himself—that this most unpretentious of American politicians is in fact quite incapable of projecting a false image—that was his own undoing. For Nixon's character, not the press, is what defeated him, just as surely as it was Governor Brown's character that brought him victory.

How to Succeed with the Backlash

October 1966

CALIFORNIA IS IN THE THROES of one of the most subtle and intensive racist political campaigns ever waged in a Northern or Western state. As Ronald Reagan admits privately, his chances of victory over Governor Edmund Brown lie in his ability to exploit overwhelming voter opposition to open-housing laws while building up and maintaining an image of moderation. The task isn't easy, but that it can be done was proved by Senator George Murphy, who two years ago defeated the Democratic candidate, Pierre Salinger, in the face of a Johnson landslide, by exploiting the muted and evasive approval of Proposition 14, the initiative measure designed to pull the teeth of the Rumford Fair Housing Act and prohibit all future open-housing laws.* Of course, Murphy wasn't quite the right-winger that Reagan is—and was publicly seen to be, until Spencer-Roberts, the public relations managers, took him under their auspices.

Reagan began his retreat from liberalism more than a decade ago, after having noisily supported Helen Gahagan Douglas in her Senatorial race against Richard M. Nixon in 1950. He stamped himself as an all-out convert to the right-wing cause when he managed Loyd Wright's forlorn primary campaign against Senator Thomas Kuchel in 1962. Wright once called for preventive war against Russia; and he sees civil rights as a part of the Communist conspiracy. Two years later, Reagan plunged into the Goldwater

---

* The goal of the Rumford Fair Housing Act was to protect renters and homebuyers from racial discrimination. In 1964 California voters repudiated it by passing Proposition 14, which the Supreme Court struck down in 1967, saying that it "expressly authorized and constitutionalized the private right to discriminate."

primary campaign so wholeheartedly that Spencer-Roberts, then managing the Rockefeller campaign in California, referred to him as an extremist. During the Presidential race, his carefully worded phrases on such subjects as voluntary social security, the United Nations, Supreme Court decisions, and violence in the streets made Reagan the darling of the right-wingers. He sent them into ecstasies with his artful radio and TV performances, and they launched his gubernatorial campaign the day after the election. Reagan was appropriately coy, but after the proper arm twisting he announced that he would yield to public demand. He tested that demand through state-wide tours, and in announcing his candidacy said that one of the prime issues was civil rights. He got the pre-primary backing of all reactionary GOP groups, including the Neanderthal Young Republicans, thus insuring victory in the primary over moderate George Christopher, former Mayor of San Francisco, but his backers knew that he would need a more moderate image for the general election. Spencer-Roberts came in to do the job, and in an enthusiastic moment, one of its executives said that the agency was going to make Reagan the John V. Lindsay of California.* That's quite an order, but the real problem is to make Reagan palatable to the middle-of-the-road voters without offending the Right.

Apparently Reagan discussed the problem with his friend and political associate, former Representative John Rousselot, the John Birch public relations man, because he confided in an unguarded moment at a pre-primary gathering that "John" was quite a good fellow who was willing to help in any way he could, from publicly denouncing the Reagan candidacy to outright endorsement. In the ensuing ruckus, Reagan dismissed the statement as a wry joke of his own making. His official position is that he will not denounce the John Birchers, nor will he solicit John Birch support, but that he will support known John Birch members who are Republican candidates. If elected, he says, he will appoint "qualified" John Birchers to office. He says that if Birchers support him it is because they subscribe to his program and not he to theirs. It is no secret that the Birch brass is lined up solidly behind him and that reactionaries such as Walter Knott and Henry Salvatori and John McCone are in his corner. He has avoided the embarrassment of having Goldwater or

* John V. Lindsay was the Republican Mayor of New York City from 1966 to 1973. He often took positions to the left of Republican Party leadership, backing civil rights legislation and refusing to endorse Barry Goldwater as Republican presidential candidate. He switched his party affiliation in 1971 in the midst of his second term.

Senator Strom Thurmond campaign for him by saying that he doesn't think it proper for out-of-state people to advise Californians on political choices.

Reagan's bid for the middle-of-the-road vote consists of taking ambiguous stands on public issues. He's all for voluntarism, including a voluntary box-office tax to be levied by theaters to help the movie industry; he sees such a tax as a way to ward off the horror of government subsidy to the producers. He approves the social security system, but thinks it is possible to "let some young men who are just starting make [voluntary] arrangements," since they won't be able to take as much out as they might put in. He approves voluntary action to stamp out pornography, but supports an "anti-obscenity" initiative measure called "CLEAN" that is so unbelievably bad it has earned the condemnation of the Council of Churches, the State Bar, all leading newspapers, the state's District Attorneys, and even that of the Republican candidate for Lieutenant Governor, who agrees with all knowledgeable lawyers that it is unconstitutional...."Constitutional or not," says Mr. Reagan, "if this measure is voted down, my opponent might take this to mean that the people of California are not opposed to pornography." What *that* means is anybody's guess.

Of course Reagan is for tax reform and against tax increases, but if we must have increased taxation, he's all for a raise in sales taxes. What he regards as turmoil at the University of California pains him; he wants an investigation of the school under the leadership of former CIA Chief John McCone. He's opposed to right-to-work laws for California, but he wants to keep Section 14(B) in federal laws so that states may have a free choice. Welfare payments are too high, in his opinion, and he would reduce them by putting relief recipients to work at tasks unspecified.

By his own say-so, Reagan is opposed to bigotry and racial prejudice, but he's also opposed to civil rights legislation. Republican Attorney General Edward W. Brooke of Massachusetts, a Senatorial candidate and a Negro, heard him try to explain his position for about an hour: "It was all vague and hazy," Brooke said later. "I don't think he thinks very well. I couldn't always make out what he was driving at except that he was trying to tell me that although he wouldn't have signed the [1964] Civil Rights Bill he was a friend of the Negroes. He seemed embarrassed." The "umbrella issue" dominating all other campaign issues, says Reagan, is that old Goldwater chestnut "morality in government"; the details are not defined, but it is apparent that morality in government will be furthered by the election of all Republican candidates.

This bland diet doesn't excite the voters, and Reagan's managers know it. But they believe that if they can present him as a reasonable man, he will win his share of middle-of-the-road votes, and the undertow of opposition to open housing will land him in Sacramento....

Reagan's tactics are simple. He insists that civil rights is a campaign issue—"one of the three or four most important issues," he says—and he rejected out of hand Brown's proposal that open-housing legislation be referred to a non-partisan committee. But he stops short after making it plain that he will propose and support repeal of existing fair-housing laws. He offers no affirmative civil rights program, a stand in keeping with the public mood of halting all further equalitarian action. The calculation of the Reagan backers is that it is up to Brown to take the initiative on civil rights issues and that the Governor dare not do so, because his every proposal will only stimulate the white backlash. As one of the actor's advisers put it, Reagan has a basic residual interest in civil rights issues "even when he is not saying a damn word about it."

Whenever civil rights problems are broached, Reagan bristles with self-righteousness, proclaims that he is not a bigot, and says that he utterly abhors racial discrimination. He stormed out of a pre-primary meeting last spring with his heart beating on his sleeve because, he said, he had been accused of bigotry. Whenever he can find an opening, he brands "bigots" as "sick people." His cure for their ailment is "voluntary action" and he said after the recent San Francisco disturbances that the Governor hasn't adequately explored voluntary action as a remedy for urban disorders. Reagan has never defined "voluntary action."...

The biggest boost to Reagan's evident attempt to win the anti–civil rights vote came on October 4, when the Republican Coordinating Committee and former President Eisenhower demanded a crack-down on what they called "rampant crime in our cities and on the streets" and on "violence and mob madness." As the *Los Angeles Times* Washington bureau chief noted, the statement "made some strong Republican campaign medicine, dispensed at a moment when reaction against racial violence and disorder is a potent factor in many congressional and gubernatorial races." Reagan took his cue quickly and rapped Brown for "failing to exhibit the leadership required to forestall riots." He added, "We must not recognize the rioters"—a code phrase which means that demands for reform made by demonstrators must be rejected out of hand....

Every informed Californian knows how deep-running is the undercurrent of racism in the gubernatorial campaign. The *New York Times* California news bureau commented on September 29 that "many California votes on November 8 hinge on feelings among electors about the racial backgrounds of their neighbors, about nondiscriminatory sale or rental of property, about the Watts riots of last year, and racial violence everywhere." The *Los Angeles Times*'s Richard Bergholz said last July 5 that there are "those in both parties who will tell you that race relations is the one campaign issue that can tip the scales against everything else." At the same time he reported that Richard Nixon told Republicans, "I want everyone in California to believe that [Lieutenant Governor] Glenn Anderson was responsible for Watts." The reference was to Anderson's supposed reluctance to call out the National Guard during the Watts disturbances. Bergholz added that Brown's refusal to back away from support of the Rumford Act "may frighten more voters who are already resentful of Negro militancy and who don't like their mandate on Proposition 14 nullified by some judges and politicians." It is to the obvious advantage of those who want Reagan elected to fish in these troubled waters and to trouble the waters to make fishing good.

The Ronald Reagan campaign is more, much more, than a mere Republican Party effort to elect a Governor. Essentially, it is a carefully contrived campaign to strengthen and perpetuate right-wing control of the GOP machinery. Top level decisions are not being made by titular heads of the party or by Spencer-Roberts. The Republican Party label is invaluable, and party leaders must be buttered up and kept content; Spencer-Roberts's job is to package the candidate and make him salable. The crafty politicians who are directing the Reagan campaign are at once stage-managing and taking full advantage of every possible racist maneuver that will benefit their candidate, not because they are bigots or racists *per se,* but because they think they have a winning issue that will cement their control of the Republican Party. They were the architects of the move to put the legislative repeal initiative of fair-housing laws on the November ballot; they now encourage and further the drive to oust the Supreme Court justices who voted to invalidate Proposition 14; they stimulated the California Real Estate Association (CREA) to put legislators on record as favoring repeal of the Rumford Fair Housing Act and engineered the association's tacit endorsement of Reagan; they helped whip up the recent national attack by the Republican Party on "crime in our cities and in our streets."

Ronald Reagan knows what's going on. But he wants to be Governor. He's willing to do whatever is necessary to achieve that ambition, no matter what his private sentiments are. On October 6, he told a cheering CREA convention that Negro complainants who alleged discrimination in housing had made "staged attempts to rent homes, when in truth there was no real intention of renting, only of causing trouble." Thereafter, he said, the "state commission acted as accuser, judge, and jury." After criticizing the courts for overruling the people's "constitutional right to put an end to" what he called these unfair practices, he wound up by saying that "the right of an individual to the ownership and disposition of property is inseparable from the right of freedom itself." He got a standing ovation from the real estate brokers. There will be more of this kind of demagogy as the campaign comes to a climax, with Reagan using code words and phrases to let the electorate know his right-wing stand on racial issues without his having to voice outright racist sentiments.

There won't be much plain talk from Californians about the racism that they know permeates the Brown-Reagan contest. Most of them won't talk about it at all if they can escape it. They don't want the nation to know— they don't want to admit to themselves—that the number-one state may elect Ronald Reagan Governor in order to "keep the Negro in his place."

Paradise Reagan-ed

December 1966

TO UNDERSTAND THE ELECTION of Ronald Reagan as Governor of California, it is important to grasp the idea of that state as "paradise." The Eden image has led millions to move there; from the Okie migrations of the thirties to the present, the state has swarmed with newcomers.

California has given us the first auto-dominated city, Los Angeles; and even within the "old and settled" city of San Francisco, people move around as though in a frenzy. All this movement to California and within it suggests that Californians are strongly motivated to escape—from the cold blasts of the Midwest or the problems of the South, or lack of opportunity, or whatever.

Thus, when an election came up during a time of rapid social change and increasing problems, the people of California fled reality. Instead, they indulged in a ritual cleansing, and brought in a totally inexperienced man who campaigned *on the basis* of being a political innocent. Brown, who campaigned on his experience, was fated to emphasize the very thing that people held against him: he reminded them that they were human, that they were part of society and had responsibilities. But now all is simple and wonderful in a land where "thinking makes it so." There is no need for government and, led by an innocent, the Californians can look forward to eternities of joy, while the rest of America, in the land of Nod (East of Eden) must continue to struggle and sweat.

AFTERWORD

Living in Five Worlds

1979

IN TERMS OF PERSONAL HISTORY, I had experienced five "worlds": the pre–World War I world with its aura of innocence; the world of the 1920s; the fervent years of the 1930s; the exciting years of World War II with their high hopes and expectations; and the thirty years of Cold War that began in 1945 and finally phased out in the spring of 1975. Despite crosscurrents and diversions, this thirty-year period was for me a "world" in the sense that the Cold War was the dominant theme; it tied these years together; it was the major obsession. One sensed this the moment Nixon left the White House and the fighting ceased in Vietnam. The Cold War had been the major force not merely in American politics and diplomacy but in the way it distorted the economy, bloated the state, played havoc with older values, generated endemic inflation, wasted resources without thought of present or future consequences, and ended with the disaster in Vietnam and the embarrassment of Watergate. Only in 1975—on the eve of the Bicentennial—did I feel that a post–Cold War period, or at least the end of a long phase of the Cold War, had finally arrived.

My "education" had consisted essentially of immersion in these five "worlds," each of which had a beginning, a development, and a finale. Once they had passed into history—and only then—could I see that they had a certain unity or at least could be thought of as entities of a sort. The contours of each had been determined, to a large extent, by the "world" that had preceded it. Over the years I came to give much more weight to the historical factors than when I set out to explore the first of these "worlds." But I never lost a feeling for the importance of idealism in keeping alive the belief that injustices can be corrected and inequalities lessened. At the same time, however, I learned early on that idealists cannot create the kind of future of which they dream, if only because they cannot agree on the form it should assume. Even if they could agree, they would find that in the shaping, their new world had assumed aspects which were not part of the original plan or vision. No future can be fully anticipated; the contingent, the unforeseeable, play hob with utopian blueprints. So I have learned to be wary of utopian projections based on rigid models. But I have also learned that some sense of ideology, or the logic of economic systems, is a prerequisite for restructuring power relationships, a task that implies an awareness that the existing economy functions as a system and that changes should be made with some alternative model in mind. The problem is to avoid becoming so imprisoned in a particular ideology that changing realities are ignored.

The past is constantly being reinterpreted and there are no infallible charts for the future; only the present is real, immediate, inescapable. No doubt this is why I have been accused of being present-oriented: I have always been much more concerned with what is happening here and now than with what happened yesterday or might happen tomorrow.

In the 1920s I was a rebel; in the 1930s I became, and I have remained, an unreconstructed, unapologetic radical. But Western radicalism is not like its Eastern counterpart in all respects. In the East, and notably in the New York City area, leftists of all persuasions are preoccupied with the theoretical correctness of their positions; with them the style factor is important. In the West radicals concentrate on issues. In the East more attention is devoted to scrutinizing the political backgrounds of one's associates; in the West agreement on issues and objectives is the prime consideration. In California I got used to being called a variety of names: fellow traveler, socialist, Communist, soft-headed liberal. I was a fellow traveler in the sense that I sponsored some committees that took positions I thought were important even though I did not always agree with the politics of the other sponsors. Some of these committees were no doubt Communist-inspired or contained names of Communist Party members on their letterheads; but at the time no other groups were raising these issues, and I have never thought it necessary or practical to screen associates when taking a political position on a specific issue of immediate importance. In a sense I have been a socialist for many years, but the fact is that I have never known a socialist party or movement with which I could identify; I have had differences with all of them. And I have never been a member of the Communist Party, although I have known individual Communists whom I respected and whose courage I admired. I would also agree with what Edmund Wilson said in a letter to John Dos Passos in 1935: that Communists, for all their shortcomings, should be given credit for having played a valuable role as agitators; they did raise some fundamental questions and worried people into trying to find answers. But had I been accused of being a radical (Western style), I would readily have pleaded guilty.

I am unable, however, to offer a pat definition of what it means to be an American radical. The radical tradition has been discontinuous, surfacing at some periods, seeming to disappear at others; it has been not so much a movement as an attitude, a tradition. In Michael Harrington's phrase, it is "part of the secret history of the United States," by which he means that there has never been a well-organized, coherent, identifiable radical movement that has persisted over any considerable period of time in the same place. The impulse has been intermittent but persistent and has been stronger in the West than elsewhere. It has found expression, at different times, in tracts, publications, manifestos, support for political underdogs—Sacco and Vanzetti, Mooney and Billings, strikers, immigrants, minorities—and in a variety of political initiatives. It has also found expression in court decisions, novels, speeches, sermons, biographies, autobiographies, editorials, histories, and critical studies. At different times in their lives, individuals have voiced radical sentiments only to disavow them at a later date; Tom Watson, the Georgia demagogue, might be cited as a case in point. And there have been a few—a very few—demagogues who ended up being radicals. One could find, I am sure, individual Socialists, Communists, Trotskyites, Republicans (a few), Democrats, and independents who could fairly be called radicals. But radicals have always been a minority within the minority of the left. Unlike liberals, they never feel part of the existing order and are invariably critical of it.

Hannah Arendt once wrote that the radical is engaged in the unbiased search for those facts in everyday affairs that contain the roots for future development. She defined "radical" in the sense of "going back and reviving much that belongs to the very roots of the American radical tradition as well as much that belongs to the radical tradition everywhere—the tradition of nay-saying and independence, of cheerful 'negativism' when confronted with the temptation of Realpolitik, and of self-confidence: pride and trust in one's own judgment. These qualities distinguish the radical who always remains

LIVING IN FIVE WORLDS ‖ 260

true to reality in his search for the root of the matter from the extremist, who single-mindedly follows the logic of whatever cause he may espouse at the moment." The radical is the perpetual outsider, the odd man (or woman) out, constantly critical of the power structure and of things as they are.

But I am also a socialist in the sense that I share the socialist critique of capitalism. But this critique does not tell us all that we need to know about socialism, precisely what it would do and how it would do it. And socialism in practice, while varied and feasible, has shown limitations that have disappointed its most enthusiastic advocates. It is easy to talk about "democratic socialism," but just how would an American socialist regime safeguard civil liberties? How could it prevent a slavish dependence on state power? How would it go about changing the structure of economic power? Could it avoid bureaucratic sloth? How would it stimulate social incentives? Could it achieve efficient management? How would it revive and sustain a sense of pride in work performed? Would it make for a more genuine public—as distinguished from bureaucratic—control of productive capacity? Would it be able to breathe new life into the constitutional concept of government of, by, and for the people?

Despite these and other unanswered questions, the socialist perspective does make it possible to see that the growth of corporate power constitutes a threat to democracy, since it focuses attention on the "bottom-line" capitalist imperatives of profits and expansion. Much as apologists prate about "corporate responsibility" and the rise of a new managerial class sensitive to public needs, the concentration of economic power can no longer, if it ever could, be adequately controlled by regulatory measures and executive directives. For one thing, the political power of the people has become increasingly diffuse and atomized with the rise of media politics. True, the people continue to elect officials, but the power remains in the board rooms, and changes in national administrations produce at best only marginal modifications in the structure of power. Nowadays even academic economists—Charles E. Lindblom of Yale is one—are disturbed by the uneasy relationship between corporate enterprise and democracy; between corporate power and democratic principles.

Over the years I have come to believe that radicals should be primarily concerned with values. If they could achieve substantial agreement on the kinds of values society should encourage, it might then be possible to proceed experimentally, tentatively, to invent new forms and institutional arrangements which would best safeguard and extend these values. Values, in a word, should take precedence over programs. This way the risks of the remedy becoming part of the problem could be minimized. This is what Henry Adams had in mind when he said of Theodore Roosevelt's trust-busting activities that the problem was "not so much to control the trusts as to create the society that could manage the trusts." But since agreement on values is unlikely and the task of altering the structure of power so formidable, the role of the radical as goad, critic, and dissenter will be needed for a long time; in fact, I cannot conceive of a society in which this function could safely be dispensed with. In the 1840s, Dostoevski believed in radicalism, basic Christian values, and the autonomy of art. My loyalties, after a rough, informal "education" in five "worlds" of politics and experience, are to radicalism, socialism (a more rational economy with a more equal distribution of power and responsibility and a more sensible use of resources), democratic principles, the kind of "Christian" humanism F. O. Matthiessen emphasized, and the autonomy of art, ideas, and values.

What it comes down to is that I am the rebel-radical I have always been (for reasons I have never fully understood) and that I still take a generous view of the future and remain basically an optimist despite much evidence that I could be wrong. On balance, however, my brand of indigenous radicalism and idealism has stood the test of time as well as or better than some of the apocalyptic ideologies of the Right and the Left. As a journalist I have learned to take all ideological projections with a grain of salt. What my "education" has given me, in brief, is some understanding of the realities of the different "worlds" I have known and what it has meant to be part of the action. Exploring these "worlds" has been my life. The past I do not purport to understand, the future I cannot fathom. But I have managed to escape the blight of boredom by exploring these five "worlds" and noting how they affected me.

Education ended for Henry Adams in 1905, the year I was born.* Only beyond some remoter horizon, as he saw it, could society's values be fixed and renewed. The new forces would educate, of that he was certain, for the

---

* The title of McWilliams's autobiography, *The Education of Carey McWilliams,* refers to another autobiography, *The Education of Henry Adams,* in which Adams detailed his lifelong search for real education in a rapidly changing nation; his lifetime (1838–1905) included the years of the Civil War, capitalist expansion, and the growth of the United States as a world power.

mind would continue to react. And the next great influx of new forces seemed near at hand. Perhaps at some point in the future—and he selected the year 1938, the centenary of his birth as a target date—he might be allowed to return with his friends to "see the mistakes of their own lives made clear in the light of the mistakes of their successors; and perhaps then, for the first time since man began his education among the carnivores," they would find a world that "sensitive and timid natures could regard without a shudder." But by 1938 the world was on the verge of war, and he and his friends, had they been allowed to return, would have had good reason to shudder at the consequences.

The centenary of my birth would be the year 2005, and I have no notion whether "sensitive and timid natures" will then be able to regard the world without a shudder. But I agree with what Oscar Ameringer, an American radical, once said to a small gathering of Socialists at one of the movement's bleaker moments. "The rank and file," he said, "is like the grass in the fields. The rains and snows beat upon it; winds and flame devour it; but one day in the early spring there is a secret stirring in the earth and behold the grass has sprung up again—green and very beautiful under a golden sun. So with you, dear brothers. You will rise again even as the grass of the field, though all men's hands be set against you, though you feel yourselves isolated and abandoned, you, the rank and file, will surely rise to spread the green mantle of democracy over this ravished American soil."

Permissions

The following material is reprinted from *North from Mexico: The Spanish-Speaking People of the United States,* by Carey McWilliams. Copyright ©1948 by Carey McWilliams. Copyright renewed 1975 by Carey McWilliams. Updated material copyright ©1990 by Matt S. Meier. Used with permission of Greenwood Publishing Group, Inc., Westport, CT.: "The Lynching of Juanita," "The Pattern of Violence," and "Blood on the Pavements."

The following material is reprinted from *Southern California Country: An Island on the Land,* by Carey McWilliams, Peregrine Smith Books (Gibbs Smith, Publisher), 1995. Used with permission of Gibbs Smith, Publisher: "The Growth of a Legend," "The Politics of Utopia," "Water! Water! Water!".

The following copyrighted material is reprinted with permission of Harold Ober Associates and the estate of Carey McWilliams:
"The Cold War Trap" [Afterword], *The Education of Carey McWilliams* (New York: Simon and Schuster, 1979).
"The Cults of California" ["Sister Aimee"], *Atlantic Monthly,* March 1946.
"Exodus from the West Coast," *Prejudice: Japanese Americans, Symbol of Racial Intolerance* (Boston: Little, Brown and Co., 1944).
"The Folklore of Earthquakes," *American Mercury,* June 1933.
"The Joads at Home," *Ill Fares the Land: Migrants and Migratory Labor in the United States* (Boston, Little, Brown and Co., 1942).
"The Long-Suffering Chinese," *Brothers Under the Skin* (Boston: Little, Brown and Co., 1964); and "Storm Signals," *Brothers Under the Skin* (Boston: Little, Brown and Co., 1951).
"Mecca of the Miraculous," *Holiday,* January 1947.
"The Wheatland Riot," *Factories in the Field: The Story of Migrant Farm Labor in California* (Santa Barbara: Peregrine Publishers, 1971).

The following selections are reprinted with permission of *The Nation* magazine:
"God Will Slap You Cockeyed," vol. 171: pp. 168–169; August 19, 1950.
Strange Doings in California, vol. 160: pp. 152–153; February 10, 1945.
The Education of Evans Carlson, vol. 161: pp. 577–579; December 1, 1945.
Mr. Tenney's Horrible Awakening, vol. 169: pp. 80–82; July 23, 1949.
Bungling in California, vol. 171: pp. 411–412; November 4, 1950.
The Old Fresno Magic, vol. 178: inside front cover; February 27, 1954.
The Kennedys Take Over, vol. 191: pp. 43–45; July 23, 1960.
Has Success Spoiled Dick Nixon?, vol. 194: pp. 487–490, 493; June 2, 1962.
Politics of Personality, vol. 195: pp. 252–253; October 27, 1962.
Mr. Nixon and the Press, vol. 195: pp. 318–19; November 16, 1962.
How to Succeed with the Backlash, vol. 203: pp. 438–432; October 31, 1966.
Paradise Reagan-ed, vol. 203, p. 596; December 5, 1966.